Biography of Sardar Vallabhbhai Patel

Biography of Sardar Vallabhbhai Patel

A.S. Pabla

CYBER TECH PUBLICATIONS
4264/3, Ansari Road, Daryaganj, New Delhi-110002 (India)
Ph.: 011-23244078, 011-43559448 Fax: 011-23280028
E-Mail: cyberpublicationsdelhi@yahoo.com
Website: www.cybertechpublications.com

BIOGRAPHY OF SARDAR VALLABHBHAI PATEL

A.S. Pabla

First Edition 2010

Published by :

G.S. Rawat for **Cyber Tech Publications**
4264/3, Ansari Road, Daryaganj, New Delhi-110002 (India)
Ph.: 011-23244078, 011-43559448 Fax: 011-23280028
E-Mail: cyberpublicationsdelhi@yahoo.com
Website: www.cybertechpublications.com

Printed at: Asian Offset Printers, Delhi-53

Preface

Sardar Patel was popularly known as Iron Man of India. His full name was Vallabhbhai Patel. He played a leading role in the Indian freedom struggle and became the first Deputy Prime Minister and Home Minister of India. He is credited with achieving political integration of India. Vallabhbhai Patel was born on October 31, 1875 in Nadiad, a small village in Gujarat. His father Jhaverbhai was a farmer and mother Laad Bai was a simple lady. Sardar Vallabhai's early education took place in Karamsad. Then he joined a school in Petlad. After two years he joined a high school in a town called Nadiad. He passed his high school examination in 1896. Sardar Vallabhbhai Patel was a brilliant student throughout his schooling. Vallabhbhai wanted to become a barrister. To realize this ambition he had to go to England. But he did not have the financial means to even join a college India. In those days a candidate could study in private and sit for an examination in Law. Sardar Vallabh Bhai Patel borrowed books from a lawyer of his acquaintance and studied at home. Occasionally he attended courts of law and listened attentively to the arguments of lawyer. Vallabhbhai passed the Law examination with flying colours.

Sardar Vallabhbhai Patel started his Law practice in Godhra. Soon his practice flourished. He got married to Jhaberaba. In 1904, he got a baby daughter Maniben, and in 1905 his son Dahyabhai was born. Vallabhbhai sent his elder brother Vitthalbhai, who himself was a lawyer, to England for higher studies in Law. Patel was only thirty-three years old when his wife died. He did not wish to marry again. After his brother's return, Vallabhbhai went to England. He studied with single-minded devotion and stood first in the Barrister-at-Law Examination. Sardar Patel returned to India in 1913 and started his practice in Ahmedabad. Soon he became popular. At the urging of his friends, Patel contested and won elections to become the sanitation commissioner of Ahmedabad in 1917. Sardar Patel was deeply impressed by Gandhiji's success in Champaran Satyagraha. In 1918, there was a drought in the Kheda division of Gujarat. Peasants asked for relief from the high rate of taxes but the British government refused. Gandhiji took up peasants cause but could not devote his full time in Kheda. He was looking for someone who could lead the struggle in his absence. At this point Sardar Patel volunteered to come forward and lead the struggle. He gave up his lucrative legal practice and entered public life. Vallabhbhai successfully led peasants revolt in Kheda and the revolt ended in 1919 when the British government agreed to suspend collection of revenue and roll back the rates. Kheda Satyagraha turned Vallabhbhai Patel into a national hero. Vallabhbhai supported Gandhi's Non-Cooperation Movement, and as president of the Gujarat Congress, helped in organizing bonfires of British goods in Ahmedabad. He gave up his English clothes and started wearing Khadi. Sardar Vallabh Bhai Patel was elected Ahmedabad's municipal president in 1922, 1924 and 1927. During his terms, Ahmedabad was extended a major supply of electricity and underwent major education reforms. Drainage and sanitation systems were extended over all the city.

In 1928, Bardoli Taluka in Gujarat suffered from floods and famine. In this hour of distress the British government raised the revenue taxes by thirty percent. Sardar Patel took up cudgels on behalf of the farmers and appealed to the Governor to reduce the taxes. The Governor refused and the government even announced the date of the collection of the taxes. Sardar Patel organized the farmers and told them not to pay even a single pie of tax. The government tried to repress the revolt but ultimately bowed before Vallabhbhai Patel. It was during the struggle and after the victory in Bardoli that caused intense excitement across India, that Patel was increasingly addressed by his colleagues and followers as Sardar. This book is intended to focus upon the life and works of Sardar Vallabhbhai Patel.

—*Author*

CONTENTS

1

Introduction

Vallabhbhai Patel (31 October 1875—15 December 1950) was a political and social leader of India who played a major role in the country's struggle for independence and guided its integration into a united, independent nation. In India and across the world, he was often addressed as Sardar which means Chief in many languages of India. He is hailed as the Iron Man of India. Raised in the countryside of Gujarat and largely self-educated, Vallabhbhai Patel was employed in successful practice as a lawyer when he was first inspired by the work and philosophy of Mahatma Gandhi. Patel subsequently organised the peasants of Kheda, Borsad, and Bardoli in Gujarat in nonviolent civil disobedience against oppressive policies imposed by the British Raj; in this role, he became one of the most influential leaders in Gujarat.

He rose to the leadership of the Indian National Congress and was at the forefront of rebellions and political events, organising the party for elections in 1934 and 1937, and promoting the Quit India movement. As the first Home Minister and Deputy Prime Minister of India, Patel organised relief for refugees in Punjab and Delhi, and led efforts to restore peace across the nation. Patel took charge of the task to forge a united India from the 565 semi-autonomous princely states and British-era colonial provinces. Using frank diplomacy backed with the option (and the use) of military action, Patel's leadership enabled the accession of almost every princely state. Hailed as the Iron Man of India, he is also remembered as the "Patron Saint" of India's civil servants for establishing modern all-India services. Patel was also one of the earliest proponents of property rights and free enterprise in India.

EARLY LIFE

Young Vallabhbhai, When a Student

Vallabhbhai Jhaverbhai Patel was born at his maternal uncle's house in Nadiad, Gujarat. His actual date of birth was never officially recorded—Patel entered 31 October as his date of birth on his matriculation examination papers. He was the fourth son of Jhaverbhai a Hindu by religion and his wife Ladba Patel. They lived in the village of Karamsad, in the Kheda district where Jhaverbhai owned a homestead. Somabhai, Narsibhai and Vithalbhai Patel (also a future political leader) were his elder brothers. He had a younger brother, Kashibhai and a sister, Dahiba. As a young boy, Patel helped his father in the fields and bimonthly kept a day-long fast, abstaining from food and water—a Hindu cultural observance that enabled him to develop physical toughness. When he was eighteen years old, Patel's marriage was arranged with Jhaverba, a young girl of twelve or thirteen years from a nearby village. As per custom, the young bride would continue to reside with her parents until her husband started earning and could establish their household.

Patel travelled to attend schools in Nadiad, Petlad and Borsad, living self-sufficiently with other boys. He reputedly cultivated a stoic character—a popular anecdote recounts how he lanced his own painful boil without hesitation, even as the barber supposed to do it trembled. Patel passed his matriculation at the late age of 22; at this point, he was generally regarded by his elders as an unambitious man destined for a commonplace job. But Patel himself harboured a plan—he would study to become a lawyer, work and save funds, travel to England and study to become a barrister. Patel spent years away from his family, studying on his own with books borrowed from other lawyers and passed examinations within two years. Fetching Jhaverba from her parents' home, Patel set up his household in Godhra and enrolled at the bar. During the many years it took him to save money, Vallabhbhai—now a pleader—earned a reputation as a fierce and skilled lawyer. His wife bore him a daughter, Manibehn, in 1904 and later a son, Dahyabhai, in 1906. Patel also cared for a friend suffering from Bubonic plague when it swept across Gujarat. When Patel himself came down with the disease, he immediately sent his family to safety, left his home and moved into an isolated house in Nadiad (by other accounts, Patel spent this time in a dilapidated temple); there, he recovered slowly.

Vallabhbhai Patel, When a Young Lawyer

Patel practised law in Godhra, Borsad and Anand while taking on the financial burdens of his homestead in Karamsad. When he had saved enough for England and applied for a pass and a ticket, they arrived in the name of "V. J. Patel," at Vithalbhai's home, who bore the same initials. Having harboured his own plans to study in England, Vithalbhai remonstrated to his younger brother that it would be disreputable for an older brother to follow his younger brother. In keeping with concerns for his family's honour, Patel allowed Vithalbhai to go in his place. He also financed his brother's stay and began saving again for his own goals.

In 1909, Patel's wife Jhaverba was hospitalised in Mumbai (then Bombay) to undergo a major surgical operation for cancer. Her health suddenly worsened and despite successful emergency surgery, she died in the hospital. Patel was given a note informing him of his wife's demise as he was cross-examining a witness in court. As per others who witnessed, Patel read the note, pocketed it and continued to intensely cross-examine the witness and won the case. He broke the news to others only after the proceedings had ended. Patel himself decided against marrying again. He raised his children with the help of his family and sent them to English-medium schools in Mumbai. At the age of 36, he journeyed to England and enrolled at the Middle Temple Inn in London. Finishing a 36-month course in 30 months, Patel topped his class despite having no previous college background. Returning to India, Patel settled in the city of Ahmedabad and became one of the city's most successful barristers. Wearing European-style clothes and urbane mannerisms, he also became a skilled bridge player. Patel nurtured ambitions to expand his practise and accumulate great wealth and to provide his children with modern education. He had also made a pact with his brother Vithalbhai to support his entry into politics in the Bombay Presidency, while Patel himself would remain in Ahmedabad and provide for the family.

Fighting for Independence

At the urging of his friends, Patel won an election to become the sanitation commissioner of Ahmedabad in 1917. While often clashing with British officials on civic issues, he did not show any interest in politics. Upon hearing of Mohandas Gandhi, he joked to Mavlankar that Gandhi would "ask you if you know how to sift pebbles from wheat. And that is supposed to bring independence." But Patel was deeply impressed when Gandhi defied the British in Champaran for the sake of the area's oppressed farmers. Against the grain of Indian politicians of the time, Gandhi wore Indian-style clothes and emphasised the use of one's mother tongue or any Indian language as opposed to English—the lingua franca of India's intellectuals. Patel was particularly attracted to Gandhi's inclination to action—apart from a resolution condemning the arrest of political leader Annie Besant, Gandhi proposed that volunteers march peacefully demanding to meet her. Patel gave a speech in Borsad in September 1917, encouraging Indians nationwide to sign Gandhi's petition demanding *Swaraj* — independence — from the British. Meeting Gandhi a month later at the Gujarat Political Conference in Godhra, Patel became the secretary of the Gujarat Sabha—a public body which would become the Gujarati arm of the Indian National Congress—at Gandhi's encouragement. Patel now energetically fought against *veth*—the forced servitude of Indians to Europeans—and organised relief efforts in wake of plague and famine in Kheda. The Kheda peasants' plea for exemption from taxation had been turned down by British authorities. Gandhi endorsed waging a struggle there, but could not lead it himself due to his activities in Champaran. When Gandhi asked for a Gujarati activist to devote himself completely to the assignment and Patel volunteered, much to Gandhi's personal delight. Though his decision was made on the spot, Patel later said that his desire and commitment came after intensive personal contemplation, as he realised he would have to abandon his career and material ambitions.

SATYAGRAHA IN GUJARAT

Vallabhbhai Patel, after his embrace of Gandhi's philosophy and a completely Indian way of life Supported by Congress volunteers Narhari Parikh, Mohanlal Pandya and Abbas Tyabji, Vallabhbhai Patel began a village-to-village tour in the Kheda district, documenting grievances and asking villagers for their support for a statewide revolt by refusing the payment of taxes. Patel emphasised potential hardships with the need for complete unity and nonviolence despite any provocation. He received enthusiastic responses from virtually every village. When the revolt was launched and revenue refused, the government sent police and intimidation squads to seize property, including confiscating barn animals and whole farms. Patel organised a network of volunteers to work with individual villages—helping them hide valuables and protect themselves during raids. Thousands of activists and farmers were arrested, but Patel was not. The revolt began evoking sympathy and admiration across India, including with pro-British Indian politicians. The government agreed to negotiate with Patel and decided to suspend the payment of revenue for the year, even scaling back the rate. Patel emerged as a hero to Gujaratis and admired across India. In 1920, he was elected president of the newly formed Gujarat Pradesh Congress Committee—he would serve as its president till 1945.

Patel supported Gandhi's Noncooperation movement and toured the state to recruit more than 300,000 members and raise over Rs. 1.5 million in funds. Helping organise bonfires of British goods in Ahmedabad, Patel threw in all his English-style clothes. With his daughter Mani and son Dahya, he switched completely to wearing khadi. Patel also supported Gandhi's controversial suspension of resistance in wake of the Chauri Chaura incident. He worked extensively in the following years in Gujarat against alcoholism, untouchability and caste discrimination, as well as for the empowerment of women. In the Congress, he was a resolute supporter of Gandhi against his Swarajist critics. Patel was elected Ahmedabad's municipal president in 1922, 1924 and 1927 — during his terms, Ahmedabad was extended a major supply of electricity and the school system underwent major reforms. Drainage and sanitation systems were extended over all the city. He fought for the recognition and payment of teachers employed in schools established by nationalists (out of British control) and even took on sensitive Hindu-Muslim Issues. Sardar Patel personally led relief efforts in the aftermath of the intense torrential rainfall in 1927, which had caused major floods in the city and in the Kheda district and great destruction of life and property. He established refuge centres across the district, raised volunteers, arranged for supply of food, medicines and clothing, as well as emergency funds from the government and public.

Patel with Bardoli Peasants

When Gandhi was in prison, Sardar Patel was asked by Congressmen to lead the satyagraha in Nagpur in 1923 against a law banning the raising of the Indian flag. He organised thousands of volunteers from all over the country in processions hoisting the flag. Patel negotiated a settlement that obtained the release of all prisoners and allowed nationalists to hoist the flag in public. Later that year, Patel and his allies uncovered evidence suggesting that the police were in league with local dacoits in the Borsad taluka even as the government prepared to levy a major tax for fighting dacoits in the area. More than 6,000 villagers assembled to hear Patel speak and supported the proposed agitation against the tax, which was deemed immoral and unnecessary. He organised hundreds of Congressmen, sent instructions and received information from across the district. Every village in the *taluka* resisted payment of the tax, and through cohesion, also prevented the seizure of property and lands. After a protracted struggle, the government withdrew the tax. Historians believe that one of Patel's key achievements was the building of cohesion and trust amongst the different castes and communities, which were divided on socio-economic lines.

In April 1928, Sardar Patel returned to the freedom struggle from his municipal duties in Ahmedabad when Bardoli suffered from a serious predicament of a famine and steep tax hike. The revenue hike was steeper than it had been in Kheda even though the famine covered a large portion of Gujarat. After cross-examining and talking to village representatives, emphasizing the potential hardship and need for nonviolence and cohesion, Patel initiated the struggle — complete denial of taxes. Sardar Patel organised volunteers, camps and an information network across affected areas. The revenue refusal was stronger than in Kheda and many sympathy satyagrahas were undertaken across Gujarat. Despite arrests, seizures of property and lands, the struggle intensified. The situation reached a head in August, when through sympathetic intermediaries, he negotiated a settlement repealing the tax hike, reinstating village officials who had resigned in protest and the return of seized property and lands. It was during the struggle and after the victory in Bardoli that Patel was increasingly addressed by his colleagues and followers as Sardar.

LEADING THE CONGRESS

As Gandhi embarked on the Dandi Salt March, Patel was arrested in the village of Ras and tried without witnesses, with no lawyer or pressman allowed to attend. Patel's arrest and Gandhi's subsequent arrest caused the Salt Satyagraha to greatly intensify in Gujarat—districts across Gujarat launched an anti-tax rebellion until and unless Patel and Gandhi were released. Once released, Patel served as interim Congress president, but was re-arrested while leading a procession in Mumbai. After the signing of the Gandhi-

Irwin Pact, Patel was elected Congress president for its 1931 session in Karachi — here the Congress ratified the pact, committed itself to the defence of fundamental rights and human freedoms, and a vision of a secular nation, minimum wage and the abolition of untouchability and serfdom. Patel used his position as Congress president in organising the return of confiscated lands to farmers in Gujarat.

Upon the failure of the Round Table Conference in London, Gandhi and Patel were arrested in January 1932 when the struggle re-opened, and imprisoned in the Yeravda Central Jail. During this term of imprisonment, Patel and Gandhi grew close to each other, and the two developed a close bond of affection, trust, and frankness. Their mutual relationship could be described as that of an elder brother — Gandhi — and his younger brother — Patel. Despite having arguments with Gandhi, Patel respected his instincts and leadership. During imprisonment, the two would discuss national and social issues, read Hindu epics and crack jokes. Gandhi also taught Patel Sanskrit language. Gandhi's secretary Mahadev Desai kept detailed records of conversations between Gandhi and Patel. When Gandhi embarked on a fast-unto-death protesting the separate electorates allocated for untouchables, Patel looked after Gandhi closely and himself refrained from partaking of food.

Patel was later moved to a jail in Nasik, and refused a British offer for a brief release to attend the cremation of his brother Vithalbhai, who had died in 1934. He was finally released in July of the same year. Patel headed Congress's all-India election campaign in 1934 and 1937 — he would collect funds, select candidates, determine the Congress stance on issues and opponents. Not contesting a seat for himself, Patel nevertheless guided Congressmen elected in the provinces and at the national level. In 1935, Patel underwent surgery for hemorrhoids, yet guided efforts against plague in Bardoli and again when a drought struck Gujarat in 1939. Patel would guide the Congress ministries that had won power across India with the aim of preserving party discipline—Patel feared that the British would use opportunities to create conflicts among elected Congressmen, and he did not want the party to be distracted from the goal of complete independence.

But Patel would clash with Nehru, opposing declarations of the adoption of socialism at the 1936 Congress session, which he believed was a diversion from the main goal of achieving independence. In 1938, Patel organized rank and file opposition to the attempts of then-Congress president Subhash Bose to move away from Gandhi's principles of nonviolent resistance. Patel considered Bose to be authoritarian and desirous of more power over the party. He led senior Congress leaders in a protest, which resulted in Bose's resignation. But criticism arose from Bose's supporters, socialists and other Congressmen that Patel himself was acting in an authoritarian manner in his defense of Gandhi's authority.

QUIT INDIA

When World War II broke out, Patel supported Nehru's decision to withdraw the Congress from central and provincial legislatures, contrary to Gandhi's advice, as well as an initiative by senior leader Chakravarthi Rajagopalacharya to offer Congress's full support to Britain if it promised Indian independence at the end of the war and install a democratic government right away. Gandhi had refused to support Britain on the grounds of his moral opposition to war, while Subhash Chandra Bose was in militant opposition to the British. The British rejected Rajagopalacharya's initiative, and Patel embraced Gandhi's leadership again. He participated in Gandhi's call for individual disobedience, and was arrested in 1940 and imprisoned for nine months. He also opposed the proposals of the Cripps' mission in 1942. Patel lost more than twenty pounds during his period in jail.

While Nehru, Rajagopalacharya and Maulana Azad initially criticized Gandhi's proposal for an all-out campaign of civil disobedience to force the British to *Quit India*, Patel was its most fervent supporter. Arguing that the British would retreat from India as they had from Singapore and Burma, Patel stressed that the campaign start without any delay. Though feeling that the British would not quit immediately, Patel favoured an all-out rebellion which would galvanize Indian people, who had been divided in their response to the war, In Patel's view, an all-out rebellion would force the British to concede that continuation of colonial rule had no support in India, and thus speed power transfer to Indians.

Believing strongly in the need for revolt, Patel stated his intention to resign from the Congress if the revolt was not approved. Gandhi strongly pressured the All India Congress Committee to approve of an all-out campaign of civil disobedience, and the AICC approved the campaign on 7 August 1942.

Though Patel's health had suffered during his stint in jail, Patel gave emotional speeches to large crowds across India, asking people to refuse paying taxes and participate in civil disobedience, mass protests and a shutdown of all civil services. He raised funds and prepared a second-tier of command as a precaution against the arrest of national leaders. Patel made a climactic speech to more than 100,000 people gathered at Gowalia Tank in Bombay (Mumbai) on August 7:

> *"The Governor of Burma boasts in London that they left Burma only after reducing everything to dust. So you promise the same thing to India?... You refer in your radio broadcasts and newspapers to the government established in Burma by Japan as a puppet government? What sort of government do you have in Delhi now?...When France fell before the Nazi onslaught, in the midst of total war, Mr. Churchill offered union with England to the French. That was indeed a stroke of inspired statesmanship. But when it comes to India? Oh no! Constitutional changes in the midst of a war? Absolutely unthinkable...The object this time is to free India before the Japanese can come and be ready to fight them if they come. They will round up the leaders, round up all. Then it will be the duty of every Indian to put forth his utmost effort — within nonviolence. No source is to be left untapped; no weapon untried. This is going to be the opportunity of a lifetime."*

Historians believe that Patel's speech was instrumental in electrifying nationalists, who had been skeptical of the proposed rebellion. Patel's organising work in this period is credited by historians for ensuring the success of the rebellion across India. Patel was arrested on 9 August and was imprisoned with the entire Congress Working Committee from 1942 to 1945 at the fort in Ahmednagar. Here he spun cloth, played bridge, read a large number of books, took long walks, practised gardening. He also provided emotional support to his colleagues while awaiting news and developments of the outside. Patel was deeply pained at the news of the deaths of Mahadev Desai and Kasturba Gandhi later in the year. But Patel wrote in a letter to his daughter that he and his colleagues were experiencing "fullest peace" for having done "their duty." Even though other political parties had opposed the struggle and the British had employed ruthless means of suppression, the Quit India movement was "by far the most serious rebellion since that of 1857," as the viceroy cabled to Winston Churchill. More than one hundred thousand people were arrested and thousands killed in police firings. Strikes, protests and other revolutionary activities had broken out across India. When Patel was released on 15 June 1945 he realised that the British were preparing proposals to transfer power to Indian hands.

Independence, Integration and Role of Gandhi

In the 1946 election for the Congress presidency, Patel stepped down in favour of Nehru at the request of Gandhi. The election's importance stemmed from the fact that the elected President would lead free India's first Government. Gandhi asked all 16 states representatives and Congress to elect the right person and Sardar Patel's name was proposed by 13 states representatives out of 16, but Patel respected Gandhi's request to not be the first prime minister. As a Home Minister, Patel merged all parts of India under federal control but Jammu and Kashmir was left out because of Nehru. After the election of Nehru as the party's president, Patel began directing the Congress campaign for the general elections of the Constituent Assembly of India.

In the elections, the Congress won a large majority of the elected seats, dominating the Hindu electorate. But the Muslim League led by Muhammad Ali Jinnah won a large majority of Muslim electorate seats. The League had resolved in 1940 to demand Pakistan—an independent state for Muslims—and was a fierce critic of the Congress. The Congress formed governments in all provinces save Sindh, Punjab and Bengal, where it entered into coalitions with other parties.

CABINET MISSION AND PARTITION

When the British mission proposed two plans for transfer of power, there was considerable opposition within the Congress to both. The plan of 16 May 1946 proposed a loose federation with extensive provincial autonomy, and the "grouping" of provinces based on religious-majority. The plan of 16 June 1946 proposed the partition of India on religious lines, with over 600 princely states free to choose between independence or accession to either dominion. The League approved both plans, while the Congress flatly rejected the June 16 proposal. Gandhi criticised the May 16 proposal as being inherently divisive, but Patel, realizing that rejecting the proposal would mean that only the League would be invited to form a government, lobbied the Congress Working Committee hard to give its assent to the 16 May proposal. Patel engaged the British envoys Sir Stafford Cripps and Lord Pethick-Lawrence and obtained an assurance that the "grouping" clause would not be given practical force, Patel converted Nehru, Rajendra Prasad and Rajagopalacharya to accept the plan. When the League retracted its approval of the 16 May plan, the viceroy Lord Wavell invited the Congress to form the government. Under Nehru, who was styled the "Vice President of the Viceroy's Executive Council," Patel took charge of the departments of home affairs and information and broadcasting. He moved into a government house on 1, Aurangzeb Road in Delhi—this would be his residence till his death in 1950.

Vallabhbhai Patel was one of the first Congress leaders to accept the partition of India as a solution to the rising Muslim separatist movement led by Muhammad Ali Jinnah. He had been outraged by Jinnah's Direct Action campaign, which had provoked communal violence across India and by the viceroy's vetoes of his home department's plans to stop the violence on the grounds of constitutionality. Patel severely criticised the viceroy's induction of League ministers into the government, and the revalidation of the grouping scheme by the British without Congress approval. Although further outraged at the League's boycott of the assembly and non-acceptance of the plan of 16 May despite entering government, he was also aware that Jinnah did enjoy popular support amongst Muslims, and that an open conflict between him and the nationalists could degenerate into a Hindu-Muslim civil war of disastrous consequences.

The continuation of a divided and weak central government would in Patel's mind, result in the wider fragmentation of India by encouraging more than 600 princely states towards independence. Between the months of December 1946 and January 1947, Patel worked with civil servant V. P. Menon on the latter's suggestion for a separate dominion of Pakistan created out of Muslim-majority provinces. Communal violence in Bengal and Punjab in January and March of 1947 further convinced Patel of the soundness of partition. Patel, a fierce critic of Jinnah's demand that the Hindu-majority areas of Punjab and Bengal be included in a Muslim state, obtained the partition of those provinces, thus blocking any possibility of their inclusion in Pakistan. Patel's decisiveness on the partition of Punjab and Bengal had won him many supporters and admirers amongst the Indian public, which had tired of the League's tactics, but he was criticised by Gandhi, Nehru, secular Muslims and socialists for a perceived eagerness to do so. When Lord Louis Mountbatten formally proposed the plan on 3 June 1947, Patel gave his approval and lobbied Nehru and other Congress leaders to accept the proposal.

Knowing Gandhi's deep anguish regarding proposals of partition, Patel engaged him in frank discussion in private meetings over the perceived practical unworkability of any Congress-League coalition, the rising violence and the threat of civil war. At the All India Congress Committee meeting called to vote on the proposal, Patel said:

> *I fully appreciate the fears of our brothers from [the Muslim-majority areas]. Nobody likes the division of India and my heart is heavy. But the choice is between one division and many divisions. We must face facts. We cannot give way to emotionalism and sentimentality. The Working Committee has not acted out of fear. But I am afraid of one thing, that all our toil and hard work of these many years might go waste or prove unfruitful. My nine months in office has completely disillusioned me regarding the supposed merits of the Cabinet Mission Plan. Except for a few honourable exceptions, Muslim officials from the top down to the chaprasis (peons or servants) are working for the League. The communal veto given to the League in the Mission Plan would have blocked India's progress at every stage. Whether we like it or not, de facto Pakistan already exists in the Punjab and Bengal. Under the circumstances I would prefer a de jure Pakistan, which may make the League more responsible. Freedom is coming. We have 75 to 80 percent of India, which we can make strong with our own genius. The League can develop the rest of the country.*

Following Gandhi's and Congress' approval of the plan, Patel represented India on the Partition Council, where he oversaw the division of public assets, and selected the Indian council of ministers with Nehru. However, neither he nor any other Indian leader had foreseen the intense violence and population transfer that would take place with partition. Patel would take the lead in organising relief and emergency supplies, establishing refugee camps and visiting the border areas with Pakistani leaders to encourage peace. Despite these efforts, estimates on the death toll vary from around two hundred thousand, to over a million people. The estimated number of refugees in both countries exceeds 15 million. Understanding that Delhi and Punjab policemen, accused of organising attacks on Muslims, were personally affected by the tragedies of partition, Patel called out the Indian Army with South Indian regiments to restore order, imposing strict curfews and shoot-at-sight orders. Visiting the Nizamuddin Auliya Dargah area in Delhi, where thousands of Delhi Muslims feared attacks, he prayed at the shrine, visited the people and reinforced the presence of police. He suppressed from the press reports of atrocities in Pakistan against Hindus and Sikhs to prevent retaliatory violence. Establishing the Delhi Emergency Committee to restore order and organising relief efforts for refugees in the capital, Patel publicly warned officials against partiality and neglect. When reports reached Patel that large groups of Sikhs were preparing to attack Muslim convoys heading for Pakistan, Patel hurried to Amritsar and met Sikh and Hindu leaders. Arguing that attacking helpless people was cowardly and dishonourable, Patel emphasised that Sikh actions would result in further attacks against Hindus and Sikhs in Pakistan. He assured the community leaders that if they worked to establish peace and order and guarantee the safety of Muslims, the Indian government would react forcefully to any failures of Pakistan to do the same. Additionally, Patel addressed a massive crowd of an estimated 200,000 refugees who had surrounded his car after the meetings:

> *Here, in this same city, the blood of Hindus, Sikhs and Muslims mingled in the bloodbath of Jallianwala Bagh. I am grieved to think that things have come to such a pass that no Muslim can go about in Amritsar and no Hindu or Sikh can even think of living in Lahore. The butchery of innocent and defenceless men, women and children does not behove brave men... I am quite certain that India's interest lies in getting all her men and women across the border and sending out all Muslims from East Punjab. I have come to you with a specific appeal. Pledge the safety of Muslim refugees crossing the city. Any obstacles or hindrances will only worsen the plight of our*

refugees who are already performing prodigious feats of endurance. If we have to fight, we must fight clean. Such a fight must await an appropriate time and conditions and you must be watchful in choosing your ground. To fight against the refugees is no fight at all. No laws of humanity or war among honourable men permit the murder of people who have sought shelter and protection. Let there be truce for three months in which both sides can exchange their refugees. This sort of truce is permitted even by laws of war. Let us take the initiative in breaking this vicious circle of attacks and counter-attacks. Hold your hands for a week and see what happens. Make way for the refugees with your own force of volunteers and let them deliver the refugees safely at our frontier.

Following his dialogue with community leaders and his speech, no further attacks occurred against Muslim refugees, and a wider peace and order was re-established soon over the entire area. However, Patel was criticised by Nehru, secular Muslims and taxed by Gandhi over his alleged wish to see Muslims from other parts of India depart. While Patel vehemently denied such allegations, the acrimony with Maulana Azad and other secular Muslim leaders increased when Patel refused to dismiss Delhi's Sikh police commissioner, who was accused of discrimination. Hindu and Sikh leaders also accused Patel and other leaders of not taking Pakistan sufficiently to task over the attacks on their communities there, and Muslim leaders further criticised him for allegedly neglecting the needs of Muslims leaving for Pakistan, and concentrating resources for incoming Hindu and Sikh refugees.

Patel clashed with Nehru and Azad over the allocation of houses in Delhi vacated by Muslims leaving for Pakistan — Nehru and Azad desired to allocate them for displaced Muslims, while Patel argued that no government professing secularism must make such exclusions. However, Patel was publicly defended by Gandhi and received widespread admiration and support for speaking frankly on communal issues and acting decisively and resourcefully to quell disorder and violence.

POLITICAL INTEGRATION OF INDIA

Under the June 3 plan, more than 600 princely states were given the option of joining either India or Pakistan, or choosing independence. Indian nationalists and large segments of the public feared that if these states did not accede, a vast majority of the people and territory would be fragmented. The Congress as well as senior British officials considered Patel the best man for the task of achieving unification of the princely states with the Indian dominion. Gandhi had said to Patel *"the problem of the States is so difficult that you alone can solve it"*. He was considered a statesman of integrity with the practical acumen and resolve to accomplish a monumental task. Patel asked V. P. Menon, a senior civil servant with whom he had worked over the partition of India, to become his right-hand as chief secretary of the States Ministry. On 6 May 1947, Patel began lobbying the princes, attempting to make them receptive towards dialogue with the future Government and trying to forestall potential conflicts. Patel used social meetings and unofficial surroundings to engage most monarchs, inviting them to lunch and tea at his home in Delhi.

At these meetings, Patel stated that there was no inherent conflict between the Congress and the princely order. Nonetheless, he stressed that the princes would need to accede to India in good faith by 15 August 1947. Patel invoked the patriotism of India's monarchs, asking them to join in the freedom of their nation and act as responsible rulers who cared about the future of their people. He persuaded the princes of 565 states of the impossibility of independence from the Indian republic, especially in the presence of growing opposition from their subjects. He proposed favourable terms for the merger, including creation of *privy purses* for the descendants of the rulers. While encouraging the rulers to act with patriotism, Patel did not rule out force, setting a deadline of 15 August 1947 for them to sign the instrument of accession document. All but three of the states willingly merged into the Indian union—

only Jammu and Kashmir, Junagadh, and Hyderabad did not fall into his basket.

Junagadh was especially important to Patel, since it was in his home state of Gujarat. The Nawab had under pressure from Sir Shah Nawaz Bhutto acceded to Pakistan. It was however, quite far from Pakistan and 80% of its population was Hindu. Patel combined diplomacy with force, demanding that Pakistan annul the accession, and that the Nawab accede to India. He sent the Army to occupy three principalities of Junagadh to show his resolve. Following widespread protests and the formation of a civil government, or *Aarzi Hukumat*, both Bhutto and the Nawab fled to Karachi, and under Patel's orders, Indian Army and police units marched into the state. A plebiscite later organised produced a 99.5% vote for merger with India. In a speech at the Bahauddin College in Junagadh following the latter's take-over, Patel emphasised his feeling of urgency on Hyderabad, which he felt was more vital to India than Kashmir: If Hyderabad does not see the writing on the wall, it goes the way Junagadh has gone. Pakistan attempted to set off Kashmir against Junagadh. When we raised the question of settlement in a democratic way, they (Pakistan) at once told us that they would consider it if we applied that policy to Kashmir. Our reply was that we would agree to Kashmir if they agreed to Hyderabad.

Hyderabad was the largest of the princely states, and included parts of present-day Andhra Pradesh, Karnataka, and Maharashtra states. Its ruler, the Nizam Osman Ali Khan was a Muslim, although over 80% of its people were Hindu. The Nizam sought independence or accession with Pakistan. Muslim forces loyal to Nizam, called the Razakars, under Qasim Razvi pressed the Nizam to hold out against India, while organising attacks with militant Communists on people on Indian soil. Even though a Standstill Agreement was signed due to the desperate efforts of Lord Mountbatten to avoid a war, the Nizam rejected deals and changed his positions. In September 1948, Patel emphasised in Cabinet meetings that India should take no more, and reconciled Nehru and the Governor-General, Chakravarti Rajgopalachari to military action. Following preparations, Patel ordered the Indian Army to integrate Hyderabad (in his capacity as Acting Prime Minister) when Nehru was touring Europe. The action was termed Operation Polo, in which thousands of Razakar forces had been killed, but Hyderabad was comfortably secured into the Indian Union. The main aim of Mountbatten and Nehru in avoiding a forced annexation was to prevent an outbreak of Hindu-Muslim violence. Patel insisted that if Hyderabad was allowed to continue with its antics, the prestige of the Government would fall and then neither Hindus nor Muslims would feel secure in its realm. After defeating Niz. m, Patel retained him as the ceremonial chief of state, and held talks with him.

Leading India

Governor General Chakravarti Rajagopalacharya, Nehru and Patel formed the *triumvirate* which ruled India from 1948 to 1950. Prime Minister Nehru was intensely popular with the masses, but Patel enjoyed the loyalty and faith of rank and file Congressmen, state leaders and India's civil services. Patel was a senior leader in the Constituent Assembly of India and was responsible in a large measure for shaping India's constitution. Patel was a key force behind the appointment of Dr. Bhimrao Ramji Ambedkar as the chairman of the drafting committee, and the inclusion of leaders from a diverse political spectrum in the process of writing the constitution. Patel was the chairman of the committees responsible for minorities, tribal and excluded areas, fundamental rights and provincial constitutions. Patel piloted a model constitution for the provinces in the Assembly, which contained limited powers for the state governor, who would defer to the President — he clarified it was not the intention to let the governor exercise power which could impede an elected government. He worked closely with Muslim leaders to end separate electorates and the more potent demand for reservation of seats for minorities. Patel would hold personal dialogues with leaders of other minorities on the question, and was responsible for the measure that allows the President to appoint Anglo-Indians to Parliament. His intervention was key to the passage of two articles that protected civil servants from political involvement and guaranteed their terms and privileges. He was also instrumental in the founding the Indian Administrative Service and the Indian Police Service, and for his defence of Indian civil servants from political attack, he is known as the "patron saint" of India's services. When a delegation of Gujarati farmers came to him citing their inability to send their milk production to the markets without being fleeced by middlemen, Patel exhorted them to organise the processing and sale of milk by themselves, and guided them to create the Kaira District Cooperative Milk Producers' Union Limited, which preceded the Amul milk products brand. Patel also pledged the reconstruction of the ancient but dilapidated Somnath Temple in Saurashtra — he oversaw the creation of a public trust and restoration work, and pledged to dedicate the temple upon the completion of work (the work was completed after Patel's death, and the temple was inaugurated by the first President of India, Dr. Rajendra Prasad).

When the Pakistani invasion of Kashmir began in September 1947, Patel immediately wanted to send troops into Kashmir. But agreeing with Nehru and Mountbatten, he waited till Kashmir's monarch had acceded to India. Patel then oversaw India's military operations to secure Srinagar, the Baramulla Pass and the forces retrieved a lot of territory from the invaders. Patel, along with Defence Minister Baldev Singh administered the entire military effort, arranging for troops from different parts of India to be rushed to Kashmir and for a major military road connecting Srinagar to Pathankot be built in 6 months.

Patel strongly advised Nehru against going for arbitration to the United Nations, insisting that Pakistan had been wrong to support the invasion and the accession to India was valid. He did not want foreign interference in a bilateral affair. Patel opposed the release of Rs. 55 crores to the Government of Pakistan, convinced that the money would go to finance the war against India in Kashmir. The Cabinet had approved his point but it was reversed when Gandhi, who feared an intensifying rivalry and further communal violence, went on a fast-unto-death to obtain the release. Patel, though not estranged from Gandhi, was deeply hurt at the rejection of his counsel and a Cabinet decision.

In 1949, a crisis arose when the number of Hindu refugees entering West Bengal, Assam and Tripura from East Pakistan climbed over 800,000. The refugees in many cases were being forcibly evicted by Pakistani authorities, and were victims of intimidation and violence. Nehru invited Liaquat Ali Khan, Prime Minister of Pakistan to find a peaceful solution. Despite his aversion, Patel reluctantly met Khan and discussed the matters. Patel strongly criticised, however, Nehru's intention to sign a pact that would create minority commissions in both countries and pledge both India and Pakistan to a commitment to protect each other's minorities. Syama Prasad Mukherjee and K.C. Neogy, two Bengali ministers resigned and Nehru was intensely criticised in West Bengal for allegedly appeasing Pakistan. The pact was immediately in jeopardy. Patel however, publicly came out to Nehru's aid. He gave emotional speeches to members of Parliament, and the people of West Bengal, and spoke with scores of delegations of Congressmen, Hindus, Muslims and other public interest groups, persuading them to give peace a final effort. The pact was approved and within a year, most of the Hindu refugees had returned to East Pakistan.

GANDHI'S DEATH AND RELATIONS WITH NEHRU

Patel with Gandhi in the Early 1940s

Patel was intensely loyal to Gandhi and both he and Nehru looked to him to arbitrate disputes. However, Nehru and Patel sparred over national issues. When Nehru asserted control over Kashmir policy, Patel objected to Nehru's sidelining his home ministry's officials. Nehru was offended by Patel's decision-making regarding the states' integration, having neither consulted him nor the cabinet. Patel asked Gandhi to relieve him of his obligation to serve, knowing that he lacked Nehru's youth and popularity. He believed that an open political battle would hurt India. After much personal deliberation and contrary to Patel's prediction, Gandhi on

30 January 1948 told Patel not to leave the government. A free India, according to Gandhi, needed both Patel and Nehru. Patel was the last man to privately talk with Gandhi, who was assassinated just minutes after Patel's departure. At Gandhi's wake, Nehru and Patel embraced each other and addressed the nation together. Patel gave solace to many associates and friends and immediately moved to forestall any possible violence. Within two months of Gandhi's death, Patel suffered a major heart attack; the timely action of his daughter, his secretary and nurse saved Patel's life. Speaking later, Patel attributed the attack to the "grief bottled up" due to Gandhi's death.

Criticism arose from the media and other politicians that Patel's home ministry had failed to protect Gandhi. Emotionally exhausted, Patel tendered a letter of resignation, offering to leave the government. Patel's secretary convinced him to withhold the letter, seeing it as fodder for Patel's political enemies and political conflict in India. However, Nehru sent Patel a letter dismissing any question of personal differences and his desire for Patel's ouster. He reminded Patel of their 30-year partnership in the freedom struggle and asserted that after Gandhi's death, it was especially wrong for them to quarrel. Nehru, Rajagopalacharya and other Congressmen publicly defended Patel. Moved, Patel publicly endorsed Nehru's leadership and refuted any suggestion of discord. Patel publicly dispelled any notion that he sought to be prime minister. Though the two committed themselves to joint leadership and non-interference in Congress party affairs, they would criticise each other in matters of policy, clashing on the issues of Hyderabad's integration and UN mediation in Kashmir. Nehru declined Patel's counsel on sending assistance to Tibet after its 1950 invasion by the People's Republic of China and ejecting the Portuguese from Goa by military force.

When Nehru pressured Dr. Rajendra Prasad to decline a nomination to become the first President of India in 1950 in favour of Rajagopalacharya, he thus angered the party, which felt Nehru was attempting to impose his will. Nehru sought Patel's help in winning the party over, but Patel declined and Prasad was duly elected. Nehru opposed the 1950 Congress presidential candidate Purushottam Das Tandon, a conservative Hindu leader, endorsing Jivatram Kripalani instead and threatening to resign if Tandon was elected. Patel rejected Nehru's views and endorsed Tandon in Gujarat, where Kripalani received not one vote despite hailing from that state himself. Patel believed Nehru had to understand that his will was not law with the Congress, but he personally discouraged Nehru from resigning after the latter felt that the party had no confidence in him.

Death

On 29 March 1949, authorities lost radio contact with a plane carrying Patel, his daughter Maniben and the Maharaja of Patiala. Engine failure caused the pilot to make an emergency landing in a desert area in Rajasthan. With all passengers safe, Patel and others tracked down a nearby village and local officials. When Patel returned to Delhi, thousands of Congressmen gave him a resounding welcome. In Parliament, MPs gave a long, standing ovation to Patel, stopping proceedings for half an hour. In his twilight years, Patel was honoured by members of Parliament and awarded honorary doctorates of law by the Punjab University and Osmania University.

Patel's health declined rapidly through the summer of 1950. He later began coughing blood, whereupon Maniben began limiting his meetings and working hours and arranged for a personalised medical staff to begin attending to Patel. The Chief Minister of West Bengal and doctor Bidhan Roy heard Patel make jokes about his impending end, and in a private meeting Patel frankly admitted to his ministerial colleague N. V. Gadgil that he was not going to live much longer. Patel's health worsened after 2 November, when he began losing consciousness frequently and was confined to his bed. He was flown to Mumbai on 12 December to recuperate at his son Dahyabhai's flat — his condition deemed critical, Nehru and Rajagopalacharya came to the airport to see him off. After suffering a massive heart attack (his second), he died on 15 December 1950. In an unprecedented and unrepeated gesture, on the day after his death more than 1,500 officers of India's civil and police services congregated to mourn at Patel's residence in Delhi and pledged "complete loyalty and unremitting zeal" in India's service. His cremation in Sonapur, Mumbai, was attended by large crowds, Nehru, Rajagopalacharya, President Prasad, and many Congressmen and freedom fighters.

Criticism and Legacy

During his lifetime, Vallabhbhai Patel received criticism of an alleged bias against Muslims during the time of partition. He was criticised by nationalist Muslims such as Maulana Azad as well as Hindu nationalists for readily plumping for partition. Patel was criticised by supporters of Subhash Bose for acting coercively to put down politicians not supportive of Gandhi. Socialist politicians such as Jaya Prakash Narayan and Asoka Mehta criticised him for his personal proximity to Indian industrialists such as the Birla and Sarabhai families. Some historians have criticised Patel's actions on the integration of princely states as undermining the right of self-determination for those states.

However, Patel is credited for being almost single-handedly responsible for unifying India on the eve of independence. He won the admiration of many Indians for speaking frankly on the issues of Hindu-Muslim relations and not shying from using military force to integrate India. His skills of leadership and practical judgement were hailed by British statesmen—his opponents in the freedom struggle—such as Lord Wavell, Cripps, Pethick-Lawrence and Mountbatten. Some historians and admirers of Patel such as Rajendra Prasad and industrialist J.R.D. Tata have expressed opinions that Patel would have made a better prime minister for India than Nehru. Nehru's critics and Patel's admirers cite Nehru's belated embrace of Patel's advice regarding the UN and Kashmir and the integration of Goa by military action. Proponents of free enterprise cite the failings of Nehru's socialist policies as opposed to Patel's defence of property rights and his mentorship of the Amul cooperative project. Among Patel's surviving family, Manibehn Patel lived in a flat in Mumbai for the rest of her life following her father's death; she often led the work of the Sardar Patel Memorial Trust — which organises the prestigious annual Sardar Patel Memorial Lectures — and other charitable organisations. Dahyabhai Patel was a businessman who eventually was elected to serve in the Lok Sabha (the lower house of the Indian Parliament) as an MP in the 1960s.

The Central Hall of the Sardar Patel National Memorial

For many decades after his death, there was a perceived lack of effort from the Government of India, the national media and the Congress party regarding the commemoration of Patel's life and work. However, Patel is lionised as a hero in Gujarat and his family home in Karamsad is still preserved in his memory. Patel was officially awarded the Bharat Ratna, India's highest civilian honour posthumously in 1991. Patel's birthday, 31 October, is celebrated nationally in India as *Sardar Jayanti*. The Sardar Patel National Memorial was established in 1980 at the Moti Shahi Mahal in Ahmedabad. It composes of a museum, a gallery of portraits and historical pictures and a library, which stores important documents and books associated with Patel and his life. Amongst the exhibits are many of Patel's personal effects and relics from various periods of his personal and political life.

Patel is the namesake of many public institutions in India. A major initiative to build dams, canals and hydroelectric power plants on the Narmada river valley to provide a tri-state area with drinking water, electricity and increase agricultural production was christened the *Sardar Sarovar*. Patel is also the namesake of the Sardar Vallabhbhai National Institute of Technology, the Sardar Patel University and the Sardar Patel Vidyalaya, which are among the nation's premier institutions. India's national police training academy is also named after him. In Richard Attenborough's *Gandhi* (1982), actor Saeed Jaffrey portrayed Patel. In 1993, the biopic *Sardar* was produced and directed by Ketan Mehta and featured noted Indian actor Paresh

Rawal as Patel; it focused on Patel's leadership in the years leading up to independence, the partition of India, India's political integration and Patel's relationship with Gandhi and Nehru.

MANIBEHN PATEL

Manibehn Patel (b. 1904-d. 1988) was the daughter of Indian leader Sardar Vallabhbhai Patel and an Indian freedom fighter. Educated in Bombay, Manibehn adopted the teachings of Mahatma Gandhi in 1918, and started working regularly at his ashram in Ahmedabad. She participated in the Non-Cooperation movement and the Salt Satyagraha and was arrested for long periods. In the 1930s, she became her father's personal aide, also caring for his personal needs. But she again participated in the Quit India movement and was imprisoned from 1942 to 1945. Manibehn Patel would serve her father closely until his death in 1950. Moving to Bombay, she worked for the rest of her life with numerous charitable organizations and for the Sardar Patel Memorial Trust, and wrote her memoirs on the freedom struggle and her father's life.

2

Sardar Patel with Gandhi

Vallabhbhai Patel was born on October 31, 1875, in a farmer's family in Nadiad, Gujarat. His father, Zaverbhai, had served in the army of Jhansi ki Rani, and his mother, Ladbai, was a deeply religious woman. Vallabhbhai's initial schooling was in Gujarati. His brother Vithalbhai, after completing middle school, had enrolled himself in English tutorial classes in a nearby town. Vallabhbhai followed suit. Vallabhbhai's superior organizational skills became evident while he was in high school at Petlad when he coordinated the entire campaign for a poor teacher who he thought deserved a seat on the local municipal committee. Vallabhbhai persuaded his fellow students to work for the campaign. So impressively was the campaign handled that the teacher was elected over the rich local businessman. Vallabhbhai matriculated from Nadiad High School in 1897. Vallabhbhai was married to Zaverbai in 1891. The couple had two children-a daughter Manibehn, born in April of 1904, and a son Dayabhai, born in November of 1905. Zaverbai died in January of 1909. Vallabhbhai sailed for England in August of 1910 to study law. He qualified as a barrister in 1913 and returned to India to a lucrative practice in Ahmedabad. He joined the Gujarat Club and took to western dressing and a comfortable lifestyle.

Gandhiji started coming to the Gujarat Club to give lectures. He came again and again, propagating the idea of his newly wielded weapon of "satyagraha" or truth force. Vallabhbhai was impressed with Gandhiji and slowly began to adopt his view. The relationship between Gandhiji and Vallabhbhai was concretely defined when Gandhiji was elected the President of the Gujarat Sabha and Vallabhbhai the Secretary, in 1917. It was a relationship of a guru (teacher) and disciple. Vallabhbhai got his first opportunity to utilize Gandhiji's philosophy of satyagraha in 1918 for the farmers of Kaira who had lost their crops to heavy rains and floods that year. The government disregarded the farmers' misery and insisted on collecting land revenue. Vallabhbhai organized the No Tax campaign on peaceful, Gandhian lines. The government held out and began confiscating land and what little crops and cattle the farmers still had. Vallabhbhai, now decked in a dhoti, kurta and cap urged the farmers not to buckle. The government eventually relented and returned the confiscated property. This was the first victory of satyagraha for Vallabhbhai. He was jubilant.

Vallabhbhai took to spinning the charkha, boycotted foreign goods and clothes and burned his foreign possessions on public bonfires. He even discarded the western dresses he once so coveted. There was no stopping Vallabhbhai. He participated in the Nagpur flag satyagraha from May to August in 1923 in protest against the stopping of a procession which carried the national flag.

On March 12, 1930, Sardar Patel left for Dandi to prepare for Gandhiji's Salt satyagraha. He went to villages to organize for the food and lodging of the marchers. In every village he went, he made stirring speeches, rousing the people to join the march to Dandi. The Government swooped down and arrested him while he was in the village of Ras. This was Sardar Patel's first prison sentence. He was released after the Gandhi-Irwin pact of March 1931. That year he presided over the Congress session in Karachi. Gandhiji sailed for London to attend the Round Table Conference in 1931. Sardar Patel regularly updated him on the situation in India. Ironically, the British Government in India stepped up repression just when the Conference was going on in London. Gandhiji was arrested on his return from the Conference. Sardar Patel and Jawaharlal Nehru were also imprisoned. Sardar Patel was imprisoned with Gandhiji in

Yeravada Jail, Pune, where they spent 16 months together. While Sardar Patel was in jail, his mother and brother died. He refused to be released to attend to their last rites.

In 1937, elections for the provincial governments were held under the Government of India Act of 1935. Sardar Patel was elected Chairman to the Parliamentary Sub-Committee which was to select Congress candidates and organize the elections. Sardar Patel's hard work resulted in the Congress forming majority governments in most Provinces. All the Congress ministries resigned when the British arbitrarily included India in the war effort against Germany and Japan. Gandhiji planned an individual satyagraha to protest India's inclusion in the war without being consulted. Sardar Patel was among the first batch of leaders to offer satyagraha. Arrests of the participants followed. On August 8, 1942, the Congress and Gandhiji passed the "Quit India" resolution, calling upon the British to withdraw from India. The Government responded with arrests of Sardar Patel, Jawaharlal Nehru, Gandhiji and other eminent Congress leaders. Sardar Patel was imprisoned in Ahmednagar Fort while Gandhiji was kept in Aga Khan Palace.

On March 23, 1946, the Labour Prime Minister of Britain arrived in India to assure independence for India. An Interim Government was proposed and Sardar Patel once again was asked to handle the campaign for the Congress. Again the Sardar delivered. The Congress won thumping majorities in almost all provinces. Jawaharlal Nehru became Prime Minister in September 1946 and Sardar Patel held the portfolios of Home and Information and Broadcasting. On August 15, 1947, India became free, but only after Pakistan was created.

When Pakistani infiltrators attacked Kashmir, Sardar Patel proposed withholding Pakistan's share of cash balances left by the British. Gandhiji felt such an act would be morally wrong and went on a fast unto death. Sardar Patel tried to prevail over Gandhiji, but he finally relented in order to save the life of the "Father of the

Nation." Sardar Patel handled the portfolio of Home Minister, Minister of States and Minister of Information and Broadcasting. As Home Minister he had to deal with communal disturbances that continued to rock the nation after partition. He transferred army units from Pune and Madras to deal with the disturbances in Delhi. He had the army move ten thousand Muslims to Red Fort to protect them from the riots.

Sardar Patel handled the integration of all the princely states into the Indian Union with great expertise. Under the Cabinet Mission, all the princely states had the right to join Pakistan, India or remain independent. The Sardar declared that "we are all knit together by bonds of blood and feelings... Therefore, it is better for us to make laws sitting together as friends." Sardar Patel dealt with Hyderabad and Junaghad firmly when these states tried to join Pakistan or remain independent. Gandhiji was full of praise.

As time passed, differences in opinion formed between Sardar Patel and Jawaharlal Nehru. Gandhiji wanted both to work together for the betterment of India. On January 30, 1948, Sardar Patel met Gandhiji who expressed his wish that Sardar Patel work side by side with Nehru. The same day Gandhiji was assassinated. Sardar Patel was crushed. He was further hurt when he was criticized for not protecting Gandhiji. Sardar Patel wanted to post plain-cloth policemen at the Gandhiji's prayer meetings, but Gandhiji had forbidden it. After Gandhiji's death, Sardar Patel acted as Gandhiji had wished and worked closely with Nehru.

Sardar Patel formed the Indian Administrative Service, Indian Police Service and other Central Services to assist in the process of nation building. The "Iron Man of India" died in Bombay in December 1950. He left behind a united India.

INDIA AND PAKISTAN 1947-50

The new border that separated India from Pakistan in the Punjab divided the Sikh population of four million in half. Nehru refused to let the British soldiers participate in the Boundary Force, and by August 15, 1947 less than 10,000 troops were in place in the Punjab. In the largest movement of people in world history about ten million Punjabis migrated in 1947. Muslims left East Punjab to go to Pakistan, and the Hindus and Sikhs departed from West Punjab to move to India. Indian intelligence estimated that at least 198,000 people were killed and that 100,000 were forcibly converted to Islam. However, Governor Francis Mudie of West Punjab estimated that half a million Muslims were killed, and the British High Commissioner in Karachi said the total was 800,000. As a result of the disruptions over the partition of India and Pakistan a total of fourteen million people lost their homes. Mountbatten and Jinnah met with the Joint Defense Council on August 29, and they abolished the Punjab Boundary Force. The soldiers went to their regiments in India and Pakistan, and these two dominions were to be responsible for law and order in their own territories. Pakistan formed the Ministry of Refugees and Rehabilitation at the beginning of September. British troops began withdrawing from India on August 17, and the last regiment left on February 18, 1948. The Indian Army was divided by religion with 270,000 soldiers going to India and 140,000 to Pakistan.

On August 15, 1947 Gandhi had fasted and prayed in a Muslim area of Calcutta instead of going to the ceremonies at Delhi. On the first of September he fasted again, and he only broke it three days later after municipal officials assured him that there had been no violence for 24 hours. While he was recovering from this fast, riots broke out in Delhi on September 7. In four days about two thousand people were killed. Gandhi went to Delhi to stop the pogroms against Muslims. When he was asked for a message, he wrote simply, "My life is my message." Meanwhile a caravan of 800,000 people was moving from West Punjab to India. The small state of Junagadh had announced its accession to Pakistan on August 15, 1947; but it is not contiguous with Pakistan, and the tiny states inside Junagadh had already acceded to India and asked for protection. India took over the administration of Junagadh on

November 9, and in the plebiscite on February 20, 1948 out of 190,870 votes only 91 favoured joining Pakistan rather than India.

In 1947 the Indian National Trade Union Congress was founded on Gandhian principles, and they represented 577 unions. Women began to be appointed to important positions. Sarojini Naidu became governor of the United Provinces. Vijayalakshmi Pandit was ambassador to Moscow and Washington.

Most of the people in Jammu and Kashmir were Muslims; but the Sikh conqueror Ranjit Singh had annexed it in 1819, and from 1846 it had been ruled by Hindu kings from the Dogra tribe. Their laws respected Hindu religion, and Muslims suffered discrimination. Maharaja Hari Singh began ruling in 1925, and he kept his capital at Jammu without going north to the summer centre at Srinagar. In 1931 the school-teacher Sheikh Muhammad Abdullah began asking for more state services for Muslims. In April 1932 the Glancy Commission reported that real grievances needed redress. A new constitution enabled Hindus and Muslims to be elected to the legislature, but the Maharaja still held autocratic power. In his presidential address to the Muslim Conference on March 26, 1938 Sheikh Abdullah called for an end to communalism, hoping that all the communities would fight for freedom. They endorsed the political struggle in June 1939 and changed their name to the National Conference.

Ghulam Abbas revived the Muslim Conference in 1941 with the support of the religious leader Yusuf Shah. Jinnah visited Kashmir for two months in the summer of 1944, and the Congress party held a conference a year later with Nehru, Azad, and Abdul Ghaffar Khan attending. The Maharaja refused to give up power and arrested the leaders of the National Conference. In 1946 Sheikh Abdullah demanded the abrogation of the 1846 Treaty of Amritsar that had established the Dogra dynasty, but the Congress party policy was not to displace Indian princes but to allow them to head constitutional democracies. The Muslim Conference did not support the Quit Kashmir campaign of the National Conference; but when they defied a ban on holding a conference in Srinagar, the Maharaja had their leaders arrested on October 25. The Government called an election for January 1947, and the National Conference with its leaders in jail boycotted the election. Only 182,000 voted out of the 707,400 who were eligible. The Muslim Conference participated and won 16 of the 21 Muslim seats. Congress party president Acharya Kripalani visited Kashmir in May. He pleaded for the release of Sheikh Abdullah and warned the Maharaja that he would have trouble if he did not join the Indian Union. Abdullah and most of the National leaders remained in jail until late September after India's Independence.

Pakistani leaders complained that Gurdaspur, which had the only road connecting India to Kashmir, had been awarded to East Punjab, and they believed that the Border Commission chairman Radcliffe was unfairly influenced by the Indians through Mountbatten. Sikhs were also upset that they lost some of their shrines to Pakistan. Sikhs and Hindus fled from West Punjab to the Kashmir Valley, and Muslims refugees went from East Punjab to Jammu. Maharaja Hari Singh signed standstill agreements with Pakistan and India, and a minister visited Delhi. The usual methods of repression by the Maharaja of Kashmir could not control the communal violence, and Muslim peasants in Poonch began a revolt. Then armed raiders from Pakistan crossed the border near Jammu, attacked villages, and stole cattle. Patel persuaded the Maharaja to release Sheikh Abdullah, and on October 3 Abdullah urged Kashmir to join India. He considered Nehru his best friend, and he revered Gandhi. Meanwhile the Muslims formed the Azad Kashmir government with the local barrister Muhammad Ibrahim as president.

Mehr Chand Mahajan replaced General Janak Singh as prime minister of Kashmir on October 15, and on that day he held a press conference and sent a telegram to Pakistan protesting the raids. One week later about five thousand tribesmen in British trucks and jeeps from the Pakistan army sacked Muzaffarabad and began pillaging and raping inside Kashmir. The Maharaja's army of 8,000 was defeated and fled. British officers in Pakistan informed their British counterparts in India of the raids. The deputy prime minister of Kashmir went to Delhi, and on October 25 he asked the Indian Defense Committee for help. That day the Pakistan army notified New Delhi that "tribal volunteers" had entered Kashmir. Sheikh Abdullah went to Nehru's house and also asked for aid. V. P. Menon flew to Jammu and persuaded the Maharaja to sign a letter of conditional accession to India; a plebiscite was to be held when conditions returned to normal. Kashmir Prime Minister Mahajan returned with Menon to New Delhi and met with Nehru and Patel. Menon later wrote that Kashmir had signed the accession papers before India sent troops, but Mahajan's report contradicted this. Nehru telegraphed Liaquat Ali Khan on October 26 that India was sending troops to Kashmir.

Governor-General Mountbatten wrote a letter to accept Kashmir's accession. More than a hundred planes carried troops and supplies from India, and 329 soldiers arrived on October 27 just in time to save Srinagar. By the end of October they had been joined by three battalions, and the raiders retreated. Jinnah ordered General Gracey to move Pakistani troops into Kashmir, but he refused to do so without the approval of Field Marshal Claude Auchinleck, who flew to Lahore on October 28 and persuaded Jinnah to withdraw his invasion order. The next day Nehru and Patel refused to go to Lahore, and Mountbatten went only with his chief of staff Ismay and met with Liaquat and Jinnah. Meanwhile Gandhi was telling his prayer meetings that the kings and maharajas of the Indian states had been puppets of British imperialism, but now the people had become the real rulers.

In a broadcast on November 2 Nehru asked how the tribesmen crossing the frontier had been "armed so effectively," but Pakistani prime minister Liaquat Ali Khan condemned the "illegal ownership" of Kashmir by the infamous Amritsar Treaty. Sheikh Abdullah inspired the popular resistance to the raiders, and by November 8 they had taken Baramulla. Pakistan refused to withdraw its forces and suggested the United Nations. Patel decided to stop honoring

India's financial commitments to Pakistan until they stopped supporting the raiders. On December 22 the Indian cabinet demanded that Pakistan stop aiding the raiders and warned that they would appeal to the UN Security Council. By the end of 1947 the Indian army had cleared the invaders out of the Kashmir Valley. India's appeal to the UN on the first day of 1948 mentioned that their forces were opposed by 34,000 raiders. At a press conference the next day Nehru asked Pakistan to withdraw their personnel from Kashmir. Pakistan replied on January 15, accusing India of genocide against Muslims in East Punjab. Two days later the UN Security Council adopted a resolution establishing the UN Commission for India and Pakistan (UNCIP). India wanted the Security Council to recognize Pakistani aggression in Kashmir; but Pakistan believed the accession was not legally valid, and they would not withdraw unless India did so too.

Gandhi was criticized for approving India's action in Kashmir; but he believed it was justified because not to stand one's ground to defend oneself against an aggressor would be cowardice. Although he may not help one retaliate, Gandhi believed that he must not let a coward find shelter behind the guise of nonviolence. However, he advised that India should transfer the money due to Pakistan. Gandhi began a fast on January 13, 1948 and said he would continue until people stopped killing each other or he died. On the third day Patel and the Indian cabinet gave in and agreed to pay the £40 million from India's assets that they had withheld from Pakistan because of Kashmir. Hindu refugees outside the gate chanted "Let Gandhi die," and the visiting Nehru angrily challenged them to kill him first, causing them to disperse. Azad learned from the physically weakened Gandhi his demands that Muslims be allowed to move freely, live where they want with no economic boycott, and that 117 mosques should be returned to them. Gandhi's kidneys were not functioning well. A Congress committee got 130 leaders that included Hindus, Muslims, Sikhs, Christians, and others to sign a peace agreement, and 200,000 people took a written pledge to protect

Muslims. So on January 18 he ended his fast. Although this religious hatred saddened Gandhi, India had gained independence, accomplishing the greatest nonviolent revolution in the history of the world.

Gandhi held open prayer meetings in Delhi for all faiths, and anyone could attend. A small conspiracy of Hindus in the extremist Rashtriya Swayam Sewak Sangh (RSSS) plotted to assassinate him, but their first attempt with a bomb on January 20 failed. Nehru and Patel urged Gandhi to accept police protection, but he refused, saying that he trusted God and would not submit to anger or fear. Police learned the names of those who would carry out the assassination, but they were unable to stop them. On January 30 at a prayer meeting Nathuram Godse shot Gandhi three times at close range; with his last breath the Mahatma chanted the name of God. More than a million people attended his funeral. Because the assassin was a Maharashtrian Brahmin, assaults in Maharashtra were made against the Brahmin and Bania communities; but most of the communal violence stopped. After a trial the assassin Nathuram Godse and one accomplice were hanged, and five other conspirators were sentenced to life imprisonment. The RSSS and other organizations of communal violence were banned.

The Eastern States merged into the provinces of Orissa and the Central Provinces. In March and April 1948 many of the smaller states were integrated into Mataya, Kathiawar, Rajasthan, and Vindhya Pradesh. In May, the Madhya States Union was formed from Gwalior, Indore, and Malwa. The Patiala and East Punjab States Union began in July. Junagadh and some adjoining states joined Kathiawar on the last day of 1948. The Greater Rajasthan Union was inaugurated as the largest union of states with 13 million people in March 1949. Baroda merged into Bombay in May, and Bhopal, Cooch Behar, Tripura, and Manipur joined the Central administration. By November all the states had become integrated except for Hyderabad and Kashmir. A total of 554 states were dissolved and integrated into the Union of India.

Hyderabad had a population of 16 million, who were mostly Hindu, but since the Mughal reign of Aurangzeb they had been ruled by the Nizam and elite Muslims. The seventh Nizam, Mir Usman Ali Khan, wanted to remain independent. When India withheld Pakistan's Rs. 550 million share of the treasury in September 1947, the Nizam approved a Rs. 200 million loan to Pakistan. Hyderabad made a standstill agreement with the Indian Union in November to maintain its status quo before independence. The Nizam's private force of Razakars were led by Kasim Razvi, and they caused border incidents with Madras, the Central Provinces, and Bombay. The Government of India demanded that the Nizam disband them, but he refused and appealed to the United Nations. Two days after a final letter of warning on September 11, 1948, Indian troops entered Hyderabad. Major-General El Edroos surrendered Hyderabad to Major-General J. N. Chaudhury of the Indian Army on September 18. Kasim Razvi was arrested, and the Nizam withdrew his case from the UN Security Council. Chaudhury became the military governor, and Hyderabad acceded to the Indian Union on January 26, 1950.

The Kashmir Maharaja appointed Sheikh Abdullah prime minister in March 1948. He was a socialist and proposed radical land reform without compensating land-owners. Pakistan's military leaders allowed soldiers to desert their army in order to raid in Kashmir, and in April their British commander-in-chief approved their sending in troops for "self-defense." India also launched an offensive in the spring, and neither side was able to advance much. On April 21 the UN Security Council resolved to send five commissioners to oversee the withdrawal by Pakistani and Indian troops. A Plebiscite Administration was to be set up to supervise the police. However, both Pakistan and India refused to accept the resolution. Mountbatten left India in June 1948, and Rajagopalacharya became the first Indian governor-general.

Mediation efforts in Kashmir failed, and the UNCIP commission did not arrive in Kashmir until July. UNCIP learned on the first day that Pakistan had sent in regular troops, but they did not inform the Security Council nor India until much later. The Commission told Pakistan that they had violated international law. Sheikh Abdullah agreed with Nehru that the best solution was to partition Kashmir, but Pakistan rejected this. On August 13 the UN Security Council proposed a cease fire. India agreed with minor modifications, but Pakistan demanded conditions that the Commission would not accept. On October 12 delegates of Kashmir passed a National Conference resolution recommending permanent accession to India. At the very end of 1948 a cease-fire agreement was signed, and US Admiral Chester W. Nimitz was appointed UN Administrator for the plebiscite.

The Maharaja passed on restricted power to his son Karan Singh when he left Kashmir for health reasons in June 1949. UNCIP invited the two governments to meet at Karachi in July, and the cease-fire line was established. The Commission proposed an arbitrator, and Pakistan accepted; but India refused, fearing they would be at a military disadvantage if Pakistan invaded again with Azad Kashmir forces. On December 17 the UN Security Council appointed the Canadian General McNaughton to mediate, but India's B. N. Rau argued that Pakistan made the plebiscite problematic by sending troops into Kashmir, occupying the northern areas, and building up the Azad forces. Pakistan's representative Zafrulla Khan pointed out that Muslims made up 77% of Kashmir. The UN Security Council appointed the Australian Owen Dixon the next mediator on April 12, 1950, but he concluded that only bilateral talks between India and Pakistan could solve the problem of Kashmir.

In January 1948 a food shortage caused the refugee camps in West Punjab to become more permanent, and in April the camps had 750,000 people. Jinnah made a broadcast to the United States in February and said that Pakistan would not be a theocratic state but would have a democratic constitution with equal rights for all religions. On February 28 Pakistan's finance minister Ghulam Muhammad presented an annual budget to the Karachi assembly calling for £27.8 million in military spending out of total expenditures of £39.4 million. A deficit of £25.1 million was expected. India also allocated more than half its budget for defense and projected a deficit of £20 million. In March the governments of India and Pakistan declared each other foreign nations in regard to customs and excise duty. Governor-General Jinnah only visited East Pakistan once, and he made his last major public address at Dacca on March 21 in English. His audience spoke Bengali, but he announced that Pakistan's official language would be "Urdu and no other language." East Pakistan was much smaller in area than West Pakistan, but it had a larger population. It would become Bangladesh in 1971.

On March 7, 1949 the Constituent Assembly of Pakistan adopted the Objectives Resolution that called for a constitution that would allow the state to exercise its power through the people's chosen representatives with principles of democracy, freedom, equality, tolerance, and social justice in accord with the teachings of Islam with provisions to protect minorities and depressed classes by guaranteeing equal rights with freedom of thought, expression, belief, faith, worship, and association, with the independence of the judiciary secured, and the rights of the Federation's territories safeguarded.

The canals in the divided Punjab were a source of dispute. When Pakistan did not renew the agreement, on April 1 the East Punjab Government cut off the water supply from the canals going into Pakistan from the Ravi and Sutlej rivers. Pakistan made another agreement on May 4; but later they complained that they had accepted it under duress. India believed that Pakistan had enough water from their rivers, and at the Inter-Dominion Conference in August 1949 they pressed for a joint survey of the water resources of the Indus rivers.

India followed the British government in devaluing the pound sterling by 30% in September, but Pakistan declined to do so. So the Indian Government refused to recognize the Pakistani rupee, and trade between the two countries stopped for seven months.

In the first three months of 1950 a half million refugees went from East Pakistan to India. The prime ministers Nehru and Liaquat

Ali Khan met, and on April 8 they made a general agreement on minorities and trade-related issues. The problem of evacuee property had not been solved yet because Hindu refugees had left behind property worth 14 billion rupees, while Muslims had left property valued at only 2 billion rupees in India. The Pakistan Ministry of Refugees calculated that West Pakistan had 7,900,000 Muslim refugees. An agreement was made at the fifth Inter-Dominion Conference at Karachi in January 1949, but the next month Pakistan ordered rent slashed on urban evacuee property by up to 80%. The Indian Government considered this a subtle way of undermining the agreement, and Pakistan accused India of not implementing the agreement. By the end of 1950 they still could not agree. That year 600,000 more refugees entered Pakistan from India.

India adopted a new constitution on November 26, 1949, and it came into force on January 26, 1950. The Constitution established a democratic republic to secure justice, liberty, equality, and fraternity and to guarantee all citizens equality before the law and freedom of speech, expression, assembly, conscience, and worship regardless of religion, race, caste, sex, and place of birth. English would continue to be the official language for fifteen years, but thereafter the official language would be Hindi. A president and vice president are elected for five-year terms. The Council of States is elected by the legislators in each state, but voters elect the House of the People directly. Governors of the states are appointed by the President for five-year terms, and the chief ministers in each state are appointed by the governors. The Supreme Court has jurisdiction over disputes between states and hears appeals from any High Court in a state. The first elections were conducted without major difficulties, and the Congress party was victorious. On January 24, 1950 Rajendra Prasad was elected the first President of India. Socialists had left the Congress party and formed their own party in March 1948. Their policy statement in October 1949 explained that they stood for democratic socialism and individual rights while they rejected totalitarian Communism. After the conservative Deputy Prime Minister Patel died in December 1950, Nehru's influence became even greater.

In a speech on foreign policy on December 4, 1947 Nehru affirmed that India stands for peace as well as freedom from imperialistic control. He began the policy that led the non-aligned movement when he stated that they avoid foreign entanglements by not joining either power bloc of the US or the USSR. He wrote in his 1949 book *Independence and After* that India's long history is significant. Although India had little military power he argued that India could have much influence because of the "world situation in which force as a factor in international affairs will be reduced to the absolute minimum." On January 18, 1950 Prime Minister Nehru wrote a letter to the Prime Minister of Pakistan proposing a joint declaration by their governments "for the avoidance of war," but the Government of Pakistan rejected his terms as "too vague

THE CONSTITUENT ASSEMBLY

The Constitution was drafted by the Constituent Assembly, which was elected by the elected members of the provincial assemblies. Jawaharlal Nehru, C. Rajagopalacharya, Rajendra Prasad, Sardar Vallabhbhai Patel, Maulana Abul Kalam Azad and Shyama Prasad Mukherjee were some important figures in the Assembly. There were more than 30 members of the scheduled classes. Frank Anthony represented the Anglo-Indian community, and the Parsis were represented by H. P. Modi and R. K. Sidhwa. The Chairman of the Minorities Committee was Harendra Coomar Mukherjee, a distinguished Christian who represented all Christians other than Anglo-Indians. Prominent jurists like Alladi Krishnaswamy Iyer, B. R. Ambedkar, Bengal Narasingh Rao and K. M. Munshi Ganesh Mavlankar were also members of the Assembly. Sarojini Naidu, Hansa Mehta, Durgabai Deshmukh and Rajkumari Amrit Kaur were important women members. The first president of the Constituent Assembly was Sachidanand Sinha later, Rajendra Prasad was elected president of the Constituent Assembly. The members of the Constituent Assembly met for the first time in the year 1946 on December 9.

Grand Finale

Thus the task of uniting the country was complete. In the history of India stretched over ages, India became one and united for the first time and that too without shedding a drop of blood. That was the marvel of the personality of Sardar. The sterling qualities of leadership he had shown as leader of Satyagraha, flowered in greater way in the administration of the country, maintenance of law and order and ensuring stability of the country and making it invulnerable. It is because of these strong steps that earned him the title of "The man of steel". Sardar Vallabhbhai passed away in Mumbai on the morning of the 15th December 1950.

PARSI SATYAGRAHA AT BARDOLI

Gujarat Anjumans Say an Emphatic no to the Cosmopolitan World Body

Who would have thought that the death knell of the infamous cosmopolitan world body would be sounded in a tiny hamlet of Gujarat, Bardoli. But then Bardoli is no stranger to fame. For it was from Bardoli that Mahatma Gandhi and Sardar Vallabhbhai Patel lead the satyagraha movement for peaceful resistance against the British, almost a hundred years ago. It seems to me that there is that something in Bardoli that inspires one to stand up for what one believes in.

How else can one explain the phenomenal success of the Community meeting organized single handedly by the Bardoli Jarthosti Anjuman, to awaken the community to the dangers of the cosmopolitan world body? This tiny Anjuman with a large heart hosted over one thousand four hundred (1400) Parsis and Iranis, on February 26th and 27th, and took upon themselves the task of creating awareness in the community about this vital matter. The silent majority of the community made their strong presence felt that day. Coming from the far corners of Gujarat they passed a Resolution (with one lone dissenter), against the Bombay Parsi

Punchayet and the Federation of Parsi Zoroastrian Anjumans of India joining the cosmopolitan world body. This was after well known scholar Khojeste Mistree had taken them through a Power Point Presentation, done in Gujarati especially for the occasion, in which he analysed and dissected the Constitution of the controversial world body. The Presentation highlighted, (1) the marginalization of the BPP and the Federation of India in the world body, (2) the absence in the Constitution of the all-important Parsi/Irani identity, 3) the cosmopolitan nature of the body, as shown by the various Clauses that would make it possible for converts to gain entry and the resultant adverse impact it would have on the community in India and elsewhere, and 4) the thus far unbroken link between the Parsi/Irani identity and the Zoroastrian religion, which they are seeking to break in this proposed world body.

Resolution after Resolution passed at various public meetings has rejected the very idea of this cosmopolitan body. At a Public Meeting organized by The Parsee Voice in Bombay, on Nov. 23rd 2003, 750 Parsis/Iranis present had passed a similar Resolution against joining the world body. At the meeting of the Federation of Parsi Zoroastrian Anjumans of India at Ahmedabad, 24 of the 29 anjuman representatives present, reiterated their opposition to it and forwarded their protest to the Chairman in writing. Since then, a remarkable fifty (50) of the 69 anjumans registered with the Federation have joined the opposition to the world body. If one considers that 13 of the 69 anjumans of FPZAI are defunct, in real term numbers this amounts to 50 out of 56 anjumans opposing the world body! If after all this, BPP spokesperson, Mr. Godrej Dotivala, says to the media, "they are in the minority", then it is obvious that Mr. Dotivala is deliberately misleading the media and through it, the community. Why doesn't Mr. Dotivala supply us with some proof of the "majority" he seems to think is for the cosmopolitan world body?

Coming back to Bardoli, what can I say? The tiny anjuman stole the show and our hearts. Their organizational skills were outstanding, their hospitality overwhelming and heartwarming, and the gaam nu bhonu, tastier than any lagan nu bhonu I've tasted this season. President of the anjuman Mr. Jamshed Mohta has wonderful ideas and big dreams for the community and has the confidence and ability to carry them through. MOHTA (meaning big) saheb's very name says it all; and his magnanimous actions match his name. Secretary of Bardoli Jarthosti Anjuman, Pervez Mehta is no less dynamic and he along with the other trustees and their families, all, opened up their homes and hearts to us.

Underlying all the hard work put in by the Bardoli team was their strong commitment and deep concern for the community and if our leaders and BPP trustees had been there with us, they would have seen for themselves that the good food and great hospitality, though greatly appreciated, were not the crowd pulling attractions they have been made out to be. The common cause at the Bardoli meeting was concern for the religion; and belittling those who had gathered at Bardoli, in a desperate attempt to dismiss the opposition to the world body, is not only in very bad taste, but also rather ludicrous. (Both the editor of Jame as well as BPP spokesperson Dotiwala have made snide remarks in the media, insinuating that 1200 community members had trooped to Bardoli solely for the food!!)

The support from Surat (Trustees and community members alike) was united and strong. Poona too was well represented and stands firmly behind tradition. The Trustees of Poona have in fact ratified the stand taken by them at the Federation meeting (opposing the cosmopolitan world body) by passing a Resolution emphasizing the same, at their AGM. These are leaders working with transparency and accountability, in consonance with the sentiments of their constituents; and one salutes them for that!

Guest of honour, Vada Dastur Cyrus Dastur of Surat spoke passionately for preserving tradition and quoted extensively from the Scriptures to make his point. Chief Guest, illustrious industrialist Mr. Areez P. Khambatta captivated the audience with personal and professional tips on entrepreneurship; and having taken the lead in emphasizing the need for the community to form a Parsi/Irani world body to safeguard Parsi/Irani interests, he announced a personal donation of Rupees one crore towards a traditionally constituted Parsi/Irani world body that would uphold and preserve the tenets and traditions of our Religion and would function under the guidance of a Council of High Priests. WORLD ALLIANCE OF PARSI IRANI ZARTHOSTIS (WAPIZ) would be the voice of the Parsis/ Iranis in the world.

18 year-old Zarvan Patvi provided a fitting finale when he requested the mike at the end of the Meet, to recite a few lines he had specially composed for the occasion. "I hope this message goes to the BPP and to all our other leaders" he said as he recited the couplets:

Na jaane din, na jaane dharam,

Na khuda no dar, na aankh maa sharam.

Nathi je-lokonaa tan per sadro, nathi je-lokunaa tan per kusti,

Evaaone laiyne vadhaarvaa chaaliya vasti.

Pasti na moole vechai jase tamaari hasti, jo khuda ni saathe kari aavi harkat sasti.

Na bujhi chhe, na bujhse jyot maaraa Jarthosti Din ni.

Na bujhi chhe, na bujhse jyot maaraa Jarthosti Din ni; Jyaa sudhi hamaaraa dil maa chhe aatash parasti,

Chhaiye hame Jarthosti.

The youth that came in large numbers to the meeting could teach many of us many a religious lesson. Gujarat has said an emphatic NO to the cosmopolitan world body. Bardoli Jarthosti Anjuman (the small anjuman with the large heart), and the Parsis/ Iranis of Navsari, Surat, Ahmedabad, Mt. Abu and a host of other anjumans in and around Gujarat, have stood up for what they believe in. Are our leaders listening?

As Congress President and the Election of 1950

In spite of being ideologically at odds with both the right-wing Vallabhbhai Patel and the left-wing Jawaharlal Nehru-he was elected Congress President for the crucial years around Indian independence in 1947. After Gandhi's assassination in January 1948, Nehru rejected his demand that the party's views should be sought in all decisions. Nehru, with the support of Patel, told Kripalani that while the party was entitled to lay down the broad principles and guidelines, it could not be granted a say in the government's day-to-day affairs. This precedent became central to the relationship between government and ruling party in subsequent decades.

Nehru, however, supported Kripalani in the election of the Congress President in 1950. The election was considered a vital battle for the party between the left, led by Nehru, and the right, led by Patel. Kripalani went up against Patel's candidate, the Hindu nationalist Purushottam Das Tandon. In an atmosphere soured by communal tension, the controversial reconstruction of the Somnath Temple, the founding of the Jan Sangh, and the Nehru-Liaquat Pact, as well as differences on economic policy, Tandon narrowly defeated Kripalani. Bruised by his defeat, and disillusioned by what he viewed as the abandonment of the Gandhian ideal of a countless village republics, Kripalani left the Congress and became one of the founders of the Kisan Mazdoor Praja Party. This party subsequently merged with the Socialist Party of India to form the Praja Socialist Party.

For a while it was even believed that Nehru, stung by the defeat, was considering abandoning the Congress as well; his several offers of resignation at the time were all, however, shouted down. A great many of the more progressive elements of the party left in the months following the election, however. Congress's subsequent bias to the right was only balanced when Nehru obtained the resignation of Tandon in the run up to the general elections of 1951.

Patel and P.Das Tandon

He and Nehru had good relations in the beginning; Nehru who commended the "No Tax" campaign started by Tandon in 1930. In the 1940s the differences between them increased. While Tandon was not perceived to be power-hungry, his relation with Nehru was not on good terms and he was believed to be a protege of Sardar Vallabhbhai Patel. In 1950, his successful election to the post of Congress President against Acharya Kriplani, who was widely believed to be backed by Nehru, put the latter in a tight spot. The relations between the party and the government suffered during that period. Subsequently, it became a sort of unwritten norm for the leader of the government to also be the party president or at the least, have a pliable candidate in the post.

A Divided Freedom

As the Second World War was moving to its final stage, the British Government released Gandhi in May 1944. On his release, Gandhi proposed to meet Jinnah and discuss the communal situation with him. As a result they held a series of parleys from 9 September till 27 September. In these parleys, the question of Partition was discussed. The discussions were centred on the Rajagopalchari or the CR formula as it was called. The principal provisions of the formula were:

- The Muslim League was to endorse the demand for independence of the country and cooperate with the Indian National Congress in forming an Interim government.
- Contiguous districts in the Northwest and East of India would be demarcated and plebiscite would be held to decide whether or not they should be separated from India.

Gandhi accepted the right of self-determination and even of secession of the two predominantly Muslim territories in India while Jinnah was demanding for Pakistan. In essence Gandhi insisted on independence first and secession later while Jinnah wanted Pakistan first and independence later. Jinnah continued to insist that the Muslims of India constituted a separate nation. This was Jinnah's trump card. In the words of Sri Aurobindo: *"The idea of two nationalities in India is only a newly-fangled notion invented by Jinnah for his purposes and contrary to the facts. More than 90% of the Indian Mussalmans are descendants of converted Hindus and belong as much to the Indian nation as the Hindus themselves. This process of conversion has continued all along; Jinnah is himself a descendant of a Hindu, converted in fairly recent times, named Jinahbhai and many of the most famous Mohammedan leaders have a similar origin".*

The talks broke down as Jinnah refused to negotiate any further. Durga Das had written earlier regarding the talks: 'Mr Jinnah will never come to an agreement during the war. While he is intransigent he is on top; the moment he settles with the Congress, the League will get merged in the nationalist movement and will never be able to dictate terms to the Congress'. Sri Aurobindo too had remarked: "Instead of doing what is necessary, the Congress is trying to flirt with Jinnah, and Jinnah simply thinks that he has to obstinately stick to his terms to get them. The more they try, the more Jinnah becomes intransigent".

In early 1945, Lord Wavell the Viceroy of India announced a plan 'designed to ease the present political situation and to advance India towards her goal of full self-government'. He proposed that a Conference be held in Simla, the summer capital of India, to which leaders of all the parties in India would be invited. This list included the Congress, the Muslim League, the Scheduled Castes, the Sikhs, and some other groups. The main topic of discussion would be the formation of a new Executive Council. It was suggested that all the members of this body would be Indians, except the Viceroy and the Commander in Chief.

Gandhi raised an objection to the classification 'Caste Hindus' whom the Congress was supposed to represent. Jinnah objected on two counts: first, that the list of members suggested by the Muslim League would be final and second that all Muslim members were to be from the Muslim League alone. Despite these objections, the Conference met and discussions were held. The Viceroy was unable to accept the demands of Jinnah; failing to convince him he announced that the Conference had failed. This act of the Viceroy gave Jinnah the veto power, which he used, to full effect in the following days.

In August 1945, the War came to an end with the dropping of two atom bombs on Japan. No doubt, Britain with the help of the Allies had crushed both Germany and Japan; but in the life and death battle it had exhausted its manpower and economic resources to such an extent that it could never again hope to recover its old power and prestige. The world situation had completely changed and it was evident that India would get her freedom as a result of new world circumstances. In the words of Leonard Mosley: "From the moment, in 1945, when war was over and the post-war world began to reshape itself, no one of clear mind had any doubt that the Indian people would achieve the independence from British rule.... After Singapore, Burma and the sinking of her finest ships by the Japanese, Britain would never again be able to demonstrate in Asia the background of strength and influence which had for so long enabled her to rule a million people with one man on the spot". It is clear therefore that it was the world circumstances and not the Quit India movement that was responsible for India's freedom. The question then predominant was no longer the attainment of freedom, which was inevitable, but the communal problem.

Some time towards the end of 1945 elections were held in the Provinces. The Congress won seven provinces, while the Muslim League won in Bengal and Sind. In Punjab it was forestalled by a coalition of the Congress and the Akalis. But one thing became clear in these elections; the Muslims were solidly behind the League while the rest of the country was with the Congress. At the same time two other factors hastened the ushering in of freedom. The first one was the trial of the INA soldiers and the second one was the revolt of the sailors serving in the Indian Royal Navy.

The soldiers of the INA were charged with committing war against the King. A Military Tribunal was set up and three officers were put on public trial; the Indian public did not know much about the INA till then, but as a result of the public trial they came to be regarded as a band of patriotic heroes who fought for the liberation of the motherland. The trial aroused great interest all over the country and popular demonstrations were held leading sometimes to violent demonstrations. The Government quailed before the storm and although the officers were convicted to sentence of transportation for life, it was soon changed to being simply cashiered.

On 18 February 1946, some ratings of the Signal School in Bombay went on a hunger strike in protest against the treatment being meted out to them by Royal Navy. Soon others in different parts of the country joined them and the situation began to get completely out of hand. They took possession of some of the ships and strikes and hartals were organised all over the country. The police had to open fire and the military had to be called in to restore order. Finally, due largely to the efforts of Sardar Vallabhbhai Patel, the ratings surrendered on 23 February.

On 19 February, one day after the Mutiny broke out, the Government announced the decision to send out a special mission consisting of three cabinet Ministers. This group known as the Cabinet Mission was made up of the following members: Lord Pethick Lawrence, Secretary of State for India, Sri Stafford Cripps, President of the Board of Trade and A.V.Alexander, First Lord of the Admiralty. They were, in association with the Viceroy, sent to find an agreement with the leaders of the different political parties on the principles and procedures relating to the constitutional issue. They arrived in India on 24 March 1946. They spent five weeks meeting the leaders of all the parties and representative groups. On 5 May, a conference of leaders of the Congress and Muslim League was held in Simla to consider the grouping of provinces, the character of the federal union and the setting up of the constitutional machinery. But it was unable to arrive at a consensus and therefore the mission issued a statement containing its own proposal on 16 May 1946. The main points of the Cabinet Mission Plan were:

- The formation of an undivided Union of India embracing both British India and the States, which should deal with three subjects: Foreign Affairs, Defence and Communications.
- The provinces would have complete autonomy with all other powers vested in them. The demands of the Muslim League would be thus met.

- A proposal for the creation of an intermediate level between the centre and the provinces. It was proposed that there could be three regional groupings – one in the northwest, one in the northeast and one consisting the rest of the country. The provinces in each group would be allowed to associate themselves in units, each having its own executive and legislature.

Both the Congress and the League seemed to be in two minds with regard to the proposals of the Cabinet Mission; they were reluctant to reject them outright and yet unwilling to accept them as they stood. The Muslim League at first accepted the Plan with the hope that it would ultimately result in the establishment of Pakistan. The Congress, despite its reservations, agreed to join the Constituent Assembly. Then followed an unfortunate incident, which changed the whole course of events. Nehru who was elected President of the Congress gave a Press conference on 10 July. In the words of Leonard Mosley: "And on 10 July after he had been elected President, he called the Press together for a conference to discuss the policy as the new head of Congress. It was a moment in history when circumspection should have been the order of the day. There was much to be gained by silence.

The fortunes of India were in the balance, and one false move could upset them. Nehru chose this moment to launch into what his biographer, Michael Brecher, has described as one of the most fiery and provocative statements in his forty years of public life". He goes on to say: "Did he realise what he was saying? He was telling the world that once in power, the Congress would use its strength at the Centre to alter the Cabinet Mission Plan as it thought fit". That was the flashpoint and soon "the Hindus and Muslims were back in two fuming camps". This was the just the thing that Jinnah was waiting for, arguing that this statement of Nehru represented the real mind of the Congress. Quite inevitably, the Muslim League decided to back out and demanded the immediate establishment of Pakistan. In order to bring this about, Jinnah called upon the Muslims to resort to Direct Action. He explained that the participation of the Muslims in the proposed constitution making machinery was fraught with danger. He said that while the British had machine guns to enforce their will and the Hindus the weapon of civil resistance, the Muslims alone remained defenceless. It followed that they must bid good-bye to constitutional methods and prepare for self-defence and self-preservation by resorting to direct action. 16 August was fixed as the day for Direct Action. While the tension was building the Viceroy decided on 12 August to invite the Congress to form the Interim Government; that proved to be the last straw for Jinnah. Nehru invited Jinnah to participate in the Interim Government but he declined the invitation. At that time, the president of the All-India-Jamaitul Ulma-I-Islam, Shabbir Ahmad Usmani declared that no power on earth can crush the Muslims. 'Living he is a Gazi and killed in action he is a martyr'.

In Calcutta, on 16 August the day began with public demonstrations, hartals and hoisting of the Muslim League flag. Soon clashes began and spread to the whole city. Utter confusion prevailed in the city and the hooligans had a field day indulging in stabbing, killing, arson and criminal assaults on women.

The mob fury continued for four days with the Government standing by and proving to be utterly ineffective to meet the situation. It is estimated that thousands were killed, tens of thousands injured, lakhs left homeless and property worth crores of rupees destroyed. Bengal was then under the Muslim League and the Chief Minister was Suhrawardy. The Statesman wrote: 'this is not a riot. For three days the city concentrated on unrestrained civil war. Upon whom the main guilt for it rests is manifest. Where the primary blame lies is where we have squarely put it – upon the Provincial Muslim League Cabinet and particularly the Chief Minister'. The rioting soon spread to other parts like Noahkali and Tipperah where the Muslims were in a majority. The Hindus were butchered mercilessly and in retaliation the Hindus in Bihar took revenge. All in all it was a sordid story of horror and cruelty. This was the way Jinnah had chosen to prove his point: *Hindus and Muslims could not live together.*

The Interim Government led by Nehru was sworn in on 2 September. The Muslim League refused to participate in it. However on 13 October, Jinnah agreed to participate and sent a list of five ministers who would be accommodated. One of the ministers was Liaquat Ali Khan who was given the important Finance portfolio. 'In the government but against it', Liaquat used his pivotal position to bring the government to a standstill. Elections to the Constituent Assembly were held in the second half of the year and were completed by December. It was decided to convene the Assembly on 9 December. Jinnah called upon the members of the Muslim League to boycott the Assembly. Naturally the Congress demanded that the League should either attend the Assembly or quit the Interim Government. This led to a complete deadlock. Jinnah knew that all that he had to do was to boycott the Assembly in order to render nugatory any decision regarding the Constitution of an Indian Union. Jinnah warned in his speeches that the only alternative to Pakistan was civil war. Under this threat, the British government decided that the decisions of the Constituent Assembly could not be implemented in so far as they affected the areas under Muslim majority. A month later, the League demanded the dissolution of the Assembly.

The country was facing a grave crisis. It was at this time that Prime Minister Atlee took a bold decision. He was of the view that it was necessary to take a clear-cut decision and he decided that the British government should fix a date for the withdrawal of British power in India. As a result, Attlee announced: "The present state of uncertainty is fraught with danger and cannot be indefinitely prolonged. His Majesty's Government wish to make it clear that it is their definite intention to take necessary steps to effect the transference of power to responsible Indian hands by a date not later than June 1948". In order to perform this task he announced that Lord Mountbatten would replace Lord Wavell as Viceroy. Immediately the political tempo was whipped up.

The Muslim League made a desperate attempt to secure control over the Provinces, which it planned to be attached to Pakistan. Direct Action was started in Assam but with little success. But in

Sind and the North-West Frontier Provinces a systematic genocide was carried on against the Sikhs and the Hindus who were in a minority. On January 27, 1947 Mian Iftikharuddin said at a Lahore public meeting of Muslims: "We have come here to tell you that if you can carry on the fight with the same determination and discipline as had been displayed during the past three days, not only will you have achieved victory in the Punjab, but you will also have reached nearer to your goal of Pakistan."

Lord Mountbatten arrived in India on 22 March. He was sent with all the powers to effect the transfer of power. Immediately he held meetings and consultations with all parties. He was soon convinced that partition was inevitable. Jinnah was determined to have even a truncated Pakistan. He said: "I do not care how little you give me, so long as you give it to me completely". Sardar Vallabhbhai Patel and Jawaharlal Nehru accepted the plan with a heavy heart. Gandhi however remained adamantly opposed to partition. He even went so far as to suggest that Jinnah could be made the first Prime Minister of a United India. The Congress rejected the proposal outright. Gandhi then not only withdrew his proposal but also withdrew himself from all politics leaving all negotiations to the Working Committee.

Mountbatten then, along with the Hindu, Muslim and Sikh leaders worked out a scheme, which was approved later by the British Cabinet. On 3 June, Prime Minister Attlee announced in the House of Commons the scheme known as the June 3rd or Mountbatten Plan. The Plan dealt with the method by which power would be transferred to Indian hands and particularly the methods by which Muslim majority provinces would choose whether to remain in India or join the new State Pakistan. The next day, Mountbatten announced that the final transfer of power would not be later than June 1948, but a few days later it was decided that the date would be 15 August 1947. On 12 June the Congress Working Committee met and passed a resolution accepting partition. An extract from the resolution: "The Congress had worked hard and sacrificed everything for the sake of unity. But there was a limit beyond which it could not go. The choice today was between accepting the statement of June 3 or committing suicide". Gandhi, who a few days back, opposed the formation of Pakistan now supported the resolution. However there were still some Congress leaders who opposed this resolution. One such person was Purushottam Das Tandon. He said: " Acceptance of the resolution will be an abject surrender to the British and the Muslim League. The admission of the Working Committee was an admission of weakness and the result of a sense of despair. The Partition would not benefit either community – the Hindus in Pakistan and the Muslims in India would both live in fear". Despite all this the plan was accepted and so in less than ten weeks, India was to be free and partitioned. The provinces of Baluchistan, Sind and the North-Western Provinces went to Pakistan. Punjab and Bengal were to be divided. East Punjab and West Bengal were to be part of India while West Punjab and East Bengal were to form part of Pakistan. Boundary commissions were set up to delineate the boundaries between these two provinces.

While all this was happening, the Princely States, which were also ruled by Britain, were left free to decide their own fate. They could become sovereign States or voluntarily join India or Pakistan. If they chose to be free, as at one time it seemed that they would, it would have meant a balkanisation of India with very grave consequences. Sardar Vallabhbhai Patel with the help of VP Menon convinced the princes that it was in their interest to join the Indian Union. By August, most of them had signed the Instrument of Accession by which they became formally part of India. Three States however held out; these were the States of Junagadh, Kashmir and Hyderabad. Soon after India attained independence, Junagadh's eccentric ruler escaped to Pakistan, while the Maharaja of Kashmir acceded to India in the month of October. The Nizam of Hyderabad held out for over a year.

As the boundary lines were being drawn, the communal hatred and cruelty that was seething for the last one year reached its crescendo. There is perhaps no parallel in the history of India to the barbarity and massacre that took place in the following days. The story may be summed up thus: six hundred thousand dead, 14 million driven from their homes, one hundred thousand young girls kidnapped, forcibly converted or sold on the auction block. The Dominion of Pakistan was inaugurated in Karachi on 14 August. On 15 August India became an Independent State. It was a moment of sorrow and destruction but at the same time millions of Indians were celebrating with great joy and enthusiasm.

Gandhi's dreams of nonviolence and Hindu-Muslim unity lay inevitably shattered in pieces, for they were built on castles of sand. On the other hand Sri Aurobindo said: "Pakistan was created by falsehood, fraud and force".

On the midnight of 15 August, Jawaharlal Nehru addressed the Constituent Assembly. Here is an extract from that speech: "Long years ago we made a tryst with destiny, and now the time comes when we shall resume our pledge, not wholly or in full measure, but very substantially. At the stroke of the midnight hour, when the world sleeps, India will wake to life and freedom. A moment comes, which comes but rarely in history, when we step out from the old to the new, when an age ends, and when the soul of a nation, long suppressed, finds utterance. It is fitting that at this solemn moment we take the pledge of dedication to the service of India and her people and to the still larger cause of humanity".

It is important to note that 15 August was the birthday of Sri Aurobindo. On the same day, Sri Aurobindo too gave a message. Here is an extract from the message: "August 15th, 1947 is the birthday of free India. It marks for her the end of an old era, the beginning of a new age.

But we can also make it by our life and acts as a free nation an important date in a new age opening for the whole world, for the political, social, cultural and spiritual future of humanity. As a mystic, I take this identification, not as a coincidence or fortuitous accident, but as a sanction and seal of the Divine Power which guides my steps on the work with which I began life. Indeed almost all the world movements which I hoped to see fulfilled in my lifetime, though at that time they looked like impossible dreams, I can observe on this day either approaching fruition or initiated and on the way to their achievement.....

India is free but she has not achieved unity, only a fissured and broken freedom.... The old communal division into Hindu and Muslim seems to have hardened into the figure of a permanent political division of the country. It is to be hoped that the Congress and the nation will not accept the settled fact as forever settled or as anything more than a temporary expedient. For if it lasts, India may be seriously weakened, even crippled: civil strife may remain always possible, possible even a new invasion and foreign conquest. The partition of the country must go,—it is to be hoped by a slackening of tension, by a progressive understanding of the need of peace and concord, by the constant necessity of common and concerted action, even of an instrument of union for that purpose. In this way unity may come about under whatever form—the exact form may have a pragmatic but not a fundamental importance. But by whatever means, the division must and will go. For without it the destiny of India might be seriously impaired and even frustrated.

3

Role in Kheda and Bardoli Satyagrahas

Sardar Patel's first major participation was during the Kheda Struggle. The Kheda division of Gujarat was reeling under a severe drought and the peasants asked for relief from the high rate of taxes. Mahatma Gandhi had approved of a struggle there, but could not lead it himself due to his activities leading a similar movement in Champaran, Bihar. Asking for one Gujarati activist to volunteer full-time to the Kheda cause, Patel raised his hand and stood up. Along with Narhari Parikh and Mohanlal Pandya, two former lawyers and students of Gandhi, Patel began a village-to-village tour, detailed grievances and asking villagers for their support for a state-wide revolt. All throughout the state, almost every villager, Hindu and Muslim backed Patel's efforts and leadership. Patel emphasized complete nonviolence despite any provocation, and unity amongst all villagers. Patel was greatly assisted by nationalists like Abbas Tyabji and the Sarabhai family of Ahmedabad.

When revenue was refused, the government sent police and intimidation squads to seize property, including confiscating barn animals and whole farms. Thousands of activists and farmers were arrested, but almost no incident of violence from the villagers was reported. Many families throughout Gujarat attempted to help the resistors by supplying them with food, clothing and other necessities. The state's people socially boycotted and segregated individuals and villages that supported the government and paid revenues. The revolt evoked great sympathy around India, but was not fought for the explicit cause of Indian independence.

The revolt ended in 1919, when the government compromised and suspended payment of revenue, even scaling back the rate. Vallabhbhai Patel emerged as an icon and hero to Gujaratis, admired and hailed by Indian leaders throughout India, especially by his mentor, Mahatma Gandhi. In the years between 1919 and 1928, Patel worked extensively against untouchability, alcoholism, ignorance and poverty. He was elected the President of the Municipal Corporation of Ahmedabad in 1922.

In 1928, Bardoli suffered from a similar predicament. In this case, the revenue hike was steeper, and the famine worse and covered a large portion of Gujarat. Patel organized the first revolt since the suspension of civil resistance in 1922, and became a hero to the whole nation. The revenue refusal was even stronger here than in Kheda, and many sympathy satyagrahas were undertaken in different parts of Gujarat.

In both cases, after the revolt had ended, Patel worked hard to make sure each farmer got his lands and property back.

It was with his work in Bardoli, that Gujaratis and people across the country began referring to him as the **Sardar**, or *Leader*. His work won him the loyalty of thousands of Gujarati freedom-fighters and the Gujarat Congress Party, and the love and adoration of millions of people in Western India.

CIVIL DISOBEDIENCE MOVEMENT

Sardar Patel became the President of the Indian National Congress in 1931, at the dawn of the Civil Disobedience Movement, or Salt Satyagraha. Patel organized Congress work before being arrested by police. He served his sentence with Gandhi in the Yeravda Jail till 1934. Gandhi and Patel grew very close, personally and spiritually in this time. Patel served Gandhi, affectionately looking after his personal needs, and Gandhi encouraged Patel to learn Sanskrit and read great Hindu epics. The two discussed many aspects of the freedom struggle, Indian history and national issues. Gandhi was especially proud of Patel's work in Gujarat, and of the inestimable help he was giving Gandhi in the work of revolution.

POWER WITHIN THE CONGRESS

Sardar Patel was Gandhiji's right-hand man, and Congress Party chief. He commanded the wide loyalty and respect of the millions of Congressmen who had fought in the hot sun and been beaten, tortured and imprisoned for many years. He was Gujarat's chief, and no other Congress leader, not even Gandhiji could have overcome his strength in his home state. His great integrity, strict discipline and adherence to core principles of the struggle, complete disinterest in office and power as such, and fatherly care for his associates and fellow Congressmen made him the only man capable of standing up to Gandhiji. Thus even though he had been Congress President only once in 1931, he remained its second-most important leader after Gandhiji, exceeding the younger and charismatic Jawaharlal Nehru in authority and influence within the party and in government. It was acknowledged by many veteran freedom-fighters and his British opponents that only Sardar Patel could stand up to Gandhiji in a contest for the loyalty of most Congressmen and Indians. No one was a stronger ally of the Mahatma. Patel would break many other bonds of power, office, leadership, friendship and family before splitting from the Mahatma. Throughout his life, he viewed himself as a "soldier in Bapu's Army." He enjoyed a close spiritual bond with the Mahatma, and the Gandhi-Patel relationship has been described as one of older and younger brothers. In Indian society, the older brother is a father-figure, with the younger brother bound with love, loyalty and respect to him.

Sardar Patel assumed a wide range of responsibilities by raising funds for the Party from businessmen and sympathizers, developing an election strategy and selecting candidates for the provincial and central elections of 1934 and 1937 under the Government of India Act 1935, and guiding the work of many Congress organizations dedicated to social upliftment and service. He was the guide and boss of the various Congress Ministries that took power in the provinces in the 1930s-never indulging in power and interfering in the work of public service, but holding an iron discipline over the ministers, preventing the British thus from dividing the leaders and ruling, and any corruption of power from hurting the purity of the overall cause for freedom.

In the eyes of some people, Patel gained infamy when he reprimanded P.F. Nariman, a Parsee Congress leader who coveted the premiership of Bombay, and Khare, another politician seeking the premiership of the Central Provinces. Both had tried to divide the party to unseat the preference of national party leaders, and to Patel, divide-and-rule was absolutely unacceptable. But his measures to oust both from were criticized as *authoritarian* and *dictatorial* by some in the press.

QUIT INDIA

Sardar Patel strongly supported Gandhi's call for a final, definitive struggle to obtain the exit of the British in India, after he realized that the British would not reward India with freedom even if India supported Britain in the World War II. Patel's support was critical, since the movement was received with criticism and caused many political divisions and controversy. Although Nehru and Maulana Azad backed the struggle, it was Patel's leadership that mobilized hundreds of thousands of Congress supporters, especially in latter-day Mumbai, Gujarat and Maharashtra. After making a fiery speech in Mumbai to a crowd over 100,000 strong, Patel energized thousands of nationalists, removing political exhaustion, division and confusion. Quit India became the most dangerous revolt in the history of the country. Hundreds of thousands of people courted arrest, and whole cities and provinces shut down. But the British did succeed, by rigorous imposition of martial law, in breaking the strength of the revolt by 1944. Thousands of protestors were killed, and over 100,000 arrested in the process.

Patel and the entire Congress Working Committee was jailed in Ahmednagar till 1946. In these years, Patel was recorded as having kept up the spirits of his comrades by constant care and service to them. Patel and the others were released by early 1946. The revolt and the war had exhausted Britain, and negotiations were about to begin for the future independence of India.

Personal Life

Vallabhbhai Patel was an extremely reserved man committed to his family and friends. After joining the freedom struggle, he would frequently live in Gandhi's ashrams, or with his close friends in Gujarat. From the 1920s till his death, his daughter Manibehn Patel would closely attend to his personal needs and often act as a right-arm.

Vallabhbhai's son Dhayabhai Patel worked for an insurance company in Mumbai, where Vallabhbhai would often live. However, Vallabhbhai was angered once by Dhayabhai's request that he use his political influence to obtain a loan crucial to his business's survival, even though he promised to return it immediately. Patel would be protective of his integrity and reputation as far as possible. His colleagues like Narhari Parikh, Mohanlal Pandya, Ganesh Vasudev Mavlankar, Ravi Shankar Vyas and Mahadev Desai would become very close and dear friends to him. Officials like V.P. Menon and H.M. Patel and his private secretary Vidya Shankar would grow a deep, personal admiration and a relationship of trust and reverence for Patel. Patel was also close to the Birla family and the family of Ambalal Sarabhai, a prominent Gujarati industrialist. His personal friends not from the political world were Dr. Kanuga and his wife, who were neighbors in Ahmedabad.

The Independence of India

Historians consider that Vallabhbhai Patel's most important contributions came in the period between 1946 and 1948, when the Congress negotiated India's independence; when the Partition of India took place, and India's independence was greeted by intensive communal violence, an exodus of 10 million people, war over Kashmir and the pending integration of 565 princely states.

THE CONGRESS PRESIDENCY

Patel famously stepped down in favour of Nehru from the 1946 election for the Congress Presidency, upon the request of Gandhi. Patel had the support of 11 out of 15 Congress Party provincial organizations, while Nehru had none. The election's importance is in the fact that the elected man would lead free India's first Government.

Gandhi is often criticized for not backing Patel, a battle-hardened leader who had the support of the entire Congress Party. But Patel respected Gandhi's judgment, and knew that he did not have Nehru's assets: health and youth, mass popularity and a likeable image with the country's Muslims and youth. But until his death, Gandhi's true wish was that Patel and Nehru head the Government together, and that the distinction be only titular. Patel took the most powerful portfolio, the Home Ministry, and retained his control over the organization of the Congress Party.

THE PARTITION OF INDIA

Sardar Patel was one of the first Congress leaders to accept partition of India as a solution to the rising Muslim separatist movement led by Mohammed Ali Jinnah. He was greatly angered by Jinnah's wrecking of attempted coalitions between his party and the Congress, and by his embrace of violence, such as the Direct Action Day, when over 5,000 people were killed in violence instigated by Jinnah. But he was also aware that Jinnah did enjoy popular support amongst Muslims, and that an open conflict between him and the nationalists could degenerate into a Hindu-Muslim civil war of disastrous proportions and consequences. When Nehru and the others had approved the idea, it was Patel who took the job of convincing a deeply saddened Gandhi of the inevitability of partition as the pragmatic solution.

Patel also represented India in the Partition Council, watching over the fairness of the division of assets and government machinery. With Pakistan being the smaller country with a smaller population, Patel made sure Jinnah did not obtain more resources for his state than was justifiable. Nehru and Patel jointly named India's first Council of Ministers. Patel took the Ministry for Home Affairs, and the title of Deputy Prime Minister. At 72, Patel assumed the *Himalayan* responsibilities of the integration of 565 princely states into the Union, advancing democracy and self-government in these fiefdoms, developing the national security apparatus and strategy, and welding Bharat into one, united country. Patel would assume a leading role in writing the free nation's Constitution as well, responsible for inculcating separation of powers, religious freedom and equality (ironically, he was often portrayed with an anti-Muslim bias) and the right to property.

GANDHI'S DEATH AND HEART ATTACK

The death of the man for whom he gave up a life of comfort to withstand 30 years of hardship, jail and overcome terrible trials of fate and history, deeply hurt Patel. At Gandhi's funeral, the Sardar gave solace, support and leadership to many Congressmen, associates, friends and the wider population. He addressed the nation with Nehru, and immediately moved to forestall retaliation against the political body that the assassin belonged to and wider violence. He also made it clear that the assassin was a Hindu, to prevent riots against the Muslim community. But within two months of the murder, he had a major heart attack that unleashed the massive bottled-up grief. Thanks to the presence of his caring daughter, his loyal secretary and nurse, his life did not end sooner than it ultimately did.

Airplane Crash

Patel also underwent a harrowing experience when a plane carrying him and the Maharaja of Patiala crashed in the desert of Rajasthan. No one was hurt, but the nation had panicked over the disappearance of Patel's plane. When he returned to Delhi, members of Parliament and thousands of Congressmen gave him a raucous welcome, and in Parliament, proceedings stopped for half an hour while the MPs gave a thunderous ovation to Patel.

Passing

Sardar Patel died in Mumbai (then Bombay) on December 15, 1950, after suffering a massive second heart attack. He was 75 years old. Just 11 months earlier, Bharat had adopted its Constitution, and become a Republic. Till his last few days, he was constantly at work as Home Minister, redeeming to his absolute last, his pledge to Mahatma Gandhi to stand by Prime Minister Nehru and provide the joint leadership that the country was crucially in need of in its first turbulent years since the birth of freedom.

Memorial

Sardar Vallabhbhai Patel is remembered across India as a man who exemplified of immense personal character, integrity, courage and determination against all odds throughout his life. In Gujarat, he is especially fondly remembered and idolized. He was officially awarded the Bharat Ratna, the nation's highest civilian honour, posthumously in 1991. His official birthday, October 31st each year is Sardar Jayanti, a national holiday in India. In 1993, the film *Sardar* was released which sketched his life and work. The film was produced and directed by Ketan Mehta and noted Indian actor Paresh Rawal played the lead role. It focused on Patel's leadership in the years leading up the Indian independence, especially the partition of India, and its political integration, and Patel's relationship with Nehru. Lionized in Gujarat, his birthplace in the village of Karamsad is still preserved in his memory. The Sardar Vallabhbhai Patel International Airport in Ahmedabad serves as the state's gateway to the world. The Sardar Patel College of Engineering in Mumbai is one of the nation's premier engineering schools. A highly prestigious school, the Sardar Patel Vidyalaya was established in 1960 by his name in New Delhi. And the major Sandhurst Road along which he lived in his family's flat on Mumbai's eastern coast, is today the Sardar Vallabhbhai Patel Road.

Family

Manibehn Patel lived in a flat in Mumbai for the rest of her life following her father's death, and often led the work of the Sardar

Patel Memorial Trust and other charitable organizations, but kept out of politics in general. Dhayabhai Patel was a businessman, and eventually went on to serve in the Lok Sabha, lower house of Parliament as an MP in the 1960s.

CHRONOLOGY OF SARDAR PATEL

Oct 31, 1875	Born in Nadiad, Kheda District, Gujarat, fourth son of Jhaverbhai Patel, a farmer of Karamsad and Ladbai Patel; primary schooling up to English Third standard at Karamsad
1893	Married to Jhaverba of Gana, a village 3 miles from Karamsad
1897	Passed matriculation exam in Nadiad
1900	Passed the District Pleader's Examination; practices in Godhra; contracts bubonic plague from a court official whom he nursed during an epidemic in Godhra
1902	Shifted legal practice to Borsad, made a name as a criminal lawyer
April 1904	Daughter Mani (later known as Manibehn) born
1905	Saved enough money to go to England to become a barrister but gave it away to his elder brother Vitthalbhai who wished to become barrister first
Nov 1905	Son Dahya born
Jan 11, 1909	Wife Jhaverba dies after a surgical operation in Bombay
July 1910	Vallabhbhai leaves for England, admitted to Middle Temple
1912	Took final examination after 6th term instead of the usual 12, ranked first in first class; won a prize of fifty pounds, left for India the day after the exam; brother Vitthalbhai elected as member of the Bombay Council
Jan 1913	Vallabhbhai becomes Barrister (Bar-at-Law) of Middle Temple Inn
Feb. 13, 1913	Returns to India; practices in Ahmedabad; becomes the foremost criminal lawyer
March 1914	Jhaverbhai, Vallabhbhai's father, dies at the age of 85
1915	Member, Gujarat Sabha, which was converted into Gujarat Provincial Congress Committee in 1919; Secretary, Gujarat Provincial Conference of which Mahatma Gandhi was the President.
1917	Elected councillor of Ahmedabad Municipality; Chairman, Sanitary and Public Works Committee

Nov 1917	First direct contact with Mahatma Gandhi
1918	Organized famine relief in Ahmedabad district; established a temporary hospital in Ahmedabad with a grant from Municipal Board to Gujarat Sabha to combat severe influenza of epidemic; successfully led "No-Tax" agitation against land revenue recovered by Government from drought affected Kheda district farmers
1920	Discards western dress and adopts khadi, dhoti, kurta and chappals; burnt all his foreign clothes; won all open seats in the Ahmedabad Municipal elections, collected one million rupees for the Tilak Swaraj Fund and enrolled 300, 000 members for Indian National Congress from Gujarat; decides with Gandhi to establish Gujarat Vidyapeeth
1921	Chairman, Reception Committee, Indian National Congress, 36th session, Ahmedabad; First Chairman, Gujarat Regional Congress Committee
1922-23	Satyagraha at Borsad, Gujarat-Against the Governments, "Haidiya" punitive tax imposed on the entire population of Borsad Taluka. Gandhi calls Vallabhbhai "King of Borsad"
1922	Leads Nagpur National Flag Agitation; collected one million rupees in Rangoon for Gujarat Vidyapeeth
1923	Elected President of Ahmedabad Municipality
1927	Unprecedented floods in Gujarat, Vallabhbhai obtained one crore (10 million) rupees from he Government for famine relief
1928	Resigned from the Presidency of Ahmedabad Municipality; presides over the Kathiawad Political Conference at Morbi
1928-29	Leads the Bardoli No-Tax Campaign Satyagraha in Kheda District; Vallabhbhai called "Sardar" by the peasants. Calcutta session of the Indian National Congress endorses the title
1929	Presided over Maharashtra Political Conference; tours Maharashtra
March 7, 1930	Arrested for canvassing Gandhi's salt Satyagraha; Lodged in Sabarmati jail, Ahmedabad. Went on hunger strike in jail requesting C class diet instead of A class provided to him because of his high status. Request granted!
June 26, 1930	Released
July 31, 1930	Rearrested in Bombay and sent to Yeravada jail for 3 months
Dec. 12, 1930	Rearrested and sentenced to 9 months imprisonment

1931	Presides over Indian National Congress, 46th session, Karachi.
Aug 1931	Joins Gandhi in talks with Viceroy Lord Irwin in Simla
Oct 22, 1933	Brother Vitthalbhai dies in a clinic near Geneva while Sardar was in prison (see below)
Jan 1932- Jul 1934	Arrested during the Civil Disobedience Movement and jailed in Yeravada Prison along with Mahatma Gandhi; later joined by Mahadev Desai from Nasik jail. Daughter Manibehn and Kasturba Gandhi also jailed but for shorter periods.
1934	Released on grounds of health-serious nose trouble.
1935-1942	Chairman, Congress Parliamentary Board; supervises Congress' ministries in eight provinces, 1937-1939; in charge of selection of candidates for elections
Nov 18, 1940	Arrested under Defense of India Act for participation in Satyagraha launched by Gandhiji to press Great Britain for a commitment on India's Independence
Aug 1941	Released from prison following a severe intestinal ailment
Aug 1942	Arrested for participation in Quit India Movement; jailed in Ahmednagar Fort along with Nehru, Azad, and other prominent leaders; shifted to Yeravada prison in early 1945
June 15, 1945	Released from prison to participate in Simla Talks
Sept 2, 1946	Sardar joins the "Interim Government," as Minister for Home, Information, and Broad-casting (headed by Nehru as Vice-President of the Viceroy's Executive Council)
April 4, 1947	Inaugurates the Vitthalbhbhai Patel Maha Vidyalaya at Vallabh Vidyanagar
June 25, 1947	Government of India decides to establish a Department of (Princely) States under Sardar Patel
Aug 15, 1947	Sardar joins Independent India's Cabinet as Deputy Prime Minister and Minister for Home, States, Information and Broadcasting
Nov 13, 1947	Visits Somnath Patan and decides to renovate the Somnath Mahadev Temple
1948	"Doctor of Laws" degree conferred on Sardar by Nagpur, Banaras and Allahabad Universities on Nov 3, 25, and 27 respectively
Feb. 15, 1948	Inaugurates Rajya Sangh of Bhavnagar
April 7, 1948	Inaugurates Rajasthan Sangh

April 22, 1948	Agreements to constitute Madhya/Bharat Sangh
Sep 13-16, 1948	"Police Action" in Hyderabad
Feb. 26, 1949	"Bharat Ratna," the highest Indian national award, conferred posthumously on Sardar Patel. The award was accepted by Sardar's grandson, Vipinbhai Patel.
Oct 7- Nov 15, 1949	Served as Acting Prime Minister of India during Nehru's visit to the U.S., UK,. and Canada
Dec. 15, 1950	Sardar Patel dies in Bombay; cremated in Bombay
1991	"Bharat Ratna," the highest Indian national award, conferred posthumously on Sardar Patel. The award was accepted by Sardar's grandson, Vipinbhai Patel.

Causes of the India–Pakistan Enduring Rivalry

The India–Pakistan rivalry remains one of the most enduring and unresolved conflicts of our times. Begun in the aftermath of the birth of the two states from British colonial rule in 1947, it has continued for well over half a century with periodic wars and crises erupting between the two rivals. The conflict has affected all key dimensions of interstate and societal relations of the two antagonists. Despite occasional peace overtures and periods of detente, it shows no signs of a permanent settlement in the near future. Since the late 1980s, the open acquisition of nuclear weapons by the two states, the increasing number of crises involving them, and the introduction of terrorist tactics into the conflict have led to the heightened possibility of a cataclysmic war breaking out in South Asia with unimaginable consequences.

What explains the persistence of this rivalry even when some other long-running conflicts in different parts of the world have come to an end? Do existing theories of enduring rivalries provide compelling explanations for this ongoing conflict? Can the rivalry and its persistence be understood on the basis of factors at the international, societal, and decisionmaker levels of analysis? Is it the convergence of these factors that keeps the conflict enduring in nature? Why do the near-and medium-term prospects of negotiating an end to this enduring rivalry look bleak? Does the answer lie in the territorial nature of the rivalry, disparate national identities of the two states, and the peculiar power asymmetry between the two parties, or the fundamental incompatibility in the strategic goals they seek? Can the extensive works on enduring rivalries and the emerging literature on asymmetric conflicts shed light on this conflict?

Theories of Enduring Rivalries and Asymmetric Conflicts

Enduring rivalries are defined as conflicts between two or more states that last more than two decades with several militarized interstate disputes punctuating the relationship in between. An enduring rivalry is characterized by a "persistent, fundamental, and long term incompatibility of goals between two states," which "manifests itself in the basic attitudes of the parties toward each other as well as in recurring violent or potentially violent clashes over a long period of time." Although there is difference of opinion among analysts on the number of disputes and interstate crises required for calling a rivalry "enduring," I accept the categorization by Paul Diehl and Gary Goertz, who treat an enduring rivalry as one that involves at least six militarized disputes during a twenty-year period. This specification, according to them, allows defining the concept along "spatial consistency, duration and militarized competition." In other words, an enduring rivalry cannot be episodic or of short duration; it should be ongoing for a reasonably long period on a continuous basis before it can be termed "enduring." Enduring rivalries are also called "protracted conflicts," but the main difference between the two concepts perhaps lies in the interstate dimension of the former. Whereas a protracted conflict can be internal or intra-state, involving state and/or non-state actors, an enduring rivalry specifically refers to interstate conflicts.

An enduring rivalry is often characterized by zero-sum perspectives on the part of the participants. The conflict can become entrenched and societal as parties view each other as highly threatening to their security and physical survival. Enduring rivalries tend to be typified by periodic interstate crises and, in some instances, war, although war is not a necessary condition for a rivalry to be categorized as "enduring." John Vasquez argues that relative equality in power capabilities is necessary for a rivalry to remain enduring, since in a highly unequal power situation the stronger party will in general be able to impose its will on the weaker side and put an end to the conflict.

Asymmetric conflicts involve states of unequal aggregate power capability, measured in terms of material resources, *i.e.*, size, demography, military capability, and economic prowess. Intangible factors such as will and morale are not included in assessing national power capabilities as these are difficult to measure. Further, these factors tend to change over time and are difficult to notice until a real military contest takes place. Weaker parties in asymmetric power dyads often use these intangible means to bolster their military and political positions during both war and peace. Within asymmetric conflict dyads one may notice wide disparity in power capabilities (as in the US–Cuba or China–Taiwan cases) or limited disparity (as in the North Korea–South Korea case).

The India–Pakistan conflict is both enduring and asymmetric, but the power asymmetry is truncated and mitigated by many factors. In particular, the weaker party, Pakistan, has been successful in reducing the asymmetry through strategy, tactics, alliances with outside powers, acquisition of qualitatively superior weapons and nuclear arms since the late 1980s, and, for over a decade, low-intensity warfare. The materially stronger power, India, is not overwhelmingly preponderant in the theater of conflict – Kashmir – and has been vulnerable to asymmetric challenges by the weaker state, Pakistan. Nor is Pakistan too small or incapable of mounting a sustained challenge, as it has proved over half a century. Pakistan, with a population of over 141 million, is the seventh largest country in the world. Its territorial size is larger than most Middle Eastern and Gulf states, except Saudi Arabia and Iran, and its elite has sufficient wherewithal and high level of motivation to sustain the conflict even if at a high cost to its society in terms of economic and political underdevelopment. The asymmetry is built into the structure of the conflict, the power balance, and the goals and objectives that the two parties seek. I argue that this peculiar asymmetry makes the conflict deadly and prolonged. This truncated asymmetry, in recent years buttressed by nuclear weapons, makes the resolution of the conflict unlikely any time soon.

Origins of the Rivalry: The Historical Legacy

A brief historical survey of the origins of the conflict is necessary at this point. The roots of the India–Pakistan rivalry lie in the two visions of statehood that arose within the context of the nationalist movement in the Indian subcontinent. The Indian National Congress, spearheaded by Mohandas Gandhi and Jawaharlal Nehru, sought a unified country built around the principles of secularism and liberal democracy. Although the majority of the Congress Party membership came from the mainstream Hindu population, the party embodied all major ethnic groups of India and had a vision of a state not supporting any single religion. Many Muslim leaders were wary of majority rule which they viewed as tantamount to Hindu rule and demanded safeguards by way of separate electorates. In order to press for their demands with the colonial rulers, they formed the Muslim League Party in December 1906. Their claim for separate electorates was accepted by the British in the Government of India Act of 1909, which offered limited political rights to the Indian subjects. The British rulers were sympathetic to separate constituencies for Muslims which they hoped would weaken the incipient nationalist movement, spearheaded by the Congress Party. However, over time this policy helped to unify the Muslim community in a communal and political sense and sowed the seeds for the idea of Pakistan. Although the Congress Party initially accepted separate Muslim electorates in 1916, it subsequently rejected the idea in the constitutional proposals it made in 1928. Alienation from both the British and the Congress Party led to the proposal for a separate Muslim homeland by the League, which was first put forward by the poet Muhammad Iqbal in 1930.

The Government of India Act of 1935 was pivotal in the rise of Muslim separatist nationalism, with the League under Mohammed

Ali Jinnah deciding to contest elections for limited self-governing provincial governments in 1937. The overwhelming electoral victory of the Congress Party in six provinces and that party's decision not to form coalition governments with the Muslim League – which had not fared well even in the separate Muslim constituencies – disillusioned Jinnah, who then began to propagate the merits of the two-nation theory. The Congress Party's rejection of Jinnah's demand that the League be recognized as the sole party of Indian Muslims (because the Congress itself had a substantial Muslim membership) and the misdeeds of some Congress provincial leaders embittered Jinnah and his followers even further.

In March 1940, at its meeting in Lahore, the League proclaimed as its goal the creation of Pakistan as a separate homeland for Indian Muslims and the Congress–League schism widened even further. The May 1944 Gandhi–Jinnah talks and the June 1945 Simla conference of top Congress and Muslim League leaders failed to break the deadlock between them. The League also benefited from its somewhat supportive position of the war effort by Britain. The arrival of the Labour Party government under Clement Atlee in July 1945 speeded up the Indian independence process. In 1946, the Cabinet Mission sent by Britain proposed that a union between British India and the princely states be established and a constitution drafted.

However, this proposal failed to resolve the divide between the Congress and the League. During this time, Hindu–Muslim communal clashes intensified in many parts of India and the last British viceroy, Lord Louis Mountbatten, came to the conclusion that the creation of Pakistan was inevitable. Accordingly, the two independent states of India and Pakistan were born on August 15, 1947, with Pakistan gaining the Muslim majority British-administered areas in the northwest and Bengal and India obtaining the rest of British India, while the fate of the 500-odd princely states remained undecided. The partition was followed by one of history's largest mass migrations– over 10 million people from both sides – and was accompanied by brutal violence.

The Indian Independence Act of 1947 contained a provision that the 562 princely states – scattered throughout the subcontinent and partially autonomous under British rule – had the option to join either India or Pakistan. Thanks largely to the efforts of Sardar Vallabhbhai Patel, almost all states within India joined the Indian Union while Jinnah succeeded in gaining the accession by the Muslim princes within Pakistan's territorial domain.

Three princely states decided to stay independent from both India and Pakistan: Jammu and Kashmir in the north, Hyderabad in the south, and Junagadh in the west. While the rulers of the latter two were Muslim, the majority of their population was Hindu and their accession to India occurred through internal revolt or Indian police actions. New Delhi legitimized these accessions through subsequent popular referenda. Only Jammu and Kashmir emerged as the most contentious, given its geographical proximity to Pakistan and a majority Muslim population (concentrated largely in the northern areas and Kashmir Valley) even as a substantial Hindu population inhabited the Jammu area and a Buddhist population lived in the Ladakh region. The Hindu ruler of Kashmir, Maharaja Hari Singh, first chose to remain independent from both India and Pakistan, but in reaction to an invasion in October 1947 by tribal forces from Pakistan's Northwest Frontier Province (which were aided by Pakistani regular troops), he sought India's help.

Following his signing an agreement to accede to India and the approval of Kashmir's undisputed leader of the time, Sheikh Mohammed Abdullah, the Indian forces intervened and managed to partially evict the intruders. Jinnah's decision to send in Pakistani troops escalated the conflict to a short war between the two states, which lasted until the end of 1948. A ceasefire agreement was reached between the two states under the auspices of the United Nations, which came into effect on January 1, 1949. A ceasefire line was established dividing Kashmir, with nearly two thirds of the state under Indian control and the rest under Pakistan, which the latter called "Azad" or "Free" Kashmir. The ceasefire line was monitored by a UN observer mission until 1972, when it was renamed Line of Control (LoC), and has been actively manned by the regular forces of the two countries, with sporadic shellings, occasional skirmishes, and limited incursions. Three major wars (1947–48, 1965, and 1971) and a minor war, Kargil (1999), have been fought over control of the territory, but neither country has succeeded in changing the line to its advantage. This military stalemate is only part of the story of the rivalry between the two states. Understanding the structure of the conflict is critical to explaining why the India–Pakistan conflict persists as an enduring rivalry.

The Structure of the Conflict: Asymmetry in Goals

The India–Pakistan conflict is simultaneously over territory, national identity, and power position in the region. The political status of Kashmir, from Pakistan's perspective, is the unfinished business of the partition of the subcontinent on a religious basis in 1947. Successive Pakistani leaders have viewed the gaining of the entire Jammu and Kashmir state from Indian control as their core national mission for identity and strategic reasons. To the Pakistanis, the Indian-controlled Muslim-majority state of Kashmir, if given full freedom to choose in a plebiscite, would join Pakistan. However, as Bose puts it: "this state-centred, legalistic interpretation of the 'right to self-determination' is significantly different from the highly populist version articulated by proponents of an independent Kashmir." Thus, despite the preference of most Kashmiri nationalist groups for independence or greater autonomy from both countries, Pakistan steadfastly holds the view that the partition of the subcontinent is still incomplete and that Pakistan's Islamic identity will not be total until the territory is unified with that country.

Gandhi advised the Congress to reject the proposals the British Cabinet Mission offered in 1946, as he was deeply suspicious of the grouping proposed for Muslim-majority states — Gandhi viewed this as a precursor to partition. However, this became one of the few times the Congress broke from Gandhi's advice (not his leadership though), as Nehru and Patel knew that if the Congress did not approve the plan, the control of government would pass to the

Muslim League. Between 1946 and 1947, over 5,000 people were killed in violence. Gandhi was vehemently opposed to any plan that partitioned India into two separate countries. Many Muslims in India lived side by side with Hindus and Sikhs, and were in favour of a united India. But Muhammad Ali Jinnah, the leader of the Muslim League, commanded widespread support in West Punjab, Sindh, NWFP and East Bengal. The partition plan was approved by the Congress leadership as the only way to prevent a wide-scale Hindu-Muslim civil war. Congress leaders knew that Gandhi would viscerally oppose partition, and it was impossible for the Congress to go ahead without his agreement, for Gandhi's support in the party and throughout India was strong. Gandhi's closest colleagues had accepted partition as the best way out, and Sardar Patel endeavoured to convince Gandhi that it was the only way to avoid civil war. A devastated Gandhi gave his assent.

On the day of the transfer of power, Gandhi did not celebrate independence with the rest of India, but was alone in Calcutta, mourning the partition and working to end the violence. After India's independence, Gandhi focused on Hindu-Muslim peace and unity. He conducted extensive dialogue with Muslim and Hindu community leaders, working to cool passions in northern India, as well as in Bengal. Despite the Indo-Pakistani War of 1947, he was troubled when the Government decided to deny Pakistan the Rs. 55 crores due as per agreements made by the Partition Council. Leaders like Sardar Patel feared that Pakistan would use the money to bankroll the war against India. Gandhi was also devastated when demands resurged for all Muslims to be deported to Pakistan, and when Muslim and Hindu leaders expressed frustration and an inability to come to terms with one another.

He launched his last fast-unto-death in Delhi, asking that all communal violence be ended once and for all, and that the payment of Rs. 55 crores be made to Pakistan. Gandhi feared that instability and insecurity in Pakistan would increase their anger against India, and violence would spread across the borders. He further feared that Hindus and Muslims would renew their enmity and precipitate into an open civil war. After emotional debates with his life-long colleagues, Gandhi refused to budge, and the Government rescinded its policy and made the payment to Pakistan. Hindu, Muslim and Sikh community leaders, including the Rashtriya Swayamsevak Sangh and Hindu Mahasabha assured him that they would renounce violence and call for peace. Gandhi thus broke his fast by sipping orange juice.

On 30 January 1948, on his way to a prayer meeting, Gandhi was shot dead in Birla House, New Delhi, by Nathuram Godse. Godse was a Hindu radical with links to the extremist Hindu Mahasabha, who held Gandhi responsible for weakening India by insisting upon a payment to Pakistan. Godse and his co-conspirator Narayan Apte were later tried and convicted, and on 15 November 1949, were executed. Gandhi's memorial (or Samadhi) at Raj Ghat, New Delhi, bears the epigraph, which may be translated as "Oh God". These are widely believed to be Gandhi's last words after he was shot, though the veracity of this statement has been disputed by many. Jawaharlal Nehru addressed the nation through radio:

Friends and comrades, the light has gone out of our lives, and there is darkness everywhere, and I do not quite know what to tell you or how to say it. Our beloved leader, Bapu as we called him, the father of the nation, is no more. Perhaps I am wrong to say that; nevertheless, we will not see him again, as we have seen him for these many years, we will not run to him for advice or seek solace from him, and that is a terrible blow, not only for me, but for millions and millions in this country.

Sardar Patel was one of Mohandas Gandhi's closest associates, and he organized and led several satyagrahas during India's struggle for freedom from British rule. When India achieved independence in 1947, Patel became Home Minister and Deputy Prime Minister, and he presided over the most difficult task facing the nascent nation-state, namely the integration of over 500 princely states into the Indian Union.

Vallabhbhai Patel was born in Nadiad in present-day Gujarat in 1875. He completed his schooling in the local area and subsequently, in his 30s, he went to Britain; like many of his generation of political leaders, he qualified as a barrister. Patel returned to India around the same time as Gandhi returned to India from South Africa, on the eve of World War I, and the two met shortly thereafter. Patel joined Gandhi in representing the weavers in the dispute with millowners in Ahmedabad in 1918, and he played a pivotal role in helping to redress the grievances of peasants in Kheda district. "I will say", wrote Gandhi in his autobiography, "that without the help of Vallabhbhai Patel, we should not have won the campaign. He had a splendid [law] practice, he had his municipal work to do, but he renounced it all and threw himself in the campaign." Patel was charged in 1928 with leading the difficult satyagraha at Bardoli, where again the colonial state was attempting to exact heavy taxes from an impoverished peasantry, and he acquitted himself brilliantly. In 1931, Patel was elected President of the Indian National Congress. Gandhi reposed great confidence in him through the three decades of their friendship.

Gandhi's assassination on 30 January 1948 at the hands of Nathuram Godse left Patel bereft of the guidance of "Bapu", his political mentor and the "Father of the Nation". [See also Vinay Lal, "'He Ram': The Politics of Gandhi's Last Words".] Patel was immensely shaken up and his own death, in late 1950, may have been hastened by the anxiety he experienced after Gandhi's death. The prevailing representations of Patel dwell almost exclusively on his political achievements, and it is not surprising that three generations of Indian school children have known Patel as the "Iron Man of India". Everyone recognized his steely determination and pragmatism, and nowhere was this more visibly on display when, as Home Minister and Minister of States, he took decisive action to consolidate the Indian Union and authorized police action to merge Hyderabad into India. It has been suggested by some people that if Patel had been placed in charge of Kashmir, a "problem" which Nehru sought to tackle himself both as Prime Minister and as Minister of External Affairs, the crisis in Kashmir would have been resolved in India's favour a long time ago.

Though a staunch Hindu, Patel had a keen appreciation of the syncretic culture of India, and he recognized that India had furnished a hospitable home to adherents of various religions over the centuries. Patel contributed very substantially to the deliberations of the Constituent Assembly, and it has not always been recognized that the protection and privileges guaranteed to minorities in the Indian Constitution under Articles 29 and 30 owe much to the vigilance of Patel. Indeed, Patel, unlike some other Hindu leaders, was insistent that the right to proselytize should be recognized as part of the right to freedom of religious worship.

With respect to the position of Muslims, Sikhs, and other religious communities in India, Patel wrote that "it is up to the majority community, by its generosity, to create a sense of confidence in the minorities, and so also it will be the duty of the minority communities to forge the past . . ."

His criticism of the use of violence to resolve political disputes bears a sharp contrast with the use of violence by religious extremists in India in recent years. In 1949, an idol of Lord Ram was surreptitiously installed in the precincts of the Babri Masjid; writing to Govind Vallabh Pant, then Chief Minister of Uttar Pradesh, on 9 January 1950, Patel encouraged him to prosecute violators of the law and perpetrators of violence. "I feel that the issue is one which should be resolved amicably," wrote Patel, "in a spirit of mutual toleration and goodwill between the two communities. . . . such matters can only be resolved peacefully if we take the willing consent of the Muslim community with us. There can be no question of resolving such disputes by force."

Patel desired nothing more than that the Indian nation-state should persevere and flourish. Nehru's biographer, S. Gopal, admitted that Patel's "major concern was national unity." Patel is still remembered as one of principal architects of Indian independence and one of the shapers of modern India. His devotion to the idea of the nation-state also points to the limitations of his thinking; unlike Gandhi, Patel could not think beyond the nation-state, and he was incapable of offering the critique of modernity that Gandhi pioneered. Nor did Patel have the kind of far-reaching and complex views of science, industrial civilization, masculinity, or a whole host of other subjects on which Gandhi pondered for a considerable portion of his life. The characterization that has sometimes been used of Gandhi, namely that he was a doer rather than thinker, is in fact far more apposite of Patel.

In recent years, Patel's name has been abused and degraded by those who purport to act in his name, or who pretend that, since Patel was a staunch Hindu, he tolerated the neglect if not mistreatment of Muslims. It is true that even in his own lifetime, there were rumours, particularly at the time of partition, that Patel was not sufficiently attentive to the plight of Muslims; and that he did not do enough in his capacity as Home Minister to ensure their safety. This view rests largely on rumours and innuendoes, since Patel's own writings, including his correspondence, lend little if any support to the representation of him as a Hindu communalist.

Gandhi himself never believed any of these rumours and, indeed, held Patel to the highest standards. Some people even held Patel ultimately responsible for the assassination of Gandhi, and he is alleged to have not done enough to unearth the conspiracy to murder Gandhi after the initial plot of 20 January 1948, where police were able to hold Madanlal Pahwa captive, was foiled. Gandhi's "love for Muslims", in the language of his most ferocious opponents, is thought, on the communalist reading, to have left the Sardar unhappy. But just how far the Hindutva appropriation of Patel, the consequences of which still remain to be unraveled, has gone can be seen in the disturbing fact that the murderous Narendra Modi, the butcher of Gujarat's Muslims, is gone on public record as having described himself as the "Chote Sardar" [small Sardar].

Unless one engages in a careful, hermeneutic, and dialectic reading of Patel, the 'iron' man who became one of the eminent followers of the preeminent practitioner and theorist of nonviolence, he too will disappear into the pantheon of martial Hindu heroes and the bottomless well of Hindutva chicanery.

Vallabhbhai was a political and social leader of India who played a major role in the country's struggle for independence and guided its integration into a united, independent nation. In India and across the world, he was often addressed as Sardar which means Chief in many languages of India.

He is hailed as the Iron Man of India. Raised in the countryside of Gujarat and largely self-educated, Vallabhbhai Patel was employed in successful practice as a lawyer when he was first inspired by the work and philosophy of Mahatma Gandhi. Patel subsequently organised the peasants of Kheda, Borsad, and Bardoli in Gujarat in nonviolent civil disobedience against oppressive policies imposed by the British Raj; in this role, he became one of the most influential leaders in Gujarat. He rose to the leadership of the Indian National Congress and was at the forefront of rebellions and political events, organising the party for elections in 1934 and 1937, and promoting the Quit India movement.

As the first Home Minister and Deputy Prime Minister of India, Patel organised relief for refugees in Punjab and Delhi, and led efforts to restore peace across the nation. Patel took charge of the task to forge a united India from the 565 semi-autonomous princely states and British-era colonial provinces. Using frank diplomacy backed with the option (and the use) of military action, Patel's leadership enabled the accession of almost every princely state. Hailed as the Iron Man of India, he is also remembered as the "Patron Saint" of India's civil servants for establishing modern all-India services. Patel was also one of the earliest proponents of property rights and free enterprise in India.

J.R.D. Tata have expressed opinions that Patel would have made a better prime minister for India than Nehru. Nehru's critics and Patel's admirers cite Nehru's belated embrace of Patel's advice regarding the UN and Kashmir and the integration of Goa by military action. Proponents of free enterprise cite the failings of Nehru's socialist policies as opposed to Patel's defense of property rights and his mentorship of the Amul cooperative project.

INDIA AFTER INDEPENDENCE

Three main problems of the independent India: The newly independent India faced three main problems in the very beginning. They were as follows:

i. The preparation of a constitution of independent India.

ii. The problem of the rehabilitation of the refugees.

iii. The problem of merging of Princely States in the Indian Federation.

Integration of Princely States:

(a) Danger of Independent Princely States after the independence of India. When India got independence on August 15, 1947, there existed the Princely States within the territories of India. The Princely states had also became independent along with India when the British ended their treaties with them. The existence of large number of Princely states became another danger for the newly independent India.

(b) Role of Vallabhbhai Patel: Steps taken by the Indian Government. Vallabhbhai Patel was the first Home Minister and Deputy Prime Minister of the newly independent India. He was quick to recognise the grave danger of the existence of Princely states within the territorial limits of India.

The Indian government drafted an agreement of integration which was to be signed with those Princely states. Vallabhbhai Patel persuaded most of the Kings, Nawabs and rulers of Princely states to sign the agreement of integration and managed to merge their territories within the Federation of India.

He was helped by the support of the subjects of the Princely states themselves who desired to integrate with the Federation of India. However, three states namely, Hyderabad, Junagarh and Jammu and Kashmir presented a problem as their ruler resisted the integration with the Federation of India.

Junagarh: Junagarh was a state in Saurashtra region of Gujarat. The people of the Junagarh state desired to join with India. The Nawab of Junagarh however started secret negotiation with Pakistan and kept his people and the Government of India in dark about his real objectives. Pakistan announced to the India that Junagarh was going to join with Pakistan. When the people of the state learned about it, they arose in strong opposition to the decision of their rulers. The neighbouring states also denounced the decision of the ruler of Junagarh. When Nawab and his Diwan found that they were being opposed from all the quarters, they fled India and took shelter with Pakistan.-A referendum was held in Junagarh state and as per the result of the referendum, Junagarh state was integrated with India.

Hyderabad: (Oct. 96; 98)

a: Nizam of Hyderabad adopted Anti-India stand: Nizam adopted anti-India stand on the independence of India.-He decided to declare Hyderabad an independent state.-He did not send the representatives of his state to the Constitution Assembly. In July 1947, he presented before Lord Mountbatten the demand to annex Madhya Prant and part of Berar which Lord Mountbatten refused to accept. In August 1947, he tried to make a deal with India on conditions but Vallabhbhai Patel refused to listen him before the integration of Hyderabad with India.-Nizam did not accept the proposal of Lord Mountbatten to ascertain the view of public of Hyderabad State on the issue of integration with India under the supervision of English officers. He tried to dupe India and the Governor General Mountbatten by simultaneously undertaking secret negotiations with Pakistan when he was negotiating with Indian government.

b: Encouragement of Razakar to Nizam: Kasim Razvi, the leader of fundamentalist group Razakar encouraged Nizam to oppose India. Kasim Razvi suggested Nizam to continue his anti-Indian activities by advising him that India which was engaged in her own problems could not take any action against him. Nizam extended the loan of 20 crore to Pakistan under the encouragement of Kasim Razvi. Nizam also banned the Indian currency in his state. Kasim Razvi stepped up his anti-Indian propaganda. Kasim Razvi along with Nizam started oppressing people. Nizam organised attacks on the India trains.

c: Police Action of September 1948 by India against Hyderabad: India government was compelled to use force against due to the anti-India activities of Nizam of Hyderabad. (Oct. 01) On September 13, 1948, Indian government undertook a police action against the State of Hyderabad. On September 17, 1948, the forces of Nizam of Hyderabad surrendered to the Indian forces. After that Hyderabad was integrated with the Republic of India.

e: Andhra Pardesh and Reorganization of Sates Act of 1956: In 1956, the Indian Parliament passed the Reorganization of States Act and Andhra Pardesh was created out of the State of Hyderabad. The Telegu speaking regions were merged with Andhra Pardesh, the Kannada speaking regions were merged with Karnatak and Marathi speaking Marathwada was merged with Maharashtra.

Three main problems of the Independent India: Preparation of Constitution, Rehabilitation of Refugees and merging of the Princely States in the Indian Federation were the three main problems of the newly independent India.

Integration of Princely States: Sardar Vallabhbhai Patel, the Home Minister and Deputy Prime Minister integrated most of the Princely States in the Federation of India. Junagarh state was integrated with India after a referendum. Hyderabad was integrated after a police action in September 1948. Jammu and Kashmir was integrated with India after the King Hari Singh signed a merger with India in 1948.

Merger of French and Portuguese Colonies (Pondichery and Liberation of Goa) : Pondichery was allowed by France to merge in India after a plebiscite. The people of Goa fought a war of liberation against the Portuguese government with the support of India and finally, in December 1961, India captured Goa with the support of people of Goa.

PATEL AND BALDEV SINGH

Independence and War

On August 15, 1947, India became an independent nation and Baldev Singh became India's first Minister of Defence, under the first Prime Minister of India, Jawaharlal Nehru. Singh was also a member of the Constituent Assembly of India. Along with Sardar Vallabhbhai Patel, the Home Minister, Singh became responsible for leading the Indian Army's efforts to curtail communal violence in the Punjab and West Bengal and the capital city of Delhi, and provide security, relief and refuge to over 10 million Hindus and Sikhs who were leaving the newly created Pakistan. Terrible violence broke loose on both sides of the frontier along the Punjab and Bengal, and to date it is estimated that over 1 million people were killed, with millions more suffering from usual acts of cruelty and great physical and personal trauma from the migration.

The Army was caught unprepared, and itself was torn apart by the conflict. Thousands of Muslim officers were leaving for Pakistan, and those still doing their duty for India were worried of their own safety. The Hindu and Sikh soldiers were committing acts of violence against Muslims leaving India as revenge for the killings of Hindus and Sikhs in Pakistan. Riots had broken out in Calcutta, Delhi and Bombay. Patel and Singh led from the front, and despite a heavy toll, the Army finally re-asserted peace and rule of law all over India and the borders of Punjab and Bengal, and organized a massive relief and aid operation for the millions of people arriving in India.

Defence Minister Singh also led the preparations and planning for war in Kashmir, which had broken out with Pakistani tribesmen and some military officers had incursed into the state with the aim of annexing it into Pakistan. Over almost two years, the Indian Army would wage battle with the militants and the Pakistan Army at the highest altitudes in the world. The Army succeeded in pushing back the raiders from Srinagar and beyond the Baramulla Pass, but with Nehru's declaration of a cease-fire under the supervision of the United Nations, a considerable portion of territory now lay under firm control of the Pakistani Army, and the Kashmir conflict was born.

In September 1948, under the instructions of Acting Prime Minister Sardar Patel Singh and his commanders prepared plans for Operation Polo, a week-long operation that annexed the princely state of Hyderabad into the Indian Union. Singh remained a close advisor to Patel on managing the Kashmir conflict and issues of the integration of India.

In 1952, Baldev Singh became a member of the Parliament of India as a member of the Congress Party when the nation held its first democratic elections under the new Constitution of India, but did not join the Nehru administration. Singh remained the major political representative of Sikh concerns and was respected by the Akali Dal, and was re-elected in 1957. Singh died in Delhi after a prolonged illness in 1961

MULTICULTURALISM IN INDIA: DIVERSE DOTS IN A MULTIPLE MOSAIC

It is an empirical reality that the majority of countries are multicultural in character. Only 10 to 15 percent of all countries can be reasonably classified as ethnically homogenous. It is also true that, even as the notion of a "global society" becomes more and more a reality, ethnocentrism and identity assertion are also on the ascendancy. In the modern world, negotiation with diverse groups within the confines of state boundaries is unavoidable.

In this regard, new concepts such as "multiculturalism" (in Europe generally referred to as "interculturalism") have evolved, been discussed, and officially sanctioned by developed societies to tackle the problems of diversity.

Canada became the first Western country to adopt multiculturalism as an official state policy in 1971, and Australia followed in 1977. But what about developing multiethnic societies such as India? How is India managing its diversities?

The Concept

To begin with, a discussion of the concept of "multiculturalism" may be useful. Multiculturalism refers to the doctrine that "cultural diversity should be recognized as a permanent and valuable part of political societies," and endorses the idea of difference and heterogeneity that is embodied in "diversity." Though it distinguishes between the majority and minority communities, it argues for the granting of equality to all within the boundaries of both the public and political arenas. In other words, "equality" and "nondiscrimination" are the watchwords of multiculturalism. The concept centers around three basic ideas:

1. Human beings live and organize their lives within a culturally structured world and their worldview will fall within that culture.
2. Since every culture presents only a limited range of worldviews, the assistance of other cultures is required not only to understand the world better, but also to enrich its own culture and expand the horizon of general understanding. The world demands "cultural interdependence" rather than "cultural autarchy."
3. No culture is wholly worthless; each carries some value for its members. This, in turn, also means that no culture is perfect enough to justify imposing its values on others.

Multiculturalism assumes that society is composed not only of individuals but also of groups, each with a particular culture. Paradoxically, one group manages to establish its cultural norms (which is termed "universalization" or "hegemony") over the others and thus tries to impose its supremacy. The role of multiculturalism here is to erode the dominance of one group and empower or give voice to the other groups that are oppressed. "It is," as Nathan Glazer puts it, "a position that rejects assimilation and the 'melting pot' image as an imposition of the dominant culture, and instead prefers such metaphors as the 'salad bowl' or the 'glorious mosaic,' in which each ethnic and racial element in the population maintains its distinctiveness." Thus, a multicultural society is one of mutual and multiple recognitions where individuals are neither subjected to the tyrannies of compulsive cultural traditions nor [are] cultural groups subjected to the oppression of either the state or a dominant group within it. It is a decent society where there is a continued effort to eliminate humiliation and institute rights and dignity in the lives of individuals and groups. It is a society, which is respectful both of its internal as well as its external "other," one which is animated by reaching out to the "other" with grace, love and participation.

In other words, it constitutes an extensive effort to cope with diversity democratically. The efforts also engenders stiff resistance to the homogenizing moves either by the state or the dominant community. Forceful assimilation, it is held, is the antithesis of willing loyalty on the part of minorities toward the state, and leads to secession. Thus, the sense of "belonging" and loyalty toward a country can only be achieved through genuine recognition—public and institutional—of the many cultural groups and their rights, rather than mere acknowledgement of their existence. In other words, providing equal space and opportunity for different cultures to sustain themselves through institutional and legal support is as important as respect for diversity. The multiculturalists argue that if every cultural group is given its rightful access to resources, opportunities to retain, express, and develop their own culture, and institutional protection, it is possible to avoid divisive frictions and ensuing conflicts.

The Context

India is a culturally diverse country. This diversity manifests itself in every respect—religion, language, caste, region, and other social particularities. The situation in India is not the same as that in developed and official multicultural societies such as Australia or Canada. Indian society incorporates a bewildering number of minorities, whose boundaries have always been fluid and overlapping. So diverse is the society that it might be more difficult to characterize the majority than the minorities. And compared to Western societies, there is not the same degree of consensus regarding a national political culture and identity. Hence, at independence many prophesized that due to innumerable ethnic, religious, linguistic, regional, tribal, and caste differences India would soon break apart, or that disunity could only be prevented by military or authoritarian rule, and certainly not in a democracy. Yet, to the surprise of all, India has defied the prognostications that it was an "historic impossibility." How has it managed to maintain what Weiner terms a "baffling democratic exceptionalism"? What factors have been responsible for this multicultural coexistence of diverse ethnicities within one political unit?

Above all, it is because of the foresight of the founding fathers of the republic that India has been able to maintain its multicultural character. While some developed Western countries pride themselves on their multicultural policies, India recognized the importance of multiculturalism as early as in 1928 when the All-Parties Conference finalized a scheme for the Indian constitution in the form of the Nehru Report. It recommended inter alia equal rights for women, freedom to form unions, and dissociation of the state from religion in any form. The character of multiculturalism was evident in the set of nineteen rights recommended by the report. Not surprisingly, ten of those nineteen rights were later included in the constitution. Thus, early on, the national leadership showed a strong desire for a postindependence polity to be based on "unity in diversity."

In the formative years, the national leadership also displayed tremendous capacity for accommodating the interests of diverse communities without any prejudice or self-interest. Decisions were arrived at by consensus on all major issues. This tact in fact was inherited during the course of the struggle for national independence. For instance, Jawaharlal Nehru, Sardar Vallabhbhai Patel, Rajendra Prasad, Vinoba Bhave, Radhakrishnan, Rajagopalacharya, Jayaprakash Narayan, B. R. Ambedkar, Shyama Prasad Mukherjee, Narendra Dev, P. C. Joshi, and many other leaders of great caliber, though belonging to different parties, ideologies, and opinions, were interested in and worked for the higher goals of unity, national integration, democracy, and development. In addition, they enjoyed tremendous support and popularity from every sector of the society.

Unconsciously, the national legacy acted as a strong force for "multiculturalism." (India's first prime minister, Jawaharlal Nehru, for instance, pronounced that "the glory of India has been the way in which it manages to keep two things going at the same time: 'infinite variety' and 'unity in that variety.'") While nation building was to be based on a common struggle against colonialism and the existing challenges confronting the nation, the country's rich cultural, linguistic, religious, ethnic, and regional diversity was acknowledged and appreciated. While the other newly independent states at that period were influenced by the "dominant model" of nineteenth-century France, Italy, and Germany in the name of building a strong nation, the Indian leadership considered "diversity" and "multiple identities" as positive features and a source of strength for Indian culture, civilization, and the emerging Indian nationhood.

The Indian National Congress, which spearheaded the Indian freedom movement, articulated a secular and inclusive nationalism in which there would be "equal respect, equal opportunities and equal liberty for all, regardless of their religious affiliations or social location." It was argued that its inclusive and syncretic character was evident in the principles of Indian civilization. In this regard, a leading congress nationalist and the first vice-president of India, S. Radhakrishnan, noted, "No religion should be given preferential status of unique distinction. No person should suffer any form of disability or discrimination because of his religion but all alike should be free to share to the fullest degree in the common life. Secularism as here defined is in accordance with the ancient religious tradition of India." It was an unstated policy that "no state is civilized except a secular state." The talk of "Hindu Raj" or a state based on one culture was considered "mad."

At the organizational level, the structure and strength of the Indian National Congress Party also provided a strong base that discouraged mobilization on multiple lines, at least in the formative years. In other words, its amorphous structure enabled it to accommodate various groups and subgroups reflecting India's diversity. Its social base extended to all religions, castes, and regions. Its all-India appeal was deeply rooted and so it wasn't difficult for the party to sustain the policy of multiculturalism during its nearly four decades in power following independence. The party allowed dissent and encouraged different views and opinions, and free discussion.

The national leadership's commitment to transforming an India that was "multicultural by accident" into an India that was "multicultural by design" was evident in the constitutional debates and the subsequent passage of a "multicultural constitution" guaranteeing to all cultural groups both "equality of treatment" as a general rule and "differential treatment" in special circumstances. For instance, constitutional recognition and protection was offered to religious, cultural, and linguistic minorities. Equal respect, fairness, and nondiscrimination were to be the guiding principles of state policies toward minorities. Article 29 of the constitution protected the right of any group "having a distinct language, script or culture ... to conserve the same." Article 30 enshrined the right of "minorities, whether based on religion or language ... to establish and administer educational institutions of their choice," and extended statutory recognition to the religious and linguistic minorities.

But it is interesting to note here that differences based on caste and class were not recognized. In fact, in this regard the constitution embraced a policy of assimilation and affirmative action. The constitution prohibited the practice of untouchability in any form (Article 17), further empowering the state to make any law "providing for social welfare and reform or the throwing open of Hindu religious institutions of a public character to all classes and sections of Hindus" (Article 25.2b). At the same time, special privileges were provided to the "Scheduled Castes" and "Scheduled Tribes," including the reservation of seats in the parliament and the legislative assemblies (such reservations, which were initially stipulated for only ten years, were later extended to further periods of ten years as a formality) and in jobs, promotions, and educational institutions. These privileges were extended on the grounds of the backwardness of the beneficiaries. Thus, the constitution was, significantly, committing the state to ensure the protection and welfare of the weaker and more vulnerable sectors of the society.

Interestingly, language assertion, which was one of the important mobilization factors in postindependence India, posing a threat to national integrity, subsequently turned out to be a source of stability. In the postindependence polity, there were two camps vis-a-vis the linguistic reorganization of states and the establishment of a single national language. Supporters of a single language and script argued, "For thousands of years one and the same culture has all along been obtaining here. . . . It is in order to maintain this tradition that we want one language and one script for the whole country." It was felt that any attempt toward linguistic reorganization might threaten national integrity and might also be administratively inconvenient, and two high-level committees recommended against linguistic reorganization.

However, the support for local languages was stronger, especially in the south, as language was closely related to culture, and therefore to the customs of the people. And so recognition was extended to regional languages. Later it was even stated that "a linguistic mosaic might well provide a firm base for national unity." A single language was also not imposed. India adopted a three-language formula— Hindi was to be the national language and English, the link language, alongside the respective languages of the states (where "state" means the federal units within the Indian Union, *e.g.*, Andhra Pradesh, Jammu and Kashmir, Manipur, Bihar, etc.).

But there was a problem of the status of linguistic minorities (those who speak a language other than the official language of the state) in each state. To avoid any integrationist or discriminatory practices by the states, certain fundamental rights were provided in the constitution itself. Article 30 provides that "all minorities, whether based on religion or language, shall have the right to establish and administer educational institutions of their choice . . . The state shall. not, in granting aid to educational institutions, discriminate against any educational institution on the ground that it is under the management of a minority, whether based on religion or language."

The contribution of a highly professional, but apolitical, civil and military bureaucracy, an effective parliament, an independent judiciary, and a free press also contributed significantly to the maintenance of diversity in Indian society. Though the bureaucracy confronted congress time and again prior to independence, in the postindependence polity congress gained the upper hand. And if the bureaucracy was by nature inflexible and conservative, it showed no favoritism toward any communal or ethnic groups in the formative years.

In parliament, though congress was dominant, the opposition parties' views were heard and even respected. The debates in the House were conducted at a high level and policies were formulated only after intensive debate and discussion. Such consensual opinions on contentious issues indirectly prevented factional infighting among the competing political groups. As far as the judiciary was concerned, except for a brief period of time during Indira Gandhi's regime, it always served to protect the vulnerable and weak. Time and again, the apex court asserted its duty to safeguard the "basic features" of the constitution. Judicial rulings, in fact, have extended the rights of minorities. For instance, in Commissioner, Hindu Religious Endowments v. Lakshmindra case (1954) it was held by the supreme court that what was guaranteed by Articles 25 and 26 was not only the right of the individual to practice and propagate matters of faith or belief, but also all those rituals and observances that adherents regard as integral parts of a religion. At the same time, in a different case (Stanislaus vs Madhya Pradesh, 1977) it was held that right of propagation was not the right to proselytize, as that would be a violation of others' rights to freedom of religion. Thus the judiciary was responsible for maintaining a balance between freedom of faith and the right to propagate. The provision of autonomous bodies such as the National Commission for Minorities, the National

Commission for Scheduled Castes and Scheduled Tribes, and the National Human Rights Commission has reinforced multiculturalism in the sense that these commissions act as vigilantes of pluralism.

As for the media, it has generally functioned without restriction and advanced informed criticism and debate on vital issues in society. In the absence of a vigilant press, it would have become difficult to gauge if multiculturalism and other policies really worked. Through the efforts of the "Fourth Estate," various attacks on the minorities in the name of "Hindutva" have been brought to light and opposed. Despite these successes in maintaining and managing diversity, why have a "million mutinies" multiplied? Why is there an impression, of late, that the intolerance of multiplicity has arisen in India? Again, this is due to the erosion of the foundations upon which the multicultural society was based.

Multiculturalism in Contemporary India

For one thing, the dominant legacy of the national movement has come to be challenged. In recent years the political discourse in India has been colored by the intense struggle for power between competing political groups. Various strategies are being pursued—the most common being "Minority Appeasement." The Hindutva forces question the Nehruvian model of secularism and multiculturalism which, they allege, posed a threat to the well-being of the nation. They stir suspicions that Indian Muslims are more attached to Pakistan than their motherland or, alternatively, they argue for "unity" rather than "diversity." In fact, they insist on Hinduism being the national character of "Hindustan" rather than videshi (foreign) cultures.

Today there is a reverse movement and the process of "othering" at work, where even those who are within the space of the nation-state-society are being excluded one by one. A "thick" notion of ethnic nationalism has gained currency. According to this perception, minorities would have to accept a formulation of "national culture" in which their contribution is not recognized, and is either assimilated or accorded very limited rights of self-determination. Equal citizenship is not extended to all (although elimination of minorities need not be envisaged). Religious majoritarianism in this context, then, should be seen as a political project for state power rather than a fundamentalist one with religious aims. Though these ethnic or cultural conflicts are very deep-rooted, they still require intensive analysis. In India it is politics that influences and fine-tunes identity. Ethnic conflicts are nothing but power conflicts. In other words, they are only a subset of larger political conflicts.

Second, a fair amount of deinstitutionalization occurred in the 1970s and the 1980s at all levels. The Indian National Congress, as a party carrying forward the traditions of the national movement, faced splits with the demise of Jawaharlal Nehru, which resulted, from 1969, in the emergence of numerous splinter groups. Thus was born the strategy of electoral appeal on the basis of identity. Later, in the 1980s, the growing weakness of the Congress Party and its exclusive appeal to Muslim electorates strengthened the parties that sought support exclusively on a Hindu plank. Various identities found expression in numerous parties, and consequently competitive politics. As the Bharatiya Janata Party ("Indian People's Party," BJP) settled for Hindu votes, the Congress, the Janata Dal, and its splinter groups sought votes among the religious minorities and the backward and lower-caste groups and divided the Hindu constituency. To strengthen their base and to fill the political vacuum left by the Congress Party, while the BJP took up the cause of Ram and Ayodhya, the Janata Dal implemented the Madal Commission Report in 1990. This further encouraged the political parties to appeal to various manufactured identities. Thus a vicious cycle of political parties and various groups based on special identities proliferated.

Third, the quality of leadership also deteriorated gradually. After Nehru and his contemporaries, many of the second-generation leadership lacked national appeal or a larger vision of the interests of the country as a whole. Instead, the new leadership appealed to the primordial emotions of the masses so as to achieve shot-term gains. Thus, for instance, Laloo Prasad Yadav is associated with the

Yadava community of Bihar, Mayawati with the Dalits of northern India, Ramdoss with the Vaniyars of Tamil Nadu, and so on. With very few exceptions, the present leadership has lacked nationwide appeal and reach. Obviously, this has hindered the efforts to assert moral authority against majoritarianism.

Fourth, though the Indian constitution has stood the test of time, it did not anticipate that one day the majority community, by virtue of its numerical superiority, might monopolize state power by collective assertion. The constitution assumed that the state would remain "neutral" and "impartial" forever. While the constitution granted wide-ranging powers to the state in reforming Hindu social practices, it included no provisions empowering such intervention in Muslim or Christian society. For instance, under Article 25.2b the state was empowered to make anv law "providing for social welfare and reform or the throwing open of Hindu religious institutions of a public character to all classes and sections of Hindus." This does not apply to other religious minorities, though Sikhs, Jains, and Buddhists were included under "Hindus."

Thus the state was placed in a unique position. Some of the objectives of the constitution are being questioned today. The present BJP-led government has even appointed a commission to review some provisions of the constitution, who submitted its report to the government in March 2002. The constitution provides no guidance for the resolution of problems such as the Uniform Civil Code, cow slaughter, national language, recognition of the identity of certain minorities like Sikhs, and religious conversions. (A proposal to include a ban on conversions was omitted from the constitution, while "the right freely to profess, practice and propagate religion" was included. One majoritarian congressman, Lokanath Misra, denounced the provision as "a charter for Hindu enslavement.") Efforts to bring some clarity to the issue via the judiciary were stymied because, without legislative endorsement, there was not the sort of mandate required in a multicultural society.

And the parliament, which is considered the watchdog of government policies, has now become a mere talking shop where effective action is impossible. Thus the government pushes its agenda at any cost, the opposition tries to disrupt them, and policies to advance the common good fall by the wayside. Deinstitutionalization has also affected the autonomy of the judiciary, which has been sensitive to social issues and social justice. In the 1970s and 1980s, previous governments pushing populist policies ignored the law of the land. When the judiciary tried to defend the fundamental rights of the people, its independence was encroached upon by the executive. However, in recent years the judiciary has had more success maintaining its independence.

The process of politicization has permeated the bureaucracy, with efforts to convert it from a "neutral" player into a "committed" body. Apart from politicization, bureaucracy has been "casteized," communalized, and regionalized. Once a highly professional force, these processes have had an increasingly divisive effect on the bureaucracy. Of late, communalism has also penetrated the ranks of the police. During communal disturbances, they either stand by as mere spectators or act against the minorities. The Krishna Commission Report, to cite one example, found that the police played a role in the communal riots in Mumbai (formerly Bombay) in the wake of the Babri Masjid demolition in December 1992. This has been the case of many such riots in the country, in Gurajat, to cite a recent example.

Concluding Remarks

To summarize, India offers the model of a multicultural developing democracy. The character of multiculturalism is derived from its legal-institutional and national legacy. It was due to this policy that the country could survive as one entity for so long, contrary to predictions that it would disintegrate. But of late, multiculturalism has been under threat, especially with the increase in political competition, and the exploitation of ethnic issues by rightist forces. The ethnic conflicts are basically power conflicts and are a subset of larger political conflicts. To regain and retain its multicultural character, India should not abandon its historical commitments. To assure the protection of India's minorities, commitment to equal rights and social justice, and the embrace and implementation of nondiscriminatory policies, may be as important as the recognition of differences. The rise of religious majoritarian forces agitating against minorities and attributing mythical threats to them makes principled adherence to the multicultural tradition a moral imperative.

Still, some shifts in approach to Indian multiculturalism are necessary. Focusing on cultural differences without exploring the possible linkages between cultural deprivation and other forms of deprivations leads to a somewhat "culturalist" and limited approach to the problem of increasing social antagonism in Indian society. Granting recognition to minority groups without addressing the other social and political causes of hostility in society, and without emphasizing the need for democratization, could increase, rather than reduce, hostility and fragmentation in society. We need to correct this anomaly immediately, given the fact that increasing conflict in society is frequently attributable to poor access to resources. In this regard, the Indian state should be prepared to devolve more power to the village communities to enable the multicultural policy to develop from below.

The building of a multicultural society calls for continued democratic struggle and spiritual strivings. Along with listening, it calls for the ability to identify with the suffering of each other and, through this, to understand each other more fully and graciously, and to contribute to the building of a common future. Identification with suffering demands much more than does the glorification of identity politics and a triumphalist approach.

At the theoretical level, if multiculturalism is to become a true conflict-prevention and management activity, then the existing political and social theories, concepts, and vocabularies are not enough. The immediate task is to find a way to forge political unity without disturbing cultural differences. While no simple formula exists, states such as India probably need to simultaneously pursue a range of objectives including freedom and equality, as well as respect for the contributions of minorities to a shared national culture.

Feminists argue that Indian society is not purely multicultural, as women continue to be discriminated against. They point out that multiculturalism is silent on the issue of implicit bias against women in society. Hence, it is also important to take into consideration, in any multicultural policy, the removal of intracultural discrimination. Provisions to reserve seats in legislative bodies for women should be passed. Such affirmative action might initially benefit upper-class women, but judging from the success of affirmative action for women in Panchayat bodies, this situation would only prevail for a short time. Multicultural education in the curriculum needs to be strengthened. Of late there has been an attempt to change the character of secular education in the name of "standardization." But such an act of manufacturing "cohesion and consent" is a way to silence dissident voices and discourage diversity and tolerance. The aim of education is not just to impart information and to equip students for their careers, but also to help make the world a better place in which to live, and to impart a sense of responsibility toward one's fellow human beings. Most importantly, studies and research on multiculturalism should be encouraged so as to facilitate the development and dissemination of more information in the field.

Rising Flames

First, Brahman priests bathed the dead man's body in holy Ganges water, placed a green tulsi leaf between his lips and marked his forehead with yellow sandalwood paste and red kumkum powder. Then, in the late afternoon, a gun carriage drawn by Indian soldiers, sailors and airmen carried the body through Bombay's streets while vast crowds mourned and planes overhead showered the procession with flowers. Finally, at the cemetery, the dead man's son poured incense and ghee (semifluid butter) over the body and lit the pyre. Watching the rising flames, Jawaharlal Nehru sobbed. It was barely ten hours since a heart attack had brought death to long-ailing, 75-year-old Sardar Vallabhbhai Patel, Deputy Prime Minister of India.

True Talent. For all its hurry (which was in conformity to Hindu custom), the funeral which focused all India's eyes on Bombay last week was worthy of a prince —a fact which would have pleased tough, bull-necked Sardar Patel. The son of a farmer, Patel was 35 before he was able to afford to fulfil his dream of studying law at London's Middle Temple. And though he quickly won a reputation as a formidable criminal lawyer, it was only after Patel joined Gandhi's movement in 1916 that he discovered his true talent—politics.

Serving as Gandhi's right hand—some Indians said "fist" was a better word—Patel first showed a genius for leadership in his organization of civil disobedience campaigns against British land taxes, thereby won the unofficial title "Sardar" which means captain or leader. It was Patel whose iron will and political savvy converted the Indian National Congress from an association of petition writers into the effective organization which ran eight of India's eleven provinces even before the end of British rule.

Shared Power. Once India was free and Gandhi dead, Patel and Nehru shared supreme power. While Nehru made speeches and handled India's foreign relations, Patel shaped much of the nation's domestic policy. As Home Minister, he used his police to suppress Communist terrorism and to "discipline" troublesome labour unions. As States Minister, he brought India's 550-odd feudal princelings to heel. (In one whirlwind 96-hour tour he pressured two dozen princes into surrendering their political powers, thus added 8,000,000 people and 56,000 square miles to the Dominion of India.) Together with his many friends among India's industrialists, he worked successfully to modify Nehru's socialist tendencies.

Differing strongly in personality and political viewpoint, Nehru and Patel worked in harness with apparent smoothness until last September. Then their differences over the proper policy toward Pakistan and India's Moslem minority—Patel favoured a tough line—led to an open struggle for control of the Congress Party. Patel won the first round, but in the end mutual dependence prompted Patel and Nehru to patch up their quarrels. Last week Indians wondered whether Nehru, the crowd-swayer, could maintain order and unity in India without his opponent and partner, Patel the organizer.

NONCOOPERATION

Non-cooperation and peaceful resistance were Gandhi's "weapons" in the fight against injustice. In Punjab, the Jallianwala Bagh massacre of civilians by British troops caused deep trauma to the nation, leading to increased public anger and acts of violence. Gandhi criticized both the actions of the British Raj and the retaliatory violence of Indians. He authored the resolution offering condolences to British civilian victims and condemning the riots, which after initial opposition in the party, was accepted following Gandhi's emotional speech advocating his principle that all violence was evil and could not be justified. But it was after the massacre and subsequent violence that Gandhi's mind focused upon obtaining complete self-government and control of all Indian government institutions, maturing soon into Swaraj or complete individual, spiritual, political independence.

Sabarmati Ashram, Gandhi's home in Gujarat in December 1921, Gandhi was invested with executive authority on behalf of the Indian National Congress. Under his leadership, the Congress was reorganized with a new constitution, with the goal of Swaraj. Membership in the party was opened to anyone prepared to pay a token fee. A hierarchy of committees was set up to improve discipline, transforming the party from an elite organization to one of mass national appeal. Gandhi expanded his nonviolence platform to include the swadeshi policy – the boycott of foreign-made goods, especially British goods. Linked to this was his advocacy that khadi (homespun cloth) be worn by all Indians instead of British-made textiles. Gandhi exhorted Indian men and women, rich or poor, to spend time each day spinning khadi in support of the independence movement. This was a strategy to inculcate discipline and dedication to weed out the unwilling and ambitious, and to include women in the movement at a time when many thought that such activities were not respectable activities for women. In addition to boycotting British products,

Gandhi urged the people to boycott British educational institutions and law courts, to resign from government employment, and to forsake British titles and honours.

"Noncooperation" enjoyed wide-spread appeal and success, increasing excitement and participation from all strata of Indian society. Yet, just as the movement reached its apex, it ended abruptly as a result of a violent clash in the town of Chauri Chaura, Uttar Pradesh, in February 1922. Fearing that the movement was about to take a turn towards violence, and convinced that this would be the undoing of all his work, Gandhi called off the campaign of mass civil disobedience. Gandhi was arrested on March 10, 1922, tried for sedition, and sentenced to six years imprisonment. Beginning on March 18, 1922, he only served about two years of the sentence, being released in February 1924 after an operation for appendicitis.

Without Gandhi's uniting personality, the Indian National Congress began to splinter during his years in prison, splitting into two factions, one led by Chitta Ranjan Das and Motilal Nehru favouring party participation in the legislatures, and the other led by Chakravarti Rajagopalacharya and Sardar Vallabhbhai Patel, opposing this move. Furthermore, cooperation among Hindus and Muslims, which had been strong at the height of the nonviolence campaign, was breaking down. Gandhi attempted to bridge these differences through many means, including a three-week fast in the autumn of 1924, but with limited success. He was the Mahatma's no-nonsense lieutenant and his "executive arm."

Mahatma Gandhi gave the nation comprehensive inspirational leadership and the technique of "war without violence"—Satyagraha with Trimoola-Mantras, three Cardinal Foundational inviolable tenets—Satya (Truth), Tyaga (Sacrifice) and Seva (Service) as the watchwords. Tens of thousands, young and the not so young, all over the country joined India's Pilgrimage to Freedom. They gave up their promising careers and cheerfully faced lathi blows, imprisonment and even the gallows. Sardar Vallabhbhai Patel is one of the most distinguished among them. He was the Mahatma's no-nonsense lieutenant and his "executive arm." He was a man of iron discipline and his forte was action. He subjugated all emotions and sentiments to the demands of reason and pragmatic idealism.

"Sardar was to Gandhiji what Lakshmana was to Sri Rama," averred Rajaji, the first among the astute of modern Indian leaders. According to Dr. Pattabhi Sitaramayya, the eminent historian of India's freedom movement and a former President of the Indian National Congress "If Gandhiji was the Christ, Sardar was John the Baptist" of Nationalist India.

Prophetic Vision

The Sardar's prophetic vision is seen clearly in his perception of the Chinese threat from across the border when the cry throughout India was "Hindi-Chini Bhai-Bhai". In a letter to Pandit Jawaharlal Nehru, the then Prime Minister, the Sardar wrote on Nov.7, 1950.

"Throughout history we have seldom been worried about our North-East Frontier. The Himalayas have been regarded as an impenetrable barrier against any threat from the north. In our calculations we shall have to reckon with Communist China in the North and North-East, a Communist China which has definite ambitions and aims and which does not, in any way, seem friendly disposed towards us." Jawaharlal Nehru wrote a note on China and Tibet that touched on some of the Sardar's points and sent a copy of Sardar.

He wrote: "I think it is extremely unlikely that we may have to face any real military invasion from the Chinese side. It is inconceivable that China should divert its forces and its strength across the inhospitable terrain of Tibet and undertake a wild adventure across the Himalayas. Thus I rule out any major attack on India by China." The attack on India by China that Sardar feared and Jawaharlal had ruled out took place twelve years thereafter.

Simplicity of Sardar

The indomitable Sardar who decided the fate of hundreds of princes, many of them fabulously rich, and habituated to lavish living and giving, was so utterly unconcerned about accumulating any money for himself or his family. When he died, he left virtually nothing, not even a will. Like his Guru, the only "personal property" he left behind was a few pieces of clothes, one or two pairs of chappals and other minor personal effects.

CHAMPARAN AND KHEDA SATYAGRAHA

The first Satyagraha revolutions inspired by Mahatma Gandhi in the Indian Independence Movement occurred in Kheda district of Gujarat and the Champaran district of Bihar between the years of 1918 and 1919.

Champaran Bihar

In Champaran, a district in the then-province, now state of Bihar, tens of thousands of landless serfs, indentured labourers and poor farmers were forced to grow indigo and other cash crops instead of the food crops necessary for their survival. Suppressed by the ruthless militias of the landlords (mostly British), they were given measly compensation, leaving them mired in extreme poverty. The villages were kept extremely dirty and unhygienic, and alcoholism, untouchability and purdah were rampant. Now in the throes of a devastating famine, the British levied an oppressive tax which they insisted on increasing in rate. The situation was desperate.

Kheda Gujarat

In Kheda, a district of villages and small towns in Gujarat, the peasants mostly owned their own lands, and were economically better-off than their compatriots in Bihar, although on the whole, the district was plagued by poverty, scant resources, the social evils of alcoholism and untouchability, and overall British indifference and hegemony. However, a terrible famine had struck the district and a large part of Gujarat, and virtually destroyed the agrarian economy. The poor peasants had barely enough to feed themselves, but the British government of the Bombay Presidency insisted that the farmers not only pay full taxes, but also pay the 23 percent increase slated to take effect that very year.

Gandhi's Solution

While many civic groups sent petitions and published editorials, Gandhi proposed *satyagraha*-non-violent, mass civil disobedience. While it was strictly nonviolent, Gandhi was proposing real action, a real revolt that the oppressed peoples of India were dying to undertake.

Gandhi also insisted that neither the protestors in Bihar nor in Gujarat allude to or try to propagate the concept of *Swaraj*, or *Independence*. This was not about political freedom, but a revolt against abject tyranny amidst a terrible humanitarian disaster. While accepting participants and help from other parts of India, Gandhi insisted that no other district or province revolt against the Government, and that the Indian National Congress not get involved apart from issuing resolutions of support, to prevent the British from giving it cause to use extensive suppressive measures and brand the revolts as treason.

In Champaran

Gandhi established an ashrama in Champaran, organizing scores of his veteran supporters and fresh volunteers from the region. He organized a detailed study and survey of the villages, accounting the atrocities and terrible episodes of suffering, including the general state of degenerate living. Building on the confidence of villagers, he began leading the clean-up of villages, building of schools and hospitals and encouraging the village leadership to undo purdah, untouchability and the suppression of women. He was joined by many young nationalists from the parts and all over India, including Dr. Rajendra Prasad and Jawaharlal Nehru.

But his main assault came as he was arrested by police on the charge of creating unrest and was ordered to leave the province. Hundreds of thousands of people protested and rallied outside the jail, police stations and courts demanding his release, which the court unwillingly did. Gandhi led organized protests and strike against the landlords, who with the guidance of the British government, signed an agreement granting more compensation and control over farming for the poor farmers of the region, and cancellation of revenue hikes and collection until the famine ended. It was during this agitation, that Gandhi was addressed by the people as *Bapu* (*Father*) and *Mahatma* (*Great Soul*).

In Kheda

In Gujarat, Gandhi was only the spiritual head of the struggle. His chief lieutenant, Sardar Vallabhbhai Patel and a close coterie of devoted Gandhians, namely Narhari Parikh, Mohanlal Pandya and Ravi Shankar Vyas toured the countryside, organized the villagers and gave them political leadership and direction. Many aroused Gujaratis from the cities of Ahmedabad and Vadodara joined the organizers of the revolt, but Gandhi and Patel resisted the involvement of Indians from other provinces, seeking to keep it a purely Gujarati struggle. Patel and his colleauges organized a major tax revolt, and all the different ethnic and caste communities of Kheda rallied around it. The peasants of Kheda signed a petition calling for the tax for this year to be scrapped in wake of the famine. The government in Bombay rejected the charter. They warned that if the peasants did not pay, the lands and property would be confiscated and many arrested. And once confiscated, they would not be returned even if most complied. None of the villages flinched.

The tax withheld, the government's collectors and inspectors sent in Pathan thugs to seize property and cattle, while the police forfeited the lands and all agrarian property. The farmers did not resist arrest, nor retaliate to the force employed with violence. Instead, they used their cash and valuables to donate to the *Gujarat Sabha* which was officially organizing the protest. The revolt was astounding in terms of discipline and unity. Even when all their personal property, land and livelihood were seized, a vast majority of Kheda's farmers remained firmly united in the support of Patel. Gujaratis sympathetic to the revolt in other parts resisted the government machinery, and helped the shelter the relatives and property of the protesting peasants. Those Indians who sought to buy the confiscated lands were ostracized from society. Although nationalists like Sardul Singh Caveeshar called for sympathetic revolts in other parts, Gandhi and Patel firmly rejected the idea.

The Government finally sought to foster an honourable agreement for both parties. The tax for the year in question, and the next would be suspended, and the increase in rate reduced, while all confiscated property would be returned. Gujaratis also worked in cohesion to return the confiscated lands to their rightful owners. The ones who had bought the lands seized were influenced to return them, even though the British had officially said it would stand by the buyers.

Success and Legacy

Gandhi's resulting fame spread like fire all over the nation. He had become a defining influence on Indian Nationalism. The proud peasantry of Gujarat still revere Gandhi and Sardar Patel, and their role in the freedom struggle. Gujarat is the most industrialized and progressive state in India today. In Bihar, poverty and social conflict pervades what was the founding of the Satyagraha movement. The Naxalite insurgency is centred around the same age-old problem of class struggle between poor farmers and rich landlords, now involving terrorism.

BARDOLI SATYAGRAHA

The Bardoli Satyagraha of 1925 in the state of Gujarat, India during the British Raj was a major episode of civil disobedience and revolt in the Indian Independence Movement. It's success gave rise to Vallabhbhai Patel as one of the greatest Indian freedom fighters.

Background

Mohandas Gandhi had led two great revolts of communities of poor Indian farmers aginst the tyranny of the British government and allied landlords in Champaran, Bihar, and Kheda, Gujarat. Success in both struggles had helped win the farmers economic and civil rights, and electrified India's people. In 1920, the Indian National

Congress under Gandhi's leadership launched the Non-Cooperation Movement. Millions of Indians revolted against the British, boycotting the courts, government services, schools and disavowing titles, pensions and British clothes and goods. The freedom fighters, known as *Satyagrahis*, peacefully protested authoritarian British laws, and called for India's independence. Many thousands were beaten, tortured and arrested. But in 1922, a mob of protestors killed policemen in Chauri Chaura. Fearing a slide into violence and anarchy, Gandhi called for the struggle to be suspended. He was arrested in the same year and sentenced to be imprisoned for six years, but released in 1924. However, many Indians were depressed by the sudden halt of the struggle.

4

Patel and Farmer's Movements

FARMERS' MOVEMENTS IN INDIA

The farmers in India had to undergo great struggle in all the states to stop exploitation by the Jagirdars and Zamindars. Some of the movements were successful, but others failed. The farmer movements in 1907 under the leadership of Sardar Ajit Singh and in 1921 under Sardar Vallabhbhai Patel were successes, but others, such as the revolts in Chauri Chaura, Avadh and Mopla, were great losses. At the global level the French Revolution had changed the course of history, as it was the working class which became the vanguard of revolution in Europe. During the first half of the 20th century, national liberation struggles started against colonisation. In these colonies, very little industry was present and their working class, if it existed at all, was still in infancy, making the impetus for these rebellions have to come from somewhere else. It was Mao's peasant revolution in China which became a catalyst for national liberation movements in many colonies, including India.

It was in Punjab that India's first farmers' movement emerged. The role played by Ghadar party, led by Raja Mahendra Pratap, in the political awakening of India was an important step. The Sikhs of Punjab were the first to migrate to the United States and Canada in the 19th century. They financed and helped the formation of Ghadar party which when gave the call to Indians abroad to return home and fight British imperialism, had its call immediately heeded to. The majority of those who did return, 8000 of them comprised Punjab's Sikhs. Despite its apparent failure, the Ghadar Movement was to have a powerful impact on Punjab politics and especially on the peasants. It established a tradition of militant and secular anti-imperialism, enriched in subsequent years by social radicalism, which was to continue to inspire subsequent generations.

The peasant conferences were held in Lahore, Faislabad, Lyallpur and other places of West Punjab—the most famous of them being 1938-39 Long Morcha in Lahore when peasants from all over Punjab courted arrests for nine months in front of the assembly building. The slogan of *Pagri Sambhal O jatta* (Hold your head high, O peasant) was first raised at a mass gathering in Lyallpur in 1907. Ten Thousand people—the Hindus, the Muslims and the Sikhs alike—attended this gathering.

Farmers' Movements in Gujarat

Mahatma Gandhi had led two great revolts of communities of poor Indian farmers against the tyranny of the British government and allied landlords in Champaran, Bihar, and Kheda, Gujarat. Success in both struggles had helped win the farmers economic and civil rights, and electrified India's people. In 1920, the Indian National Congress under Gandhi's leadership launched the Non-Cooperation Movement. Millions of Indians revolted against the British, boycotting the courts, government services, schools and disavowing titles, pensions and British clothes and goods. The freedom fighters, known as *Satyagrahis*, peacefully protested authoritarian British laws, and called for India's independence. Many thousands were beaten, tortured and arrested.

Bardoli Satyagraha

Bardoli Satyagraha of 1925 in the state of Gujarat, India during the British Raj was a major episode of civil disobedience and revolt in the Indian Independence Movement. In 1925, the taluka of Bardoli in Gujarat suffered from floods and famine, which hurt the crop produce, leaving farmers facing great financial troubles. However, the Government of the Bombay Presidency had raised the tax rate by 30% that year, and despite petitions from civic groups, refused to cancel the rise in face of the calamities. The situation for the farmers was grave enough, that they barely had enough property and crops to pay-off the tax, let alone for feeding themselves afterwards.

The Gujarati activists Narhari Parikh, Ravi Shankar Vyas and Mohanlal Pandya talked to village chieftains and farmers, and solicited the help of Gujarat's most prominent freedom fighter, Vallabhbhai Patel. Patel had previously guided Gujarat's farmers during the Kheda struggle, and had served recently as Ahmedabad's municipal president. He was widely respected by common Gujaratis across the state. Patel and Gandhi decided that the struggle be left entirely to the people of Bardoli taluka.

Governor of Bombay ignored the request made by Patel to reduce taxes but reciprocated by announcing the date of collection. Patel instructed all the farmers of Bardoli taluka to refuse payment of their taxes. Aided by Parikh, Vyas and Pandya, he divided Bardoli into several zones-each with a leader and volunteers specifically assigned. Patel also placed some Gujarati activists close to the government, to act as informers on the movements of government officials. Patel instructed the farmers to remain completely nonviolent, and not respond physically to any incitements or aggressive actions from officials. He reassured them that the struggle would not end until not only the cancellation of all taxes for the year, but also when all the seized property and lands were returned to rightful owners.

The Government declared that it would crush the revolt. Along with tax inspectors, bands of Pathans were gathered from northwest India to forcibly seize the property of the villagers and terrorize them. The Pathans and the men of the collectors forced themselves into the houses, took all property, including cattle. The government began to auction the houses and the lands. But not a single man from Gujarat or anywhere else in India came forward to buy them. Patel had appointed volunteers in every village to keep watch. As soon as he sighted the officials who were coming to auction the property, the volunteer would sound his bugle. The farmers would leave the village and hide in the jungles. The officials would find the entire village empty. They could never find out who owned a particular house.

Members of the legislative councils of Bombay and across India were angered by the terrible treatment of the protesting farmers. Indian members resigned their offices, and expressed open support of the farmers. Even many in the Raj's offices heavily criticized the Government. In 1928, an agreement was finally brokered by a Parsi member of the Bombay government. The Government agreed to restore the confiscated lands and properties, as well as cancel revenue payment not only for the year, but cancel the 30% raise until after the succeeding year. While Patel credited Gandhi's teachings and the farmers' undying resolve, people across the nation recognized his vital leadership. Gandhi and his fellow satyagrahis called him *Sardar* for the first time, which in Gujarati and most Indian languages means *Chief* or *Leader*. It was after Bardoli, that Sardar Patel became one of India's most important leaders.

Farmer Movements in Rajasthan

Rajasthan is known as the land of kings and palaces and whose history is replete with encomium of their kings, the land known for "Sati", the land known for its vast tracts of deserts was witness to a history in making, the successful agitation of farmers and peasants for their right to livelihood.

The twenty-two princely states of erstwhile Rajputana state did not form a common political collectivity which can be termed as a unified political action model. Each state had its own territorial area, which was exclusive politically in that it had its separate administration nag and army. Each state retained its cultural and linguistic distinctiveness. Political authority varied from ruler to ruler depending upon the terms of contract or covenant with the paramount power dating back to the period of subsidiary alliance of Lord Wellesley. Obviously in a state like this, the freedom movement was bound to be divided and segmented, depending upon the degree of unity and cohesiveness among political players in each state. The two states of Jaipur and Jodhpur provided differential patterns of political movements.

Justice Kan Singh Parihar, the retired Judge of High Court of Rajasthan, has written about exploitation of farmers by Jagirdars prior to Independence as under: "Every thing that the Kisan had, never treated as his own. In Jagir areas all cultivators were really landless. There was no tenancy law and one could be thrown away from the land one cultivated at the pleasure of Jagirdar, his "malik". In most of the Jagirs a Jagirdar would in the first instance be taking fifty percent of the produce. This would be taken by actual division of the produce on the thrashing floor or by appraisal of the standing crop (*kunta*).

Then over and above the share of the produce the Kisan had to pay numerous "lags" or cesses. Together with the share of the produce known as "Hasil" these cesses meant that the Kisans had to part with more than eighty percent of their produce. The findings of the Sukhdeonarain Committee in the years 1940-42 bear this out. If a Kisan had to marry his daughter he had to pay "Chavri Lag", if he held a dinner then a "Kansa Lag"; if members of the family separated then "Dhunwa Lag" and so on. If the Jagirdar had a guest then fodder for his mount had to be supplied. Then there was "begar" that is forced labour, for tilling the personal lands of the Jagirdar. The homestead in which the Kisan lived in the Abadi had to be vacated in case he ceased cultivating the land. He could not alienate the plot to anyone."

Shri Kan Singh Parihar played a great role in drafting and enactment of Marwar Tenancy Act of 1949 and Marwar Land Revenue Act of 1949. Shri Parihar's idea of fixing all tenants in cultivatory possession as Khatedars thus making all of them almost the proprietors of all their fields, wells etc. without paying any premium or compensation and further being relieved from paying any lag bag (Cesses) etc., impacted these documents. This Marwar Tenancy Act of 1949 and Marwar Land Revenue Act of 1949 became a role model for the Rajasthan Assembly in 1955 and similar laws were passed based on these Acts, thus greatly benefiting the farmers of Rajasthan.

Shekhawati Farmers' Movement

The farmers of the Sekhawati region are considered to be the most advanced in the state of Rajasthan. The Shekhawati region has the highest literacy in the state. The most dominating farmer community in the rural areas of Shekhawati is Jat. The Jats are politically and economically very sound. The major land holdings in the present times are with Jats. Then comes the Rajput community who were the jagirdars before independence. The farmers of the region have done great struggle to come to the present status.

Before independence the conditions of the farmers were worst. The farmers of the Shekhawati region were exploited and oppressed by the Jagirdars during British Raj. They were deprived of fundamental rights. They were given inhuman treatment when the Jagirdars did not get cesses known as *lag* (tax) or *begar* (unpaid work) in time, they were given hard punishments and their crop used to be destroyed. There were 37 kinds of *begars* (work without pay) prevalent in Shekhawati. A newly married bride was forced to go first to Jagirdar.

The Shekhawati Jat farmers' movement had its genesis in the Jat Praja Pati Maha-Yagna a socio-religious festival held in January, 1934. It lasted ten days and was the biggest of its kind in Rajputana. It facilitated a widespread involvement of Jats in a community festival. Each Jat household attending it was to contribute some cash and an unspecified quantity of ghee. A total of two hundred maunds of ghee were used in the sacrificial flame. The function concluded with a triumphal elephant ride hitherto prohibited by the rules of Sikar Thikana. The success of this movement encouraged the Jats to hold more meetings on local levels and print literature to glorify Jat history.

The Yagna became a dominant symbol of folklore which glorified it as the beginning of an anti-feudal struggle. The peasants demanded remissions in taxes and finally a Jat-Sikar Thikana Agreement was signed on August 23, 1934, by which the Thikana authorities conceded to abolish various lags (taxes) and agreed to provide for a mobile dispensary. The following year, the Kisan Sabha formally came into existence and under its aegis the famous Sikar Andolan of 1935 was launched. With outside mediation efforts of Jamnalal Bajaj, Sir Chhotu Ram-a renowned Jat leader of Punjab and Ratan Singh of All India Jat Mahasabha, a settlement was arrived at and the Jats were promised remissions of rent, abolition of internal cesses and an introduction of fixed rent tenure. The Jats were also promised equal opportunities in Thikana administration and were permitted to ride elephants and horses and to construct schools for their children.

The formation of a Jat Kisan Panchayat was officially sanctioned and the right to agitate for redressal of grievances in non-Khalsa areas was conceded. Much however, could not be made out of these agreements for two reasons. First, the subordinate Thikanedars of Sikar did not fully cooperate with Sikar authorities to ensure compliance with the terms of these agreements. Secondly, the beginning of settlement operations and reform of revenue administration was a time-consuming process which entailed enormous delay. This was interpreted by the Jats as a breach of agreement and hence, they indulged in acts of disorder and violence, which were perceived by Thikana authorities as signs of bad faith. In the meanwhile two unsavoury incidents led to a termination of agreements. The first, occurred at Khudi village, where the sight of Jat bridegroom riding a horse incensed the local Rajputs and the two sides readied themselves for an armed combat. The state authorities asked the two parties to disperse but the Jats refused. The state police charged and in the melee that followed, several people were injured. The second incident took place at Kudan village, where about one hundred armed Jats attacked Sikar revenue officials. The police fired upon the armed mob, which resulted in several casualties and injuries. A total of 104 Jats were arrested.

Farmers of the Shekhawati, mainly the Jats, united against oppression of Jagirdars by forming 'Sikar Jat-Kisan-Panchayat' and stopped giving "lags" or cesses to the Jagirdards. The 'Jaipur Praja-

Mandal' also supported the Shekhawati farmers' movement against abolition of Jagirdari system. The leaders of 'Bijoria-Kisan-Movement' of 1922, 1931, and 1932 supported the movement of Shekhawati farmers. The Jagirdars tried to suppress the movement in many ways. Many farmers were killed and a large number were sent to jail. A Jat farmer was beaten to death in the market of Sikar town; his dead body was thrown and insulted. This movement got support from famous Kisan leaders like, Baldev Ram Mirdha, Nathuram Mirdha and Kumbharam Arya. After a long struggle the farmers got rid of oppression and got the ownership right over the land they were cultivating.

The leading Jat farmers of Shekhawati region, who played important role in the movement for abolition of the Jagirdari system, were:

- Sardar Har Lal Singh, Mandasi
- Iswar Singh Bhamu Bhairupura,
- Hari Singh Burdak and Hardeva Palthana,
- Prithvi Singh Gothra,
- Ganeshram Kudan,
- Panne Singh Bataranau,
- Goru Singh Katrathal,
- Deva Singh Bochalya,
- Chandrabhan Singh,
- Hardev Singh Nehra Harsawa.

Shekhawati farmers' movement against abolition of Jagirs got great support from outside Kisan leaders like Sir Chhotu Ram from Haryana, Kunwar Ratan Singh and Thakur Deshraj from Bharatpur, Kunwar Hukum Singh from Aangai.

Marwar Farmers' Movement

The farmers of the Marwar region are considered to be the most simple in the state of Rajasthan. The most dominating farmer community in the rural areas of Marwar is Jat. The Jats are politically and economically very sound. The major land holdings in the present times are with Jats.

Though the position of *Kisan* (farmer) in what was *Khalsa* (under the direct control of the state) was better in comparison to a Kisan of the Jagir areas, he was only a little above a beast of burden. In Jagir areas of Marwar state before independence all cultivators were really landless. There was no tenancy Law and one could be thrown away from the land one cultivated at the pleasure of Jagirdar, his "malik". In most of the Jagirs a Jagirdar would in the first instance be taking fifty percent of the produce. This would be taken by actual division of the produce on the thrashing floor or by appraisal of the standing crop (*kunta*). The latter method proved at times more onerous as the appraisal depended on the whims of the *Kamdar.* Then over and above the share of the produce the farmer had to pay numerous "lags" or cesses. There were 64 kinds of *begars* (work without pay) prevalent in Marwar. Then the bigger Jagirdars had judicial powers including magisterial powers. Further they had their own police force besides the revenue staff. This enabled them to keep their stronghold on the farmers. Over and above this policy of divide and rule was fully practiced. By offering the temptation of giving better land for cultivation one farmer would be set against another. There were no schools worth the name in rural areas and the masses were steeped in ignorance.

The oppression of the public by traditional Samantas (chiefs) and Jagirdars (feudatories) of Marwar state made their life difficult, which led to a class war. In urban areas, Jaynarayan Vyas started agitation against oppression, under the banner of "Marwar Lok Parishad" founded on 16th May 1938. This movement was supported by National Congress. The persons who played important role in "Marwar Lok Parishad" were: Shiv Dayal Dave and Jorawar Singh Oswal of Nagaur, Rajpurohit Manji Jagarwal of (Bagra, Jalore), Kishanlal Sahu, Manak Chand Konari and Sari Mal of Kuchaman City, Tulsiram of Didwana, Srikishan Pandit of Kolia and Sukhdev Dipankar of Ladnu.

Rural masses of Marwar were united by Kisan Kesari-Baldev Ram Mirdha under the banner of "Marwar Kisan Sabha" founded in 1940. After the formation of Rajasthan, Baldev Ram Mirdha who had by then retired from Government service formed the "Rajathan Kisan Sabha" and unified the *Kisans* of Rajasthan under its banner. He was its first president. Since the broad objectives of the *Kisan Sabha* and the congress were identical the congress leaders approached Baldev Ram Mirdha to unite the Rajasthan *Kisan Sabha* with the Congress. Baldev Ram Mirdha was a visionary and he realized that the two could not and should not remain separate. Therefore, he just made one demand from the national leaders that the Jagirs be abolished forthwith in Rajasthan. This was agreed to by the Congress high command with the result that the Jagirs were soon abolished. A tenancy law was passed and the cultivating farmers were made the owners of the land.

Gharsana Farmers' Movement

The tehsil town of Gharsana and the neighbouring Raola in Sriganganagar district of Rajasthan is currently site of clashes between the police and the farmers agitating for irrigation water. The farmers, and their leaders who led the agitation under the banner of Kisan Mazdoor Vyapari Sangarsh Samiti, were either nursing their injured or in hiding. About 20 injured have been admitted to the Gharsana hospital and the district hospital in Sriganganagar. The authorities said curfew was clamped in Raola as a precautionary measure as in the previous agitation by the farmers on the same issue in October-November 2004 both Raola and Gharsana had witnessed serious violence.

Earlier in October 2004, Defying prohibitory orders, hundreds of farmers had gheraoed the SDM's office at Gharsana town in Sriganganagar district, reviving their agitation for irrigation water after the October 27, police firing which claimed five lives. With a view to appeasing the agitating farmers, the Vasundhara Raje Government ordered the removed of the Divisional Commissioner of the region, Mr Ramavtar Raghuvanshi, and Superintendent of

Police, Mr Sunil Dutt, while two officers of the Rajasthan Administrative Service, Mr Indra Singh Rao and Mr Hitesh Kumar, have been placed under suspension. The farmers' agitation led the Government to impose curfew in July 2005 also.

Farmers of Gharsana, at Ganganagar in Rajasthan, are on path of confrontation with the BJP government for the release of water from Pong Dam to the Phase I areas of Indira Gandhi Canal, the lifeline of farmers in the Gharsana-Raola agriculture belt. At a juncture when India is importing wheat from other countries, the state government is dissuading farmers in the region from cultivating wheat during the rabi season. The farmers have been told to sow barley or mustard, rather than wheat, which is a water-intensive crop. The movement has gained momentum with the Kisan Mazdoor Vyapari Sangharsh Samiti, the committee of farmers, labourers and agro-traders of the region deciding to go ahead with sowing wheat. The strife over water has seen the peasants and the state administration clash often in the past three years. Seven farmers were killed and many were injured when police fired at protesters in 2004.

UNIFICATION OF PRINCELY STATE AND PATEL

Rajputana Under British Paramountcy

The Failure of Indirect Rule : When India became independent in 1947, nineteen princely states and three chiefships of Rajputana were amalgamated into a single political unit, Rajasthan, that became a state within the Indian union. The special form of indirect rule, paramountcy, which Britain exercised in the princely states had not prepared Rajputana for independence. Princely rule and legitimacy, based on birth, was abruptly replaced by parliamentary government and the authority of democracy. Institutional changes which had taken place in British India over more than one hundred years were brought into being in Rajasthan in less than five. This work was accomplished not by those who stood at the head of the old regime but by those who had opposed it from within and by the new men of the central government in Delhi.

Rajasthan succeeded states which, after the making of treaties with Britain in 1818, had lived under that ambiguous conception of sovereignty which deprived the princes of their foreign powers and left their domestic powers subject to certain supervision. The gentle breezes of change and British political influence modified Rajput monarchial and feudal institutions but did not replace or even fundamentally transform them. The princes and their administrators learned what makes a respectable modern state and began, often with British guidance to construct new institutions. Sometimes these were effective and meaningful; more often they had the insubstantiality of stage setting. The political community expanded very little, but newly aware groups did take shape and hover near its boundaries waiting to assert their claims. The gradual extension of the rule of law and a growing appreciation for modern administration began but did not complete the separation of the state and its public offices and finances from the private estate, retainers, and income of the prince. These changes contributed to a consciousness of political rights and liberties but failed to make them constitutional. Until the crises and traumas of 1947 revealed their hollowness and fragility, the traditional ideas and practices of legitimacy and rulership, which paramountcy was designed to protect from external and internal dangers, continued intact.

Vagueness concerning the limits of power is likely to be helpful to those who exercise it. The British Government studiously avoided precision in defining paramountcy, the exercise of power over princely states. Its meaning derived from a wide variety of treaties concluded with different princes and a system of case law and precedent whose interpretation lay with the paramount power. The Butler Commission concisely summarized the deliberate ambiguity of paramountcy in 1928 when, in response to a request from the princes to define the concept, it merely stated: "Paramountcy must remain paramount." Paramountcy implied that the governor-general of India would exercise power in the field of foreign affairs, defense, communications, and coinage on behalf of the princely states. It left the states internally autonomous while guaranteeing the rulers protection against enemies foreign and domestic. The guarantee against domestic enemies brought with it unsystematic intervention in domestic affairs to insure that there would not be too many of them. An agent or a resident drawn from the special administrative cadre known as the political service represented the governor-general in the state and exercised these powers.

The influence of the British on the states depended on the overall policy espoused by the governor-general and the respective qualities of the political agents and the princes. A hands-off policy toward the princely states followed the rebellion of 1857, which frightened the British government away from strong interventionism. This policy ended at the turn of the twentieth century when Lord Curzon began to impress the princes with their responsibilities. The example of Maharaja Ganga Singh of Bikaner, who in 1899 sharply protested against the political agent's desire to review the dismissal of two petty state officials, was not exceptional in the Curzon era. "Nothing is further from my mind [the agent wrote] than interference with your orders, and I trust there will never be any greater need than there is now for contemplating such interference. It is, however, the duty of every political agent to satisfy himself that the state with which he is, is well and justly governed, or how it is governed, and he can only do this by occasionally asking for reports on selected petitions." Lord Minto's easy-going policy eased the pressures for reform and intervention that Curzon had applied, but Lord Linlithgow's viceroyalty in the 1930's once again brought an emphasis on administrative modernization and reform, and hence greater intervention.

The British exercised influence through numerous channels even in areas beyond the ordinary concerns of paramountcy. The crown drew to itself the right to recognize the successor to the *gaddi* (throne) of any state, and thus became involved in settling succession disputes. Since legitimate successors were often minors, and since during succession disputes unprotected minors sometimes expired prematurely, the crown took some responsibility for the minority administration. It appointed the regent, often making its selection within the state, sometimes sending in a member of the political service to conduct the administration. Minority rule provided the occasion for strong, often creative, intervention and laid the basis for subsequent influence. At the end of a twenty-year minority administration exercised on behalf of Maharaja Umed Singh of Kotah by the political agent to that state, he offered the following "advice" to the newly invested ruler: "Your Highness will in all important matters consult the political agent, be guided by his advice, and obtain his concurrence before introducing any important change in the measures carried out during your minority." Similar "advice" was given at Bikaner at the same time, although in later years the maharaja of that state became notoriously independent.

The channels of British influence were both direct and indirect. The political agent advised in the matter of the prince's education. In the twentieth century especially, English tutors were often employed, unless the prince attended one of the princes' and nobles' schools established with Government of India blessings to transmit the more superficial trappings of English public school education. Less superficial traits, like the dutiful asceticism of ruling classes trained at Eton, Harrow, and Winchester were more difficult to transmit to heirs who arrived with retinues of ten servants. In the twenty years before independence, the larger states often appointed Englishmen from the political department as *dewans* (chief ministers) and ministers. In the latter years of the British *Raj*, when Indian members of the Indian civil service began to control provincial administration under the direction of Indian ministers in British India, a senior member of the political service observed: "The administration in so-called Indian India was sometimes more under the control of British officers than it was in British India." The emergence of nationalism in British India had a curious effect on both the British attitude toward the princes and on the princes themselves. To the extent that the princes were a bulwark of British power, particularly when it began to be challenged in British India, the Government of India was inclined to treat them generously. To the princes, generosity meant being left alone. Yet the need for internal improvements became more apparent as nationalism and reformist sentiment grew. Improvement meant interference.

The chamber of princes was established on a permanent basis in 1921, the year after Gandhi turned the nationalist movement in British India in a popular direction. The chamber provided a forum in which princes could protest against efforts by the government to intervene and hurry them along and a context in which they became more conscious of one another and of the requirements that accompanied being a "modern ruler". The chancellor of the chamber of princes in 1927 circulated a memorandum summing up some of the most significant reforms on which he hoped they might all agree; suggested reforms included limitation of the privy purse to 10 per cent of state revenues, an independent judiciary, security of tenure for state civil servants, a promulgated code of law, and the maintenance of an efficient and honest police force. The chamber began to create an environment in which good government became more fashionable. Princes vied with one another to secure the services of one of the four or five men who had built all-India reputations as able chief ministers in princely states. Paramountcy did, then, affect the structure and quality of government in the princely states. But the channels of British influence were too irregular and undefined to exploit consistently the available opportunities. Imperial policy, which varied with the outlook of the viceroy, his agents, and the developments in British India, never achieved the direction or firmness necessary to make it otherwise.

Caste, clan, land, and chivalric reputation had legitimized rulership in the old princely states ruled by Rajputs, members of the warrior-ruler caste (Kshatriyas). After conclusion of the subsidiary alliances in 1818, British recognition and support were required as well. The addition did little, however, to change explicitly the way most Rajastbanis understood the legitimacy of their maharajas or nobles; ascriptive factors justified the exercise of power in 1947 as they had done in 1818.

Yet the old ideas about what made government legitimate were subtly undermined during the period of paramountcy by a tentative new concern with effectiveness and consent. The example of events in British India and British pressures suggested that a prince justify his rule by performance. As Lord Curzon, who was wont to lecture the princes on this subject, put it: A ruler's "*gaddi* (throne) is not intended to be a divan of indulgence, but the stern seat of duty", and "by this test will he, in the long run, as a political institution, perish or survive." Princes were pressed to convert their courts into more "public" institutions and to orient their rule towards public rather than personal and familial benefits. The differentiation of the princes' privy purse from the public revenue, incomplete as it was in many states, and reports on administration that provided a rudimentary accounting of how government had discharged its task were the chief manifestations of this shift. The same influences affected the bureaucracy, which was urged to consider itself a public and professional service, not a body of private retainers.

The idea that greater public service would not only add luster to the name of the maharaja—that idea had already existed in pre-British days—but also become a condition of legitimate rule was by no means universally understood. Only a few, some of the new-style court bureaucrats and members of a tiny educated class, saw its relevance and import. But a good many maharajas, affected by their English tutors or schools, pressure from the political department, the communications spill-over from British India or far-seeing ministers, began to believe that they should serve as well as rule. Their consciousness of themselves as public men was affected by this idea even though they failed often to act on it. At the time of independence, the maharajas' feeble resistance to the challenge of democratic authority and leadership arose in part from an awareness of their failure to meet the new standards.

Traditional ideas of legitimacy were modified in another and more subtle respect. Ordinarily the maharaja sought not to offend and listened to the grievances and advice of the limited political community of the twice-born castes, the Brahmans, Kshatriyas and Vaishyas who could help or hinder him spiritually, militarily, and financially. Most Rajasthanis were politically irrelevant and thought that they should be. Before 1935, only a tiny circle of intellectuals and modern nationalists without status and power thought otherwise. After 1935, the potential political community, those seeking to share power in the state and to influence government, expanded. A handful of schoolmasters, lawyers, and journalists began to awaken the urban and rural common people by telling them that their interests and aspirations were relevant for government and that its authority should rest on their will. They made little progress; only after independence during the first general election of 1952 did Rajasthanis begin to perceive a connection between popular sovereignty and legitimacy. If some maharajas accepted the notion that their right to rule depended in a measure upon performance and service, none conceded that it depended upon the support of organized public opinion. Some used means to consult public opinion, such as great annual *durbars* (royal public audiences), to inform themselves and their governments of public grievances and aspirations, but none entertained the notion of reigning rather than ruling by transforming the state into a democratic constitutional monarchy. Only toward the end of World War II, when the signs of the times pointed to the loss of British support and a more democratic future, did some princely states introduce elections based on limited franchise for legislatures to be dominated by an official or appointive majority.

The presence of the idea of democratic authority, though it lacked a large social base and effectively organized political support, weakened older beliefs and paved the way for its own ultimate realization. The strongest safeguard for any concept of legitimacy is for it to appear as natural; without rivals, its self-evidence stands unquestioned. The innocence of alternatives, which was traditional legitimacy's most powerful safeguard, was shattered by knowledge of the growing influence of organized public opinion in British India and its nascent expression within Rajasthan.

Prior to the British arrival, power in the Rajput states was shared by a territorial nobility and a maharaja, who was often their clan chief. The initial effect of British paramountcy in the nineteenth century not only sustained this diffusion of power but also undermined the attempts of some rulers to centralize power at the expense of their nobility. Sir Alfred Lyall in the late nineteenth century saw the nobles as a countervailing power of the kind that had created feudal liberties in the West. This belief persisted into the twentieth century when it was challenged but not replaced by a British policy of centralization designed to create financial viability and orderly and efficient administration. In the small states, the new policy was resisted by the maharajas since it involved partial if not total surrender of sovereignty, but in the larger states modest advances were achieved.

The pattern of decentralization in the nineteenth century had not been uniform. In Kotah, Dewan Zaiim Singh virtually replaced the maharaja and reduced the independent territorial power of the nobility by making them dependent on the crown. In Dholpur and Bharatpur, two eastern states of Rajasthan ruled by Jats rather than Rajputs, territorial nobility on the Rajput pattern never existed. Formally classified as a peasant caste, the Jats had a recent history of military prowess and local rulership. Their states were centralized in the negative sense that they lacked strongly articulated local power, but not in the positive one that they possessed a vigorous central government. The Rajput states confronted a dual task: to reduce the power of the nobility and to strengthen state government.

Maharaja Sawai Man Singh's efforts in Jaipur throughout the 1930's to strengthen his hand against his feudality illustrates one of the more successful attempts to reduce feudal power. It did not produce striking results. His effort to diminish the extensive financial, civil, police, and judicial powers of the state's great nobles in Shekhawati began in 1932 with his appointment of C.V. Wills, a British Indian official, to investigate the historical and legal relations between the maharaja and his nobles. The proceeding itself, utilizing Western legal concepts, departed from traditional methods. Wills' findings, perhaps not surprisingly, established that the nobles' claims to a separate and quasi-autonomous status had no legal or historical justification. Not until 1939, seven years after Wills began his labours, did the Jaipur *durbar* venture to assert the powers which his investigations had persuaded it that it could claim: to vary the assessments of the *thikanas* (nobles' estates) which, by remaining fixed, had rendered the state revenue inelastic; to treat the state as a single economic and commercial unit by extending its customs cordon to include the *thikanas*; to abolish residuary civil and criminal powers reserved by some *thikanedars*. Only in 1939, then, did Jaipur clearly claim the minimum fiscal and legal powers characteristic of a modern state. Having done so, the *durbar* announced that in practice it would insist on only some of them. The *durbar* was "graciously pleased," it announced, for example, "to order that the *muamla* (assessments) be declared to be permanently fixed at the existing figure in all cases," foregoing, thereby, that enhancement of revenues so vital for substantial expansion of state functions.

The paramount power's responsibility for external security rendered the military forces of the states less significant, but they too reflected the diffusion of power. State forces were maintained to keep law and order and for ceremonial purposes and, from the 1890's, as imperial service troops to aid the Government of India in foreign wars. The *thikanas* kept armed retainers to satisfy their obligations to the maharaja and for their own purposes. Only in 1925 was the end of feudal military relations in Jaipur formally recognized. At that time the *thikanedar's* obligation to provide mounted and foot soldiers to the Jaipur *durbar* was commuted to cash. After this change some, nevertheless, continued to maintain military units. In 1937, the Jaipur *durbar* confronted the last gasp of feudal military power when its forces faced ten thousand armed retainers in Sikar, the state's largest *thikana*. Bikaner, more forward in this respect, faced its last significant challenge in 1905.

It is possible that, but for British intervention, effective centralization might have gone further in such vigorous and forward-looking states as Bikaner and Jaipur. The political department tried, on the one hand, to encourage modernization and on the other, to prevent an efficient autocrat such as Bikaner or a gentler one such as Jaipur from running roughshod over his nobility. The two aims were incompatible. Effective centralization could not proceed without reducing or transforming the civil and judicial power of the nobles, as well as the immense economic power they exercised over their estates, which covered over half the territory of most Rajput states. Crucial to control of the *jagir* (nobles' grants) areas were settlement operations that would establish occupancy rights and revenue payments, and state intervention to enforce these and other relationships between peasants and nobles. But vigorous efforts to restrict and control the landed nobility, such as in Bikaner in the first decade of the century, Jaipur in the 1930's, and Jodhpur in the 1940's, invariably generated resistance and raised the possibility of the paramount power having to fulfil its pledge to protect rulers from internal rebellion.

The political department considered risking such difficulties. In 1942 it prepared to press for fair rent, occupancy rights, and records of rights in Rajasthan, especially in Jaipur. But the advice of officers familiar with the area persuaded the department that the proposal was too risky. The political department's desire to avoid the difficulties that economic or social or administrative changes entailed, especially when the Congress in British India was prepared to use such difficulties for its own purposes, was buttressed by a solicitude for the property rights of the nobility. The result was a policy of marginal and limited changes in land relations. On the other hand, without British supervision most Rajput princes would not have pressed for radical change. Efforts to amalgamate police, judicial, and certain administrative functions of some of the smaller Rajasthan principalities, for example, ran into resolute opposition from princes concerned to preserve their dynastic and territorial sovereignty and individuality. The political department considered centralization and greater administrative efficiency desirable but was not prepared to risk much on their behalf by forcing the princes or coercing the nobles.

Most states sought to rationalize government in such a way that central power could reach further as it became stronger. The establishment of specialized government departments with defined responsibilities and jurisdictions strengthened executive control. A letter by the twenty-one-year old Maharaja Ganga Singh of Bikaner illustrates the early efforts of an able Rajput ruler: There is nothing laid down as to the limits of power which each Member [of Council] or the Dewan [chief minister] can exercise over the departments under their control. The result is that sometimes important things are decided and settled by officers above mentioned, whereas some trifling things are sometimes referred to the full Council or to me. In fact, owing to there being no rules everything is done in a haphazard way. There is also a general tendency to shirk responsibility as much as possible, and for everybody to try to have a finger in the pie whenever they have a good opportunity. The result is unsatisfactory and injurious to the interests of the state while much extra work is thrown on my shoulders.

Ganga Singh eventually became the ablest Rajput ruler in the twentieth century, but he too opposed the development of regular procedures where they interfered with his personal rule. He saw that bureaucratization itself, even without responsible government, involves a restraint on power. For years he resisted appointing a permanent and responsible chief minister to direct the government even though he was often out of the country. Ganga Singh also resisted the establishment of competitive civil service recruitment. On the other hand, Bikaner state was divided into districts and subdistricts for purposes of revenue administration as early as 1872, strengthening crown control. Not until 1945, and then only for the crown lands, did Jaipur establish district officers responsible for revenue, law, and order and give them powers approximating those of British Indian officers.

The competence of the bureaucracy in many states increased during the era of paramountcy. Academic qualifications, reflecting the growth of educational opportunities in the twentieth century, were added to those of caste and heredity, but since they were no guarantee of competence, the state administrative cadres remained something less than merit services. The qualifications, however, did represent a concession to recruitment by achievement rather than by ascription. The increasing emphasis on educational qualifications can be seen from a comparison of princely state officials recruited in the 1920's, 1930's and in 1940-47. Among 143 *tahsildars*, chief administrative officers for *tahsils* (subdivisions of a district), selected from princely state services for positions in the administration of post-independence Rajasthan, 10 per cent of those recruited in the 1920's, 56 per cent of those recruited in the 1930's, and 94 per cent of those recruited in the 1940's had B.A. degrees.

Apparently no state recruited through competitive examinations before 1940, and none established security of tenure. In 1941 Udaipur established a formal civil service, recruited competitively; Jodhpur began competitive recruitment in 1942, Jaipur in 1943 (judicial) and 1944 (civil), but Bikaner never did. Thus, while professional competence was more highly valued, the states did not, until World War II, give bureaucrats the job security nor insist on the merit which might have strengthened them against accepting irregular subventions from below or currying favour above. Taken as a whole, the princely state civil servants selected for the post-independence services of Rajasthan showed the marks of patrimonial service and court relations in their manners and style. These years also saw the growth of new ideas of financial and administrative accountability. Their realization, however limited, played a significant part in the conversion of princely rule from private and familial estate management to rule directed toward public concerns and benefits. The demand that princes give some public account of their administration first came from the paramount power toward the end of the nineteenth century. In response, the states began to issue annual reports on public administration which gave abbreviated statements of the fiscal situation of the state and of programmes and policies. They provided even less enlightenment than the dullest British Indian provincial reports. But the need to publish a rudimentary budget encouraged the modern-minded maharajas to differentiate their privy purses from public funds. This led in turn to a sense that purses should have a known and regular relationship to state revenue. In time, 10 per cent came to be considered the correct proportion. This limit was not always observed.

Thus Kotah, in 1935-36, allocated 16 per cent of state revenues to palace expenses, and Bikaner allocated about 17 per cent in 1935-36. States often conveyed the impression in annual reports that they observed the 10 per cent limit when they did not, hiding major palace construction in the figures for the public works department. In 1937-38 Jaipur reported a Rs. 1,428,255 palace expenditure but did not choose to report how much of the Rs. 1,586,649 public works department figure had gone to the splendid Jaipur House then being built in Delhi, or the George V Solarium, also under construction. (One wonders to what extent princes protected themselves against criticism from the political agent by naming some extravaganza "Prince of Wales Hall.") The reports did not circulate widely but did provide the basis for some public scrutiny. Spokesmen for the sporadic democratic movements in the states liked to point out that the maharaja of a million people ought not, perhaps (as in Bikaner), receive a privy purse of approximately $450,000 when his state spent only about $50,000 for education.

Princes gave such accountings as they did because they were anxious to win approval of the political department. A "red tick" put opposite their names by the political agent was thought to be most undesirable. The remarks by the viceroy, Lord Irwin, addressed to the maharaja of Jaipur at the maharaja's formal assumption of office in 1932 indicate the steps taken by the Government of India to insure a ruler's concern with administrative performance, and also illustrate the benignly paternal atmosphere from which that concern took its meaning. For the last six months you have been receiving administrative training in your own State under the personal supervision of Mr. Glancy. In that time, short though it is, you have had an opportunity of studying the working of all principal State departments, have regularly attended the meetings of the Council and have made several tours of inspection in more distant portions of the State. It is a great pleasure to have received from Mr. Glancy such favourable reports of quick understanding displayed by your Highness of State affairs and of your appreciation of duties of your high position.

The more educated princes were also eager to win respect in the world of modern-minded maharajas. Enough of the twentieth-century rulers had been abroad or had received a cosmopolitan education to know what was expected of a modern state and to develop some aspirations to build one. Democratic movements, made up of individuals whom the princes considered inferior or *declasse*, were probably least influential among those to whom the maharajas felt accountable.

All of these reforms, from the known and limited privy purse to departmental reorganization, while they did introduce elements of rationalization and reduce the scope of personal government, were more formal than substantive. If an annual report bore witness that the appurtenances of contemporary administrative practice had been achieved, they also contained more aspirations than accomplishments. The larger states did more than the smaller, and of the larger, Bikaner, Jaipur, and possibly Jodhpur progressed farther than traditional-minded Udaipur. The quaint accounts of visiting political agents and the quainter language of the administrative reports sometimes give a more reliable impression than the administrative reports' facts. In Udaipur, for example, according to Sir Arthur Lothian who had occasion to know it well as resident, the attempt to maintain personal rule in the literal sense continued to recent times. His account of the maharana of Udaipur, who died in 1930, illustrates how thin a veneer reforms could be:

I have never seen a finer or more dignified countenance than that of the old Maharana. Kindliness and nobility were written all over it. He was the quintessence of courtesy, and an excellent Ruler, according to his lights. He, old-fashioned however, attempted to control the administration of his big state in every detail himself, which under modern conditions was beyond the capacity of any human being. Although, therefore, he wore himself out with his constant labours, the arrears became so great that the administration got hopelessly clogged. . . . One instance of the arrears into which things had fallen came to my personal knowledge. The return of prisoners in the State Jail happened to be shown to me one day, and

I noticed that two men had been confined in jail under sentence of death for twelve years. On enquiry into what had happened, it transpired that the death sentences, which required the Ruler's confirmation, had been sent to the late Maharaja twelve years before for this purpose, but had got mislaid somewhere amid the masses of papers awaiting his attention, and the prisoners were, therefore, kept on indefinitely as if they had been under trial. In the outcome this redounded to their advantage as they were sentenced to twenty years rigorous imprisonment in lieu of the death penalty and the years they had already served in jail were deducted from this.

Changes in the relationships between princes and noblemen, the degree of public accountability, and administrative and financial reforms were paralleled by movements to expand the political community, to make government popularly accountable, and to secure the rights of subjects through settled legal and administrative procedures. The Rajputana states had insulated themselves with remarkable success from the social and intellectual ferment that affected British India in the mid-nineteenth century. What is sometimes (and curiously) referred to as the Indian "renaissance," that mixture of English liberal and Indian nationalist ideas which captured the consciousness of the burgeoning professional and business middle classes, affected Rajasthan hardly at all. Nor did changes in the economy, communications, and education touch it substantially. Control of the press and bad communications conspired to prevent the excellent British Indian papers from circulating regularly in Rajasthan. Jai Narayan Vyas, later chief minister in post-independence Rajasthan, had to print nationalist literature in Ajmer, a British Indian enclave set in the midst of the Rajasthan states, and to smuggle it out. Some of the princely states insisted that not merely presses but even typewriters be registered. Education lagged, and so did the emergence of a modern economy and modern middle classes. Urbanization was insignificant. Political associations were few and usually ephemeral and severely restricted.

The feebleness of modern associational life until the mid-1930's was in part due to the lack of interest or the timidity of subjects. Also responsible was the Indian National Congress decision, taken in 1920 when it laid plans for the mass organization of nationalism, not to include the princely states. In its Nagpur Constitution of 1920, Congress assigned responsibility for particular princely states to established provincial Congress committees. Political activists from the princely states could belong to the nearby provincial committees, but Congress failed to take the same interest in their activities as it did in those of British India. Both practical and ideological considerations shaped this policy of self-restraint. Many members feared, Patabhi Sitaramayya wrote, "Congress [would] be embroiling itself with the local vagaries and idiosyncracies of a variety of states, 562 in number, a task obviously beyond the pale of the practical politics of Congress." Gandhi went further: "That part of India which is described as British has no more power to shape the policy of the states than it has (say) that of Afghanistan or Ceylon,"His views were representative of the conservative wing of Congress. To its adherents foreign autocracy was more reprehensible, apparently, than was indigenous autocracy. The Congress Left, including Nehru, opposed "this hush-hush policy [of non-interference] . . . adhered to by [Gandhi] in spite of the most extraordinary and painful occurrences in the States." Nehru pictured Gandhi's views as most welcome to the rulers.

Gandhi's attitude toward Indian princes, under whom his father and grand-father had served as chief ministers, was indeed positive. Their benign autocracy did not disturb him, although specific abuses might. If (for certain purposes and in certain contexts) he supported democracy, he never fully committed himself to the principles of popular or representative government over those of responsive autocracy. In line with important aspects of Indian traditional thought, which looks to inner virtue rather than institutional restraints as the guarantor of public morality, Gandhi was more concerned in the 1920s with the personal debauchery of princes, where it existed, than with their failure to grant political liberty:

My ideal of Indian states is that of *Rama Rajya* [the rule of the epic hero Rama] ... By abandoning his kingdom and living in the forest for the sake of truth Rama gave to all kings of the world an object lesson in noble conduct. By his strict monogamy he showed that life of perfect self-restraint could be led by a royal householder. He lent splendour to his throne by his popular administration and proved that *Rama Rajya* was the acme of *swaraj* [self-rule]. Rama did not need the very imperfect modern instrument of ascertaining public opinion by counting votes. He had captivated the hearts of the people. He knew public opinion by intuition, as it were. . . Such *Rama Rajya* is possible even today.

Although the All-India States Peoples Conference was formed by prominent Congressmen in 1927, and thereafter acted as a kind of sister organization to Congress, it was hardly militant in its early years. Some of its leaders, moderates in Indian politics like C.Y. Chintamani and Ram Chandra Rao, former chief minister of Mysore, were not involved with the more radical nationalist movement and steered the conference conservatively. Only in the later 1930's under the leadership ofPattabhi Sitaramayya and eventually Nehru, did the States Peoples Conference take a more militant turn. At the same time, both Gandhi and Congress shifted to a more active interventionism.

They did so partly because pressure by popular movements in some non-Rajput princely states, notably Mysore, forced them to. As Sardar Patel, the Congress's great organizing talent, put it: "The policy of non-intervention by the Congress was, in my opinion, a perfect piece of statesmanship when the people of the States were not awakened. That policy would be cowardice when there is all-round awakening among the people of the States." Congress also changed its policy following the passage of the Government of India Act of 1935 because the prospect of a federal government under it, including representatives from the princely states, spurred Congress on. So long as government in the princely states was autocratic, the princely states' delegations could be counted upon to be nominees of the princes, who in turn could be expected to support conservative and anti-nationalist policies in the federal legislature.

Faced with a coalition of princely state representatives and other non-Congress elements. Congress could expect to be a minority. By devoting more attention to the movement for freedom in the princely states. Congress hoped to soften or neutralize if not capture their representatives. In the event, the princely states could not make up their minds to join the federation, and a federal legislature never met. Before this result became apparent, however, the prospect of it so doing affected associational life and political consciousness in the princely states.

The policy of the Congress began to shift in 1936, and the Haripura session in 1938 sanctioned the organization of Congress committees in princely states provided they undertook neither parliamentary activity nor direct action in Congress's name. By 1939, Gandhi personally backed the States Peoples Freedom Movement, as it became known, to the extent of reviewing and guiding all the activities of the Jaipur Praja Mandal (Jaipur People's Society), the popular movement's organization in that state. He was drawn into its activities by his close friend and disciple, a wealthy Rajasthan businessman, long-time Congressman, and treasurer of the Indian National Congress, Jamnalal Bajaj. Bajaj, as president of the Jaipur Praja Mandal, was refused entry to the state, and the Mandal was forbidden to bold public meetings and proceedings. Bajaj and his followers offered civil resistance and were sent to jail. One brief letter exchange illustrates Gandhi's close but conservative interest in Jaipur affairs. Bajaj wrote to Gandhi on January 29, 1940: "I showed you the letter I received from the Home Minister of Jaipur. I enclose a draft of the reply I propose to send him. You will kindly return it to me with the necessary corrections." Gandhi replied: "Your draft is not properly worded. Your complaint is directed against the Maharaja. I don't consider it advisable to bring him in."

Most of the larger princely states had active movements toward the end of the 1930's, though some had them much earlier. The movements were led mostly, though not exclusively, by Brahman and Kayasth (caste of scribes) schoolmasters, such as Hiralal Shastri in Jaipur, Haribhau Upadhyaya in Ajmer, Bhogilal Pandya in Dungarpur,

Manikyalal Verma in Udaipur, and Master Bhola Nath in Alwar, and by the new profession of lawyers, generally also Brahman or Kayasth, and were supported by some members of the merchant castes. That the literate castes should have been leaders in the movement is not surprising, since their literacy made available to them currents of thought other than those generally accepted in Rajasthan. On the other hand, it is not self-evident that their leadership should have been directed toward social and political change. One of the most fascinating features of Indian political and social development has been the role of the Brahmans, guardians per excellence of tradition and the sacred order, as the bearers of the new political and social ideas. The vicarious authority which Brahmans and members of the other twice-born castes lent to innovation may help explain the relative ease with which India has taken to social and political change over the past 150 years.

Most of the prominent members of the literate castes in Rajasthan were attached to the bureaucracies of the princely states, or dependent on the court for trade and other patronage.. But those who led the freedom movement had, almost without exception, some independent occupational base: as school-masters and lawyers they were not directly dependent on court patronage. If they were dependent, like Shastri (office superintendent under Finance Member Atal in Jaipur State) they left their posts before becoming active in the Praja Mandal. For the most part they were city men; the peasant castes and rural people were scarcely represented.

Members of the merchant castes were active in the freedom movement, especially in Jodhpur. Jamnalal Bajaj, one of Gandhi's most important financial supporters, was an important figure in Jaipur State as well as on the national scene. Gandhi's efforts to organize and encourage non-political social service organizations and through them his campaigns to prevent the sale or consumption of alcoholic drinks and even to aid untouchables appealed to the merchant castes, already attached by religion and custom to teetotalism and nonviolence. In the mid-1930's members of merchant castes were particularly prominent as officers of the Harijan Sevak Sangh

(Service Society for Untouchables). Formally apolitical, it had strong reformist over-tones and was explicitly connected to Gandhi's programme.

Some of those who joined the freedom movement did so because of their mobile sensibilities, their capacity to imagine themselves and others under circumstances other than those which the traditional society prescribed; some joined because they had fallen from favour; some because a rebellious disposition made them unable and unwilling to "succeed" under the conditions of courtierly behaviour required in a princely state. Even Rajasthanis who did not join the nationalist movement speak with bitterness of remembered humiliation, of being made to "feel small" in the presence of ministers, of not being offered a seat by those in authority, or of being required to express themselves in ways they foqnd degrading. Some joined because they were idealists prepared to take risks. The Gandhian appeal made sense to these men because it did not demand the martial style which was incompatible with their non-Kshatriya aversion to violence. Instead, it proposed self-suffering of a kind long familiar to Brahmans, whose ancestors had fasted or immolated themselves in response to unjust exactions. It appealed to the instincts for pedagogy of the traditionally literate castes now in the roles of schoolmasters or lawyers, who were asked to carry their Gandhian and nationalist teachings to rural people, bringing the message of moral and material conditions as they were elsewhere and might be here too. Still others, having been educated in British India, found the political climate in Rajputana incompatible with what they had learned.

The earliest activities of the freedom movement are difficult to isolate and identify. A variety of local issues just after World War I and, subsequently, during Gandhi's first civil disobedience campaign, took on added meaning from national events and concerns. In 1918, Manikyalal Verma and Vijay Singh Pathik organized a peasant *satyagraha* (nonviolent resistance campaign) against forced labour at Bijolia, Udaipur. Verma's arrests in 1918 and 1922 vaguely united the political consciousness arising out of protests over local grievances with that of the larger nationalist movement. The Marwar Hitkarni Sabha (Marwar Improvement Society) formed in the early 1920's in Jodhpur State by Jai Narayan Vyas and other Jodhpuri political activists, aimed at freeing the state from the rule of "aliens": a chief minister and other non-Jodhpuri officials both Indian and English. Its motto was "Marwar [Jodhpur] for the Marwaris" and its design to protect local interests from the effects of administrative reform. The maharaja, happy to free himself from the implicit restraints which outsiders represented, gave the Sabha his blessing, while Vyas saw his role in it as his first contribution to the freedom movement. Such political ambiguity was not unique to Jodhpur.

In the "Sikar rebellion" of 1937, the backward looking Rao Raja of the largest estate in Jaipur asserted the claims of feudal liberty against those of centralizing absolutism in resisting the maharaja's British-officered armed forces. In this struggle between prince and feudal aristocrat, the middle-class Jaipur Praja Mandal to a degree backed the claims of Sikar in an effort to advance the fortunes of representative government and public liberties. At the same time, the maharaja was inclined to be more sympathetic to the Praja Mandal under the Jaipuri leadership of Bajaj than was his government under the direction of a British chief minister. Freedom movements affected by local patriotism and susceptible to palace influence were sometimes useful in dealing with pressures for administrative reform from the political department and a maharaja's own government.

Freedom organizations of a clearly anti-princely cast, however, faced grave obstacles. Jai Narayan Vyas, whose first organization, the Hitkarni Sabha, was banned in 1924, became adept at shaping new ones as those he created were outlawed. He formed in quick succession the Jodhpur Praja Mandal, the Youth League, and the Marwar Lok Parishad. Whenever Vyas had trouble in his home state of Jodhpur, or was ordered out of other states in the areas, he guided his movements from Ajmer, the British enclave in the middle of Rajasthan, or from Bombay. Ajmer played an important role throughout the nationalist years since British administration made it a haven for agitators expelled from the princely states. In 1921 and again in 1930-32, the civil disobedience movement of British India found its counterparts there.

The less political Rajasthan Sevak Sangh, a Gandhian non-political service organization, fared better, although its leaders sometimes engaged in political activities. It began at Ajmer in the late 1920's and even employed paid workers in some states. Early activities in Bikaner, Kotah, and other states coincided with the civil disobedience movement of 1931-32 in British India. In Kotah, the Haravati Praja Mandal imitated the British-Indian agitation by picketing liquor and foreign-cloth shops in 1931 and 1932. But even these associations tended to lead precarious lives since most states disapproved of any association which, in the words of the Bikaner Public Safety Act of 1932, was "likely to create disaffection against the Maharaja or his government." Assembly, publication, and speech were more restricted than in British India. But the pattern of restriction varied: Kotah reports meetings of up to three hundred persons in 1937-38, not insignificant for a small (population 700,000) state, and successive meetings through at least 1941 favouring responsible government, federation of princely and British India, compulsory education, and temperance. In Bharatpur, the Praja Mandal sought "to secure responsible government under the aegis of His Highness the Maharaja." When it attempted to organize a campaign to withhold payment of land revenue from the state, the Mandal was declared unlawful in April 1937. Four hundred and seventy-three individuals were detained in connection with the campaign and 212 were arrested-again, not a small agitation in a state containing only 500,000 people. Jaipur and Jodhpur alternately forbade and permitted Praja Mandals and Lok Parishads to function. In Jodhpur in 1937, the Civil Liberties Union and the Praja Mandal were declared unlawful and their president, A.P. Sharma, arrested. Since Seth Jamnalal Bajaj, the Jaipur leader, was a man of national stature and treasurer of the Indian National Congress, the Jaipur *durbar* was in constant embarrassment regarding methods of dealing with him, but eventually admitted both him and the Praja Mandal to public activity. In Bikaner, the Public Safety Act of 1932 acted as a strong deterrent. Udaipur banned the Praja Mandal in 1938, as soon as it was founded, and expelled its founder. Sirohi and Alwar also had active movements, while Dungarpur and Banswara had developed a tiny but impressive service organization working in a Gandhian spirit among the Bhil tribes.

The life of the "old nationalists" was not always easy, Manikyalal Verma came out of the nonviolent resistance movement at Bijolia badly beaten, as did Gokulbhai Bhatt out of a Sirohi meeting in 1939. Mrs. Verma was imprisoned for two years in 1934. Narottamlal Joshi, later speaker of the Rajasthan legislature, was beaten twice on the same day by Rajput landholders of small estates for the effrontery of campaigning for political freedom and tenant rights in Jaipur's first election in 1945. He was attacked near a police station, the occupants of which remained inactive throughout the assault, and believes he escaped death only because his assailants stuck at Brahman killing. Unable to walk, he was tied to a camel and abandoned in a forest.

The attempt to win responsible government did not succeed. In 1913 Maharaja Ganga Singh established what he liked to call the "Bikaner Representative Assembly." The organization had the power to pass bills. In reality, however, it provided no forum for criticism, much less for the exercise of power by representatives independent of the crown, since the assembly was dominated by a majority nominated by the maharaja, and the climate of the institution was courtierly and placating. "I have nothing special to mention in connection with the budget," a representative said in speaking in the budget debate, "except that this year's budget is an occasion of great delight for us as it contains a provision for the estimated expenditure of the celebration of His Highness Sri Maharaj Kumarji Sahib's auspicious marriage, which auspicious marriage celebration has come after many years, and it would be an occasion of great delight for every loyal subject of the state." The budget had been delivered to members on the day previous to the debate, and it passed in a few hours. The assembly met for three days in the year. Similar bodies were introduced in Jaipur and Jodhpur in the 1940's, but until after the war their powers were insignificant. The Jaipur assembly saw a budget for the first time in 1946. After the war, as independence rushed ominously closer and democracy began to loom as a real possibility, most of the states moved swiftly toward popular governments, which were soon superseded by the amalgamation of Rajasthan's twenty-two princely states into one.

In British India, the political associations and representative institutions of the nationalist era served as an important recruiting ground for post-independence political leadership. In Rajasthan this function was indifferently performed. The experience which British Indian Congressmen developed in the Swarajist days of the 1920's when they joined legislatures, or in the short-lived provincial governments of the 1930's, or in district boards and municipalities was missing altogether in Rajasthan, where there were no meaningful representative institutions, unless a few municipalities deserve the title. And the Praja Mandals too were inadequate training grounds for later state politics. The small movements required devotion and idealism, but they did not develop new organizational and administrative skills on the part of their leaders. Because they were personal, comradely organizations, each coinciding with a princely state, they resembled the small state governments in that no high professional competence was required to manage them.

The British Indian political movements, because they covered large linguistic areas, developed in their leaders a capacity to build rational and effective political structures, to coordinate diverse political interests, and to formulate and communicate policies. The Rajasthan political organizations, because they were very small operations, developed few qualities that would equip their alumni in later years to take over the large-scale unified government of the twenty-two states of Rajasthan. In fact, this early political experience may even have disqualified them for their later tasks.

They carried the narrow horizons of parochial princely states into the politics of the larger state, failing to shift easily to the more abstract general perspectives required in the new circumstances. Many remained small-town politicians when faced with the responsibility of governing fifteen million people in new Rajasthan. Yet, when independence came and the old order was superseded, they were the only ones available for the new politics.

Apart from the freedom associations, Rajasthanis did not form voluntary organizations of the kind that grew in British India and structured its emerging middle classes' turn to politics. The Rajasthan middle classes, such as they were, developed few modern institutional channels for action. The universities, the chambers of commerce, the bar, and a host of social, literary, cultural, and political associations had given focus to the organized interests of British Indians in the days before a mass movement gave new strength to nationalism. Higher education in the princely states was feeble and dependent on the maharaja. The bar was weakly developed since much legal practice rested with the traditionally trained *vakils* (pleaders), and a modern legal profession had still to emerge. The merchantry was organized in caste associations, but not into any association cutting across caste on the basis of economic or civil interests. Such associations as existed were mostly natural groups congruent with the old society and polity and felt no special reason to upset them. Thus, in 1912, at the silver jubilee of the maharaja of Bikaner, addresses were offered by the following groups: officials of the government, Maheshwari Sahukars (a merchant caste), Oswals (a merchant caste), Brahmans, Pushkarna Brahmans, Jain Swetamber Yatis (Jain holy men), Mohammedans, Sikhs, the Nagri Society, two secondary educational institutions, and the bar association. They made no political demands, restricting themselves to requesting traditional favours, such as the maharaja's intervention in a serious caste dispute among the merchants or support for some new building or educational enterprise.

Neither the old corporate groups nor the new political associations explicitly demanded expansion of the political community, although that was sometimes a long-range objective. The cry for responsible government amounted rather to a demand for institutions that would make effective the influence of those who already had some claim to be *de facto*, though not *de jure*, part of the political community-the literate, the twice-born. For the most part, the Brahmans and Vaishyas (merchant castes) and Kayasths in the Congress appealed to others like themselves. But there were exceptions. In a few areas, for example in Jodhpur and Jaipur in the early 1940's, members of the peasant caste ofJats began to develop political consciousness, and elsewhere Congressmen who took seriously Gandhi's guidance went to the rural areas to preach social reform if not political participation.

The 1930's, however, brought one additional sign that the times were changing and that new groups were emerging at the edge of the political community. Census reports as far back as 1891, and other official records of much earlier vintage, record that in the British Indian provinces certain lower and middle castes were beginning to organize themselves to press courts, temples, and administrative bodies for recognition of rights, privileges, and higher status than tradition assigned them. These efforts foreshadowed attacks on the traditional order of castes. The censuses of Rajasthan in the twentieth century, on the other hand, reported very few developments of this sort before 1930. In 1911, a Kayasth group tried to list itself as Brahman, as did the Bhargavas (another caste). Some individual members of castes made up of illegitimate descendants of Rajputs tried to have themselves listed as Rajputs. But the efforts were sporadic and apparently involved very few people.

The main agricultural caste in Rajasthan is the Jats: they comprise the largest single caste in the state (9 per cent), and were, in the 1930's and even earlier, the most self-conscious and prosperous among the peasant castes. In 1935 their claims to certain privileges led to a series of clashes between them and the Rajputs, who resisted their attempts to revise accepted signs of status. The clash of 1935 is reminiscent of similar ones in other areas between lower castes on the rise and higher established castes. The Jat demonstrations broke out in Sikar, the largest *thikana* in Jaipur State, and involved both economic and social issues. The Jats in the area had formed two associations, the Sikarwati Jat Panchayat and the Jat Kisan Sabha, and had received some help and encouragement from the British Indian province of Uttar Pradesh. Some of these "outsiders" were organizers for the socialist-oriented Kisan Sabha which attempted to mobilize the peasantry in the 1930's in response to radical pressures in the Congress.

The initial demonstration in Khuri village on March 27, 1935, was occasioned by a social issue, whether a Jat bridegroom should be allowed to ride to his bride's house on a horse, a ceremonial act asserting higher station than Rajputs were prepared to concede. The Rajputs objected, the Jats insisted, fighting broke out, and an old Jat was killed. The incident led to further clashes, and the *thikana* police, the Sikar Lancers, under command of the English chief of the Sikar police, charged the Jat crowds with *lathis* (quarter-staffs), injuring many. This incident was followed by others as Jats in the area protested against the revenue collections and resisted and attacked Sikar revenue officials on April 22 at Bhaironpura and at Kudan village on April 25. The Sikar police killed four Jats while putting down this last demonstration and arrested 104 persons. The anti-rent agitation eventually involved some twenty-one villages, and local headmen were as active as any outsiders. A school where, according to the Jaipur *durbar*, unlawful doctrines were being preached by a Jat teacher from outside the state, was knocked down. The agitation had some effects. The Rao Raja of Sikar remitted all arrears of revenue previous to 1934 and promised to open schools, provide loans where needed, and embark on a permanent land settlement that would introduce some certainty into the vagaries of the *thikana's* revenue demand.

There was some evidence that the more advanced peasantry were beginning to insist on some regulation of their land rights. Beginning as early as 1872 in Alwar, most states undertook survey and settlement operations in *khalsa* (crown lands), that is, they prepared records of rights and established regular revenue demands. In the judgment of an inquiry committee of high civil servants from

British Irdia that reported on tenant rights at the time of independence, "the tenant (of *khalsa*) has his rights defined and secured, and there is, on the whole, little cause for him to complain." But in the *jagir* (nobles' estates) lands, which made up a substantial part of most states (about half), records were rarely kept, collection procedures remained arbitrary, and peasants had no protection. Only 32 per cent of the 16,7 80 *jagir* villages in all of Rajasthan had been settled (their revenue obligations officially specified and limited) by 1947. A number of *durbars* tried to press settlement, but their efforts were strongly resisted by the *jagirdars*. No one doubted that tenants had customary rights, including in many cases rights of inheritance, mortgage, and fixed rents. But so long as these rights were not established by enforcible laws and administrative procedures, they were subject to the *jagirdars* discretion; the nobles rightly regarded settlement as a diminution of his own powers. But it was a limitation that would in turn have conferred upon tenants rights most fundamental in a peasant society-rights in land.

Most *durbars* did not undertake *jagir* settlement before the 1930's and 1940's. Such operations as were undertaken in *jagir* lands proved dangerous, especially in small holdings where the landlord and tenant were not very far apart economically. In 1937, the Jaipur *durbar* pressed settlement in Udaipurwati, an area adjoining Sikar, where the Jat agitation had taken place, only to see its revenue officials chased out by irate small *jagirdars*. In 1947, the Jaipur *durbar* passed enabling legislation for laying down rules concerning rights in land and for establishing procedures and principles fixing land rent in *jagir* areas, a clear indication that the 1937 effort had not advanced far.

Legal procedures were regulated, at least as far as the maharaja's hand reached, by taking over British Indian legal codes with only minor alterations and by establishing courts at various levels to administer that law. A graduated court system with defined jurisdiction existed at Jhalawar and Jaipur in the 1870's, and written codes were taken over, at least formally,. in most states by 1910-20. These changes marked an advance toward promulgated law which could be anticipated. It is difficult to say just how meaningful the adoption of the codes and the creation of courts was. Most states were reluctant to have defendants bring in lawyers from British India to argue before these tribunals, a policy which may have been due to a feeling that the local system would not stand scrutiny, or to provincial fears that the local judiciary might be made to look foolish by "slick" Bombay barristers, or both. In any case, the new law impinged less than in British India on the local, pluralistic caste and customary law, a circumstance that may have been congenial to Rajasthanis but that illustrates the restricted development of the legal power of the state.

The new conceptions of government were compelling enough to teach some maharajas how a respectable ruler conducts himself. Responsibility to the public welfare and effective performance were added to birth in judging the legitimacy of rule. Public reports of government action implied that princely expenditure amounted to a public budget, not merely a private household account, and thus favoured the differentiation of the public and private roles of the prince. They also implied that the prince in his public capacity was accountable to someone other than himself.

Associations developed enough to introduce, at least in the minds of the literate, ideas of representation and consent and to undermine the self-evident quality of princely rule. Advances in administration, particularly fixing of the revenue demand, introduced the principle that government action ought to follow certain rules. The prince often consulted his fellow princes, or the political department, or his now more modern conscience. But his new sense of public responsibility, of effective performance, and regular procedures fell short of establishing a modern state or constitutional rule in Rajasthan. The emergence of a modern state, the revision of traditional notions of legitimacy, and the growth of popular politics progressed too slowly under paramountcy to be of any real help to Rajasthan when it became part of India. The attempts to centralize authority and regularize administration did not carry very far and were often more formal than substantive. Compared to

British India, the development of associational life in Rajputana was slight. No real concessions were made to political participation and institutional restraints on autocratic power. Important changes did occur, but, without roots in society and consciousness, they lacked substance

Ahmedabad: Piping hot bhajiyas with tea! Who can resist them? Not even the iron-willed Sardar. Patel's passion for this delicacy has found a mention in the Ahmedabad Municipal Corporation's booklet ' Amdavad ni Krantiyatra' . So much so, that during his early days as a lawyer, Patel was an active member of a 'Bhajiya Club' in the city. In 1913, when Sardar began his practice as a barrister in Ahmedabad, it was a ritual to meet friends over a cup of tea and bhajiyas. This gathering came to be known as the 'Bhajiya Club'. The sessions provided food for thought too.

Narayan Desai, in his book 'Agnikund Man Khilelu Gulab' on his father and Gandhiji's secretary Mahadev Desai, has quoted an incident referring to this club. The book quotes a letter by Mahadevbhai to Pyarelal, a senior Congress leader, which mentions Sardar's love for bhajiya. He wrote, "When Vallabhbhai came to Ahmedabad after the successful Bardoli Satyagraha, he received a grand welcome in the city. And surprisingly, he forgot all his fatigue when he mingled with his own bhajiatmak club.

We should thank Jugatram for the word bhajiatmak." This letter clearly spoke of Sardar's affiliation towards 'Bhajiya Club'. Initially, the club members gathered at Krushnalal Desai or Dr. Kanunga's house.

Later, it shifted to Dr. Kanunga's dispensary on Gandhi Road where bhajiyas and tea were ordered from a nearby hotel. Dr. Kanunga, Chimanlal Thakor, Maganbhai Patel, Krushnalal Desai, Jivanlal Barrister, Dr. Chandubhai and Dr. Hariprasad Desai were the members of this club.

Many government officers and professionals were a part of this gathering. Everything except politics was discussed here. Adarsh Prakashan on Gandhi Road today is where Dr. Kanunga's dispensary used to be. After Sardar become a national leader in 1935, this club rarely gathered. Leaders like Mahadev Desai, Pyarelal and Jugatram knew of Sardar's love for the bhajiya

Gandhiji and Patel at Gujarat

Such simple food made Gandhiji a experience mental purity and really became a real aspirant after 'moksha'. This increasing religious attitude and spirit of renunciation created a bitter disharmony In Gandhiji's domestic and family life. The ideal of the Ashrama at Phoenix and on the Tolstoy Farm was of community life and as such Gandhiji looked more after the need of others than of Kasturba and his sons. This led to a deep sense of dissatisfaction in them. Gandhiji was opposed to the-then prevalent system of education So, he had not sent his sons to any school and he himself could not find time to teach them because he was always busy with public affairs. This distressed the sons and in May 1911 his eldest son, Harilal left his father's house. Gandhiji tried hard to win him back and even permitted him to stay in Ahmedabad and prosecute his studies at an. English school. But with the passage of time the gap between the father and the son increased and Hairball's life was proved to be a sort of painful atonement for Gandhiji and he bare it without blaming Harilal, Gandhiji had a life of spiritual disciple at the Phoenix Ashram and on the Tolstoy Farm bore fruit in 1913, In 1910 the four colonies of South Africa had amalgamated themselves into an Union of South Africa, The Union Government did nothing to remove the Indian's complaints, So, in September 1913 Gandhiji resumed his movement, The movement was against two new grievances.

In addition to the two old grievances relating to the law of registration certificates and the law based on racial prejudice and Indian from entering South Africa. Court had given a decision declaring illegal all those marriages not performed according to Christian rites and registered in the country. This decision of the Supreme Court made illegal all the marriages performed according to Hindu and Muslim rites' and reduced Hindu and Muslim wives to the position of concubine. This was an insult to the Indian women. Gandhiji inspired the women residing in the Phoenix Ashram to oppose this decision. Kasturba became the leader of these women. The second issue was about the 'indentured labourers. According to the agreements these labourers were to return to India after five years. A tax ok three pounds on each adult of those labourer's families who did not do so had been imposed since 1893. Then in 1902 a law was passed requiring indentured ,Indian sons above the age of 16 and daughters, above the age of 13 were also made liable to pay the same tax of 3 pounds if they refused to return to India. Gopal Krishna Gokhale had visited South Africa in 1912. At that time South Africa's Ministers had promised him that this tax would be withdrawn. But they did not keep their promise. So, during this last movement the women residents of the Tolstoy Farm, acting with Gandhiji's consent, inspired the indentured labourers to go on strike.

Thousands of labourersmen and women joined the strike. Gandhiji collected all of them together and marched from Natal towards the Transversal. After Gandhiji had been arrested the police and the army let loose a reign of terror on the workers When the news about this reached India, the whole country was agitated. The Viceroy, Lord Harding, made a speech sympathizing with the Indians in South Africa. As a consequence, the South African Government was compelled to arrive at a settlement with Gandhiji. The Government released Gandhiji and appointed an Inquiry Commission to inquire into the grievances of the Indians and recommend measures to remove them. The commission made recommendations which removed all the grievances of the Indians and the Union Parliament in June 1914 passed a law to implement these recommendations After the successful conclusion of the struggle, Gandhiji left for India after meeting Gokhale in London. Before his departure, different classes of Indians presented him addresses. The Indentured Indians had also arranged one such meeting.

Gandhiji was impressed by these labourers' sacrifice during the struggle and after his release from the jail he had adopted their mode of dress. In reply to their address of honour, too Gandhiji took them a pledge to dedicate his whole life in the service of the afflicted and the oppressed. He said, "your indenture is for five years with one man. I will be an indenture with you for the whole of my life" After returning to India, he kept that pledge both in letter and spirit. When Gandhiji reached London to meet Gokhale, the first world war had already started and in London he inspired the Indian students there to offer their services in the cause of the injured soldiers.

But in London Gandhiji became afflicted with pleurisy and he could not stay there longer. He launched at the port of Bombay on January 9, 1915, overflowing with joy and dreaming to give himself to the service of the motherland. Thus started a new stage of service in his life. When Gokhale had visited South Africa in 1912 he had made Gandhiji a promise that he would not express opinion about any issue in public for one year after his return to India. So, Gandhiji passed his first year in India in travelling in the different parts of the country and in understanding the situation. But before doing so, in May 1915, he established the Satyagraha Ashram at Ahmedabad with the object of bringing about a total regeneration of the country He introduced strict vows to be observed by the inmates in the Ashram. These vows included, the traditional five vows of truth, nonviolence 'Brahmacharya' 'non-stealing' and 'non-possession' Together with these, keeping in mind the then prevailing conditions in the country, he had added removal of untouchability, equal respect for all religions, swadeshi and manual labour and some others. A few months after the Ashram had been established Gandhiji admitted an untouchable family to the Ashram, and so invited the opposition of the orthodox in the city.

Thus began his career in India as a reformer. When the year of silence on public affairs was over Gandhiji seized the first opportunity to express his views. Banaras Hindu University was inaugurated in February, 1916. Gandhiji was invited to speak on that occasion. He used the opportunity to make a moving speech describing the sad state of the country. He strongly castigated the region of fear prevalent in India. This led to an uproar in the audience. All the princes as well as Annie Besant had been sitting on the dais left it before Gandhiji had ended his speech. This speech of Gandhiji raised a çountry wide controversy. This was the first occasion in the public life of the country when anyone had voiced such views fearlessly at a function at which the Viceroy was the chief guest and in the presence of the ruling Princes, After one year Gandhiji got an opportunity of practicing fearlessness in public and with that started his active public life in India. In the Champaran district of Bihar the white landlords compelled their tenant-peasants to cultivate indigo one some portion of their and the peasants were oppressed in the process. 'Gandhiji went to Champaran to study the peasant grievances at the request of a farmer named Raj kumar Shukla. The collector of Champaran asked him to leave Champaran but Gandhiji disobeyed the order. In defending his action, Gandhiji said in the court that he was ready to accept the punishment for disobeying the Collector's order.

The Government withdrew the order and allowed Gandhiji to make his inquiries, This incident had a miraculous effect in the whole district and crowds of peasants started visiting Gandhiji fearlessly to give statements of their grievances. Kaiendrababu who was practicing in Patna and other educated persons joined Gandhiji in this work, While Gandhiji's inquiry was proceeding, the Bihar Government appointed a commission for solving the problem and nominated Gandhiji as one of its members. The commendations of this Commission removed most of the grievances of the peasants, Thus, Gandhiji gave his first lesson in India of nonviolent Satyagraha. Gandhiji derived another great benefit in the course of inquiry, and that was that he saw the poverty of Indian villages and started thinking how to remove it. This sowed seed of the Khadi programmes which he later presented to the people. He also started in the villages of Champaran district the constructive programmes of cleanliness and primary education. This programme did not succeed fully but he followed in India, the policy he had done in South Africa that resistance against injustice should be accompanied with the purification of people's life. From this programme developed in the course of time the multifarious constructive activities that he inspired later on. After the work of the inquiry was over, Gandhiji presented his original views on two important question in his presidential addresses to two conferences in Gujarat.

The first of these was the Second Gujarat Educational Conference held at Bharuch on 20th October, 1917 and the second was the first ever Gujarat Political Conference held at Godhra on 3rd November of the same year. He laid stress on the use of the mother-tongue as the medium of education at the Bharuch conference and gave a picture of the educational system, which was later to be adopted by national 'Vidyapeeths': In the political conference, he presented his policy, according to the principles of Satyagrahee bringing about a change of heart among Englishmen through nonviolence and explained the need for a comprehensive programme of public service in that connection. Soon after the work in Champaran was over, Gandhiji took up, at the suggestion of the request of Ansuyaben Sarabhai, the problem of the textile workers of Ahmedabad. He undertook a fast for three days in this connection and got mill-owners to appoint an arbitrator to inquire into the demands of the mill workers. With this he also continued his efforts to purify the internal life of these workers. Thus he gave an example of the policy of arbitration and mutual cooperation in place of class-war in regard to the issues between industrialists and workers. Inspired by this experiment of Gandhiji, many provinces and the centre later passed laws to solve the issues between the employers and employees. Such laws were also enacted and implemented in the field of education. No sooner had the problem of Ahmedabad workers ended, the issue of the farmers of the Kheda district arose.

The crops had been less than the normal owing to excessive rains in the previous year. So, the farmers had requested the Government for remission of revenue or postponement of its collection. The Government had rejected this demand. So at the request of Vallabhbhai Patel, Gandhiji took up the issue, made an on-the-spot study and advised the farmers not to pay the revenue and bear the consequences. This was the first experiment of direct resistance to Government's injustice. It was not totally successful but it created some sense of confidence in the farmers of the Kheda district that, if necessary, they could resist the Government. Thus during the year 1917-1918, Gandhiji put before the public his concept of Satyagraha in three different contexts. This experience made him one of the front-rank leaders of the country. After that within a year he became the centre of its political stage.

In August 1918 he had an attack of dysentery which had resulted in piles. In January, 1919 he underwent an operation to get the piles removed and on Kasturba's insistence he compromised with his vow of not taking milk and started taking goat's milk. But before he could regain his strength after the operation, a very serious problem cropped up for the country. Sporadic terrorist activities were being indulged in certain parts of the country and particularly in Bengal and the Punjab. These activities were not such that they could not be controlled by ordinary laws in force in India. But in February, 1 91 9 Government introduced two Bills in the Central Legislature giving extraordinary powers to police and civil officials to suppers these activities.

Indian members of the Legislature strongly opposed these Bills but the Government ignored their opposition, Gandhiji felt that the people would be much humiliated and a rule of terror would prevail in the country if these bills were allowed to be passed. He decided to oppose these bills through Satyagraha and for that purpose formed the Satyagraha Sabha. The movement started with a call for a nationwide strike and it met with an astonishing success. But during the strike there were some riots in Delhi and Amritsar. Gandhiji was taken into custody at the Punjab border when he was going there to stop them. The people in Bombay, Ahmedabad and Viramgam got excited when they heard this news and there were large-scale riots at all these three places. There were disturbances in Punjab also. On 13th April General Dyer, a military officer fired on a peaceful assembly of people at Jallianwala Bag in Amritsar killing more than 300 men and women, wounding more than a thousand people. Immediately after the incident, Martial Law was imposed in the Punjab rule and the people were subjected to inhuman torture.

The whole country was agitated. Gandhiji was deeply pained but he did not lose his balance of mind. Following his concept of Ahimsa he withdrew his satyagraha and went to Punjab to console the people there after the restoration of peace in that province. There he had the first experience of the people's love for him which later they were to shower upon him. The Government had appointed a committee to investigate the causes of the disturbances and measures taken by the Government to suppers them. But the Government was not prepared to give enough facilities to the leaders sent to jail in tendering their evidence. So, the Congress appointed its own committee. Gandhiji, as a representative of that committee visited the Punjab villages and took statements of uncounted number of men and women and exposed the unbelieveable tyranny of the Punjab Government in his report. Though Gandhiji thus had an experience of the high-handedn8ss of the Government, he still had faith in the sincerity of the British Government so at the annual session of Amritsar Congress held at the end of the year, he advised cooperation with the Government. In August, 1917, Mr. Montague, Secretary of state for India had announced that the British Government's aim was to take India in the direction of 'Responsible' Government. A new constitution was to be framed in accordance with that policy and with that aim in view Montague visited India in 1918 to consult the Indian leader.

In accordance with the joint recommendations of Montague and Lord Chelmsford, the then Viceroy a law was passed by the British Parliament in December 1919 giving limited self-rule to provincial governments. Signing this law king George had issued a proclamation on 24th December appealing the Indian people and the British officials in India to have mutual trust and cooperation. Gandhiji was impressed by this appeal and so he advised the congress to have trust in the sincerity of the British Government and to accept that law. The Congress accepted this advice and passed a resolution accordingly. But within only five to six months after this

Gandhiji's faith in the British Government received shock. Turkey had fought on the side of Germany in the first world War and this gave rise to the possibility of the powers of Sultan of Turkey might be curtailed and the Allies under the peace treaty to be made after the War. So, when the War was in progress, Muslim leaders in India had demanded promise from the British Government that the Sultan of Turkey would not be humiliated. The British Prime Minister had replied to that demand in ambiguous terms. As the time of the peace treaty drew near the Indian Muslims began to press their demand more strongly and sent a deputation to the Viceroy in that connection. Gandhiji felt that Muslim leaders demand to be just. So, he urged the Hindus and the congress to extend their cooperation to the Khilafat committee set up by the Muslim leaders.

The Muslin leaders' demanded was that the authority of the Sultan as the Khailfa over the sacred Muslim place in Arabia should remain in act, and hence their movement was called 'Khailfat' When the terms: of the peace treaty were published in May 1920, it became known that Turkey was deprived of some of its territories and that the Sultan was also deprived of his authority over the holy Muslim places in Arabia. At about this time, the report of the inquiry committee set up by the Government about the disturbances in the Punjab was also published. Gandhiji felt that the report covered up the atrocities committed by the Government and that it did not contain a recommendation for adequate punishment of General Dyer. The General was retired from the Army but his pension granted by the Indian Government was continued. These two measures of the British Government shocked Gandhiji and his faith in the sense of justice of the British Government was shaken. So, he called upon the country to start a nonviolent agitation against the Government and thus started the first country-wide fight of direct action against British rule. In the noncooperation movement, the programme included the four-fold boycott of courts, Government's educational institutions, legislatures and foreign cloth.

Together with these, there was the constructive programme of communal unity, abolition of Untouchability, Swadeshi, Knaaiana

National education. Gandhiji toured the whole of India to spread the message of this struggle. In his speeches during this tour, he poured out the pain he had felt in his heart at the country's poverty and holding the British Government responsible for that poverty described as Satanic. To bring about Hindu-Muslim unity he undertook a joint tour of the country with the Khilafat, leaders, Maulana Mohammed Ali and Shaukat All. The Khilafat movement also brought him into friendly relationships with Hakim Ajmalkhan, Dr. Ansari and Maulana Abul Kalam Azad. While carrying on propaganda for the abolition of untouchability he described the practice as Hindu 'Dyerism', thus inviting the unity of the orthodox Hindus. The noncooperation movement of Hindus produced a country-wide awakening. The boycott of courts was not very successful from the point of numbers, but it got for Gandhiji able leaders like Motilal Nehru, Jawaharlal Nehru, Chittaranjan Das, Vallabhbhai Patel, Vitthalbhai Patel, Sarojini Naidu and Chakravarti Rajagopalacharya as colleagues even the constructive programme did not meet with great success.

But it firmly planted in the minds of the people the idea that Swaraj was not only for political power but also for the amelioration of conditions of the poor in the village, It is possible the it the whole programme would have been successful to a greater extent had not there been violent disturbances in the wake of the movement. But in August 1921, the Arbas in Malabur known as the Moplas indulged in violent riots against the Government and as a result even the local Hindus had to suffer much. The Congress gave a call to boycott the Prince of wales when he visited India in November. In that connection there were disturbances first in Bombay in November 1921 and then in Madras in January 1922. Gandhiji ignored these disturbances and continued the agitation. But finally in February 1922, an excited crowd in place called Chauri Chaura the Gorakhpur district. Uttar Pradesh burnt alive about twenty policemen in their station. Gandhiji, ignoring the opposition of other leaders called off the 'no-tax' movement which was to be started at Bardoli and stopped aggressive propaganda against the Government though the constructive programme was continued. The Government took advantage of the changed situation. Arrested Gandhiji and had prosecuted him in a court of law.

The judge sentenced him to a six year imprisonment. Till that day the people of India had called him the Mahatma. Now, thanks to this strict adherence of the principle of nonviolence he came to be reputed as the Mahatma even in Western countries. French philosopher, Remain noiana him by writing his biography. Miss Madeleine step daughter of British Admiral on reading that book was fascinated by Gandhiji and in November 1925 she became Gandhiji's disciple and became an inmate of his Satyagraha Ashram. Gandhiji gave her the name Miraben. She continued to take an active part in Gandhiji's missions of service till his death. Because of illness Gandhiji was realised from jail by the Government in February 1924, before he had completed his term but at that time the nationalist forces of the country were in disarray. Some leader like Motilal Nehru, Chitaranjan Das and Vithallbhai Patel had given up the boycott of the legislatures and had formed the Swaraj Party to participate in the elections which were to be held at the end of 1923. On the other hand Rajgopalachary, Vallabhbhai Patel, and Rajendrababu advocated complete adherence to the policy of noncooperation. In Turkey Kemal Ataturk had deposed the Sultan and declared the country a republic. So, the Khilafat movement in India had also collapsed. The bond of cooperation between the Hindus and the Muslims having thus sapped the old animosities between the two communities became intensified and communal riots started at many places. In protest against them Gandhiji undertook a fast for 21 days at the residence.

Patel and 1946 Episode

Waves of anti-imperialist struggle rose one after another in different parts of India – from North to South, from East to West and lashed at the regime of the imperialists. The most spectacular and most significant among them was the uprising in Bombay which began on 18 February 1946. The ratings of the Royal

Indian Navy (R.I.N.) rose in revolt first in Bombay and then in Karachi, Calcutta and Madras. The rebel navymen, who had various grievances – bad food, racial discrimination, insults meted out by British officers and so on – were inspired by the deeds of Subhash and the example of the I.N.A.

By 22 February 1946 the rebel sailors were in control of about 22 vessels in Bombay, including the flagship of the British Vice-Admiral. A total of 78 ships of the R.I.N., 20 shore establishments and 20,000 ratings were involved in the struggle. Over a thousand men in the Royal Indian Air Force camps in Bombay came out on a sympathy strike. When ordered, Indian soldiers refused to fire on the R.I.N. ratings in Bombay as well as in Karachi. On 21 February the strike by the navymen developed into a pitched battle between them and British troops who had been called in as Indian soldiers refused to fire. And Bombay's workers and youth, irrespective of the community to which they belonged, stood by the heroic men of the navy, carried food to them, erected barricades and fought pitched battles with armed policemen and several British battalions equipped with armoured cars and tanks. On 22 February, Bombay observed a general strike in the teeth of the opposition from big Congress and Muslim League leaders.

Ignoring the Congress and League leaders, the entire working class of Bombay came out at the call of the Naval Central Strike Committee, which was supported by the CPI. For two days there were pitched battles on the city's streets, in which, according to official estimates, there were about 1,500 casualties including more than 200 dead. "The British tanks could clear the streets", wrote B. C. Dutt, one of the leaders of the revolt, "only after hundreds had been shot down. This was the first time in the turbulent history of India's freedom movement that the rulers were forced to use tanks to battle with unarmed and leaderless people.... February 21 had been the ratings' day. February 22 belonged to the workers of Bombay." In his 'Foreword' to Dutt's book, S. Natarajan wrote: "What was impressive among the ratings was their complete freedom from communal or sectarian prejudices and their staunch loyalty to each other." To quote Dutt, "The R.I.N. mutiny was the one conspiracy against the crown in which there was no king's witness. They tried their best. They drew blank".

Besides Bombay, Karachi was the scene of actual fighting between navymen and British soldiers. Gurkha soldiers refused to obey orders to fire on the *Hindustan*, an old sloop, which put up a brave fight. The Gurkha soldiers had to be replaced by British soldiers. Not only did the Indian army units refuse to obey orders to fight the navymen, they went on strike in several places in sympathy with the rebel navymen. We have noted that one thousand men of the Indian Air Force went on sympathy strike in Bombay. So did the men of the Air Force in Poona, Calcutta, Madras and Ambala. To quote Dutt, "An R.I.A.F. squadron, which had been ordered to proceed to Bombay, was grounded at Jodhpur; every aircraft had mysteriously developed engine trouble." Hallett, then Governor of the U.P., informed Wavell on 19 November 1945 that soldiers of the Air Force stationed in Allahabad, Bamrauli and Cawnpore had sent their contributions to the I.N.A. Defence Fund. The Indian Air Force stationed in Calcutta opposed the court martial of the I.N.A. men. It sent its subscription to the I.N.A. Defence fund with the words: "for the defence of the brave and patriotic sons of India." Penderel Moon noted: "There was also unrest at this time in the R.I.A.F. and in some of the technical units of the Indian Army." Not only was there unrest in some technical units of the army but army units, as pointed out before, disobeyed orders in Bombay and Karachi.

In the Jabalpur cantonment soldiers staged a revolt in March 1946 and in Dehradun Gurkha soldiers went on strike. In some places the police also rose in revolt. In March 1946 the police in Allahabad and Delhi went on hunger-strike. In April 10,000 policemen struck work. In September the military police went on strike in Patna and Begusarai. There was a widespread strike by policemen in Bihar in March 1947. The wall sedulously erected by the British Raj to segregrate the armed forces from the people crumbled down. At no time since the First War of Indian Independence in 1857-8 did the regular armed forces come out to defend the cause of freedom as they did now.

The brave men of the navy refused to be cowed by any threat – not even the threat of Admiral Godfrey (who had flown in bombers) to sink the navy. They appealed to political parties to lead them, promised to hand over to them the navy which they had renamed the Indian National Navy. But no political party, not even the CPI, responded to their appeal though they could have access to the rebel men of the navy.

Jinnah's appeal to them, *especially the Muslims among them*, to surrender came in the early hours of 23 February when their representatives were meeting to decide their future course of action. Dutt wrote: "... the overwhelming majority were for a fight to death and not for surrender." The Naval Central Strike Committee ultimately took the decision to surrender, stating that they were surrendering not to the British Raj but to the Congress and the League. In their last message to the people, they said: "For the first time the blood of the men in the services and the people flowed together in a common cause. We in the services will never forget this. We also know that you, our brothers and sisters, will never forget. Long live our great people. Jai Hind." After the surrender the manhunt began. More than two thousands of the rebels were arrested and kept in detention camps; about five hundred were sentenced to prison terms to serve as common criminals. The top Congress leaders, who had given the pledge that "no disciplinary action" would be taken, did little to keep their pledge. What role did the Congress leaders play during the historic naval revolt? Sardar Patel, Abul Kalam Azad, S.K. Patil (secretary of the Bombay Provincial Congress Committee, and later, minister of the central government), Jinnah and Chundrigar of the Muslim League openly opposed the call for a strike on 22 February issued by the Naval Central Strike Committee and advised the navymen to surrender to the British. Patil had secret confabulations with the Bombay governor and the Congress and the League placed 'volunteers' at the service of the Raj to "assist the police" and British army units to fight the people. Colville wrote to Wavell that on 22 February he "saw several of these volunteers... and they did useful though limited work".

Bombay observed a successful general strike in the teeth of the bitter opposition of the Congress and the League leaders. Workers and students of Bombay fought pitched battles in the streets with British army units and the armed police, who were assisted by Congress and League volunteers.

At a mass meeting held in Bombay with the permission of the Bombay government on 26 February, Nehru and Patel strongly condemned "the mass violence in Bombay", that is, the resistance of the navymen and workers who had dared to raise the banner of anti-imperialist revolt. Addressing the press next day, Nehru thundered: 'The R.I.N. Central Strike Committee had no business to issue such an appeal [to the city of Bombay to observe a sympathy strike]. *I will not tolerate this kind of thing*." The Nehrus alone had the right to issue calls for strikes!

Gandhi, the prophet of nonviolence, condemned the rebels for their thoughtless orgy of violence – not the real orgy of violence by the Raj, of which the people were victims. To him the "combination between Hindus and Muslims and others for the purpose of violent action is unholy..." He went on denouncing those who disbelieved in British professions that they would grant freedom to India. It was a country-wide anti-imperialist revolt. Wavell noted in his diary on 7 March 1946 that the victory parade that was organized in Delhi was boycotted and crowds of men burnt down the Town Hall.

Workers were on the march everywhere despite the opposition of Congress and League leaders. The number of workers who went on strike in 1946 was 1,961,984 and in 1947, 1,840,784. There was an unprecedented upsurge of anti-imperialist struggle throughout the country, in which workers, peasants, students, other youths, office employees, navymen and sections of the Indian army, air force and police and lower rungs of the bureaucracy took part, and armed confrontations were frequent. Peasant revolts took place in different parts of India. In the Thana district in Maharashtra the struggle of the Warlis broke out. In the Alleppey district of the native state of Travancore (now a part of Kerala) peasants and workers launched a united struggle. In several districts of Bengal, especially in North Bengal, the Tebhaga struggle broke out under the leadership of the Communist Party. It was a struggle of the peasantry, mainly sharecroppers (who bore the expenses of cultivation) for a two-thirds share of the produce. Peasants fought heroically. In the undivided district of Dinajpur, forty peasants became martyrs. In 1946 began the historic struggles of the peasants in Telangana districts of the native state of Hyderabad (Telangana, now a part of Andhra Pradesh) under the leadership of the Andhra State Committee of the CPI. It developed into a struggle for land and power. Large areas were liberated. The struggle continued even after the march of troops of the Indian government in 1948 to suppress it, until it was withdrawn unconditionally by the CPI leadership in 1951. In several other native states ruled by princes, puppets of the British Indian government, there were revolts of the people, especially in Travancore and Kashmir.

Imperialism Unable to Rule in the Old Way

We have noted Commander-in-Chief Claude Auchinleck's appreciation, of 24 November 1945, of the Indian situation, with which Viceroy Wavell generally agreed. On 19 February 1946, Wavell recorded in his diary that he had seen Porter, Secretary, Home Department, who was all for capitulation to the I.N.A; that he had discussed with Bewoor, Secretary, Posts and Air Department, about a postal strike; that he had talks with Carr, A.O.C-in-C, about R.I.A.F mutiny; with Griffin, Chief Commissioner of Railways and Conran Smith, Secretary, War Transport Department, about a railway strike; and "finally the C-in-C, most gloomy of all, about R.I.N. mutiny in Bombay and the I.N.A trials; What a cheerful day – prospect or reality of three mutinies and two strikes", commented Wavell.

After referring to the "serious rioting in Bombay", "a mutiny in the R.I.N., much indiscipline in the R.I.A.F., some unrest in the Indian Army" and "threatened strikes on the Railways, and in the

Post and Telegraphs", Wavell wrote to King George VI on 22 March 1946: "Perhaps the best way to look at it is that India is in the birth-pangs of a new order..."

When in late March 1946, the Cabinet Mission with Secretary of State Pethick-Lawrence, Stafford Cripps and A.V. Alexander came to India to negotiate, mainly with Congress and League leaders, a settlement of the constitutional issues and met the Viceroy's Executive Council, Edward Benthall said on behalf of it that "*the Council was unanimous that a change of Government at the Centre was imperative...* It [the Council's lack of confidence] is due to the uncertainty of Indian troops and police to whom they must look for defence and support in the future."

Champaran, Kheda, Khilafat and Amritsar

Mahatma Gandhi had shown in South Africa and in 1918 in Champaran, Bihar and Kheda, Gujarat that the only way to earn the respect and attention of British officials was to actively resist government activities through civil disobedience.

Now in Champaran and Kheda in 1918 he led impoverished farmers, mired in social evils like unhygienic conditions, domestic violence, discrimination, oppression of women and untouchability. On top of their miseries, these people were forced to grow cash crops like indigo, tobacco and cotton, instead of food, and virtually not compensated. In addition, they would have to pay taxes despite a famine.

The Governments of the affected regions signed agreements suspending taxation in face of the famine, allowing the farmers to grow their own crops, releasing all political prisoners and returning all property and lands seized. It was the biggest victory against the British Empire since the American Revolution.

Mahatma Gandhi was assisted by a new generation of Indian revolutionaries like Rajendra Prasad and Jawaharlal Nehru. In Kheda, the entire revolt had been led by Sardar Vallabhbhai Patel, who was to become Gandhi's lieutenant.

Millions of India's Muslims were also antagonized by the Government's support of Mustafa Kemal of Turkey, who had overthrown the Sultan of Turkey, considered the Caliph of Islam. Muslim leaders formed the Khilafat committee to protest the actions and find a way to effectively stop the British authorities from neglecting their concerns.

A public meeting of unarmed civilians at Jallianwala Bagh in Amritsar was fired upon by troops under the command of Reginald Dyer. Hundreds of people died and perhaps thousands were injured. Women, children and the elderly were not spared. The outcry in Punjab led to thousands of arrests, beatings and more deaths at the hands of police and some violent protesters. The Amritsar Massacre became the most infamous event of British rule in India. To Gandhi and many others, it became clear that a reckoning with the British was not far off.

Satyagraha

Gandhi's idea was a nationwide protest against the Rowlatt Acts. All offices and factories would be closed. Indians would be encouraged to withdraw from Raj-sponsored schools, police services, the military and the civil services, and lawyers to leave the Raj's courts. Public transportation, English-manufactured goods, especially clothes would be boycotted.

Veterans like Bal Gangadhar Tilak, Bipin Chandra Pal, Mohammed Ali Jinnah, Annie Besant opposed the idea outright. The All India Muslim League also criticized the ideas. But the younger generation of Indian nationalists were thrilled and backed Gandhi. The Congress Party adopted his plans, and he received extensive support from Muslim leaders like Maulana Azad, Mukhtar Ahmed Ansari, Hakim Ajmal Khan, Abbas Tyabji, Maulana Mohammed Ali and Maulana Shaukat Ali. Gandhi was elected President of the Indian National Congress in 1919 and 1920, as well as the All India Home Rule League-the latter erstwhile dominated by Gandhi's critics like Jinnah, Besant and Tilak.

Success and Suspension

The success of the revolt launched was a total shock to British authorities and a massive encouragement to millions of Indians. Then on February 4, 1922, in the Chauri Chaura, after violent clashed between the local police and the protestors in which three protestors were killed due the insuing police firing, Gandhi felt that the revolt was veering off-course. He did not want the movement to degenerate into an orgy of violence where police and angry mobs attacked each other back and forth, victimizing civilians in between. Gandhi went on a fast lasting 3 days, appealing to the Indian public for all resistance to end, and called off the mass civil disobedience movement.

Aftermath

Non-co-operation movement was withdrawn because of the Chauri-Chaura incident. Despite stopping a national revolt single-handedly, on March 10, 1922, Gandhi was arrested, and on March 18, 1922, he was imprisoned for two years for publishing seditious materials. The British judge who passed the sentence was shaking with emotion of admiration, and said he would himself be the happiest if the government released Gandhi. Although most Congress leaders remained firmly behind Gandhi, the disillusioned broke away.

The Ali brothers would soon become fierce critics, and Motilal Nehru and Chittaranjan Das formed the Swaraj Party, rejecting Gandhi's leadership. Many nationalists had felt that the Non-Cooperation Movement should not have been stopped due to isolated incidents of violence, and most nationalists, while retaining confidence in Gandhi, were depressed. Contemporary historians and critics suggest that the movement was successful enough to break the back of British rule, and possibly even result in the independence most Indians strove for till 1947.

But many historians and Indian leaders of the time also defend Gandhi's judgment. If he had not stopped the revolts, India would probably have descended into an anarchy-style rebellion which would alienate common Indians and impress only violent revolutionaries

SUCCESS AND LEGACY

Gandhi's resulting fame spread like fire all over the nation. He had become a defining influence on Indian Nationalism. People in Gujarat still revere Gandhi and Sardar Patel, and their role in the freedom struggle. Gujarat is the most industrialized and progressive state in India today. In Bihar, poverty and social conflict pervades what was the founding of the Satyagraha movement. The Naxalite insurgency is centred around the same age-old problem of class struggle between poor farmers and rich landlords, now involving terrorism.

The Issue

In the district of Kaira, the crops for the year 1917-18 have, by common admission, proved a partial failure. Under the revenue rules, if the crops are under four annas, the cultivators are entitled to full suspension of the revenue assessment for the year ; if the crops are under six annas, half the amount of assessment is suspended. So far as I am aware, the Government have been pleased to grant full suspension with regard to one village out of nearly 600, and half-suspension in the case of over 103 villages. It is claimed on behalf of the ryots that the suspension is not at all adequate to the actuality. The Government contend that in the vast majority of villages, crops have been over six annas. The only question therefore at issue is, whether the crops have been under four annas or six annas, as the case may be, or over the latter figure.

Tyrannical Talatis

Government valuation is in the first instance made by the Talatis assisted by the chief men of the villages concerned. As a rule, no check on their figures is considered necessary, for it is only during partial failure of crops that Government valuation of crops may have to be challenged. The Talatis are as a class obsequious, unscrupulous and tyrannical. The chief men are especially selected for their docility. The Talatis, one aim is naturally to collect full assessment as promptly as possible. We sometimes read accounts of assiduous Talatis having been awarded 'pugree' for making full collection. In applying to the Talatis the adjectives I have given, I wish to cast no reflection on them as men. I merely state the fact. The Talatis are not born; they are made; and rent-collectors all the world over have to cultivate a callousness without which they could not do their work to the satisfaction of their masters. It is impossible for me to reproduce the graphic description given by the ryots of the rent-collectors which the Talatis chiefly are.

Government Estimate Biased

My purpose in dealing with the Talatis is to show that the Government's valuation of the crops is derived in the first instance from the tainted source and is presumably biased against the ryots. As against their valuation, we have the universal testimony of ryots, high and low, some of whom are men of position and considerable wealth, who have a reputation to lose and who have nothing to gain by exaggeration except the odium of Talatis and possibly higher officials. I wish to state at once that behind this movement there is no desire to discredit the Government, or an individual official. The movement is intended to assert the right of the people to be effectively heard in matters concerning themselves.

Careful Inquiry

It is known to the public that the Hon'ble Mr. G. K. Parekh and Mr. V. J. Patel, invited and assisted by the Gujarat Sabha, carried on investigations, as also Messrs. Deodhar, Joshi and Thakkar of the Servants of India Society. Their investigation was necessarily preliminary and brief and, therefore, confined to a few villages only. But the result of their inquiry went to show that the crops in the majority of cases were under four annas. As their investigation, not being extensive enough, was capable of being challenged, and it was challenged, I undertook a full inquiry with the assistance of over

20 capable, experienced and impartial men of influence and status. I personally visited over 30 villages and met as many men in the villages as I could, inspected in these villages most of the fields belonging to them and after a searching cross-examination of the villagers, came to the conclusion that their crops were under four annas. I found that among the men who surrounded me there were present those who were ready to check exaggerations and wild statements. Men knew what was at stake if they departed from the truth. As to the rabi crops and the still standing kharif crops, I was able by the evidence of my own eyes to check the statements of the agriculturists. The methods adopted by my co-workers were exactly the same. In this manner 400 villages were examined and with but a few exceptions, crops were found to be under four annas, and only in three cases they were found to be over six annas. The method adopted by us was, so far as the kharif crops were concerned, to ascertain the actual yield of the whole of the crops of individual villages and the possible yield of the same village in a normal year. Assuming the truth of the statements made by them, this is admittedly an absolute test, and any other method that would bring about the same result must be rejected as untrue and unscientific; and as I have already remarked, all probability of exaggeration was avoided in the above-named investigation. As to the standing rabi crops, there was the eye estimate and it was tested by the method mentioned above.

The Government Method

The Government method is an eye estimate and, therefore, a matter largely of guess-work. It is moreover open to fundamental objections which I have endeavoured to set forth in a letter to the Collector of the District. I requested him to treat Vadthal—a well-known and ordinarily well-to-do village of the district with the railway line passing by it and which is near a trade centre—as a test case and I suggested that if the crops were in that village proved to be under four annas, as I hold they were, it might be assumed that in the other villages less fortunately situated, crops were not likely to be more than four annas. I have added to my request a suggestion that I should be permitted to be present at the inquiry. He made the inquiry but rejected my suggestion and, therefore, it proved to be onesided. The Collector has made an elaborate report on the crops of that village which, in my opinion, I have successfully challenged. The original Government valuation, I understand, was twelve annas, the Collector's minimum valuation is seven annas. If the probably wrong methods of valuation to which I have drawn attention and which have been adopted by the Collector are allowed for, the valuation according to his own reckoning would come under six annas and according to the agriculturists it would be under four annas.

Need for Impartial Inquiry

Both the report and my answer are too technical to be of value to the public. But I have suggested that, as both the Government and the agriculturists hold themselves in the right, if the Government have any regard for popular opinion, they should appoint an impartial committee of inquiry with the cultivators' representatives upon it, or gracefully accept the popular view. The Government have rejected both the suggestions and insist upon applying coercive measures for the collection of revenue. It may be mentioned that these measures have never been totally suspended and in many cases the ryots have paid simply under pressure.

The Talatis have taken away cattle and have returned them only after the payment of assessment. In one case I witnessed a painful incident—a man having his milch buffalo taken away from him; and it was only on my happening to go to the village that the buffalo was released; this buffalo was the most valuable property the man possessed and a source of daily bread for him.

Scores of such cases have already happened and many more will no doubt happen hereafter, if the public opinion is not ranged on the side of the people. Every means of seeking redress by prayers has been exhausted. Interviews with the Collector, the Commissioner and His Excellency have taken place. The final suggestion that was made is this :

Proposals to the Government

Although in the majority of cases, people are entitled to full suspension, half suspension should be granted throughout the district except for the villages which show, by common consent, crops over six annas. Such a gracious concession may be accompanied by a declaration that the Government would expect those who have already means voluntarily to pay up the dues, we, the workers, on our part undertaking to persuade such people to pay up the Government dues. This will leave only the poorest people untouched. I venture to submit that acceptance of this suggestion can only bring credit and strength to the Government. Resistance of popular-will can only produce discontent which, in the case of fear-stricken peasantry such as of Kaira, can only find an underground passage and thus demoralize them. The present movement is an attempt to get out of such a false position, humiliating alike for the Government and the people.

Law Abused

And how do the Government propose to assert their position and so-called prestige? They have a Revenue Code giving them unlimited powers without a right of appeal to the ryots against the decisions of the Revenue Authorities. Exercise of these powers in a case like the one before us, in which the ryots are fighting for a principle and the authorities for prestige, would be a prostitution of justice, of a disavowal of all fair-play. These powers are :

1. Right of summary execution.
2. Right of exacting a quarter of the assessment as punishment.
3. Right of confiscation of land, not merely Royatwari but even Inami or Sanadi.
4. Right of keeping a man under lock-up.

These remedies may be applied singly or all together, and unbelievable though it may seem to the public, it may be mentioned that notices of the application of all these remedies but the last have been issued. Thus a man owning several hundred acres of land in perpetuity and valued at thousands of rupees, paying a small assessment rate, may at the will of the authority lose the whole of it, because for the sake of principle he respectfully refuses voluntarily to pay the assessment himself and is prepared meekly but under strong protest to penalities that may be inflicted by law. Surely vindictive confiscation of property ought not to be the reward for orderly disobedience which, properly handled, can only result in progress all round and in giving the Government a bold and a frank peasantry with a will of its own.

Appeal to the Public

I venture to invite the Press and the public to assist these cultivators of Kaira who have dared to enter on a fight for what they consider is just and right. Let the public remember this also that unprecedentally severe plague has decimated the population of Kaira. People are living outside their homes in specially prepared thatched cottages at considerable expense to themselves. In some villages mortality has been tremendous. Prices are ruling high of which, owing to the failure of crops, they can but take little advantage and have to suffer all the disadvantages thereof. It is not money they want so much as the voice of a strong, unanimous and emphatic public opinion.

A Letter by Gandhi and Patel to Kheda People

To,

The Brothers and Sisters of Kaira District,

The struggle that the people of the district of Kaira entered upon on the 22nd of March last, has come to an end. The people took the following vow on that day:

"Knowing the crops of our village are less than 4 annas, we requested the Government to suspend the collection of revenue assessment till the ensuing year, but the Government has not acceded to our prayer. Therefore we, the undersigned, hereby solemnly declare that we shall not, of our own accord, pay to the Government the full or the remaining revenue for the year. We shall let the Government take whatever legal steps it may think fit and gladly suffer the consequences of our non-payment. We shall let our hands rather be forefeited, than by voluntary payment allow our case to be considered false or our self-respect compromised. Should the Government, however, agree to suspend the collection of the second instalment of the assessment throughout the district, such amongst us as are in a position to pay will pay up the whole or the balance of the revenue that may be due. The reason why those who are able to pay still withhold payment is that, if they pay up, the poorer ryots may in a panic sell their chattels or incur debts to pay their dues, and thereby bring suffering upon themselves. In these circumstances, we feel that for the sake of the poor, it is the duty even of those who can afford to pay, to withhold payment of their assessment."

The meaning of this vow is that on the Government suspending collection of the revenue from the poor, the well-to-do should pay the assessment due from them. The Mamlatdar of Nadiad at Uttersanda, on the 3rd of June issued such orders, whereupon the people of Uttersanda, who could afford, were advised to pay up. Payments have already commenced there.

On the foregoing order having been passed at Uttersanda, a letter was addressed to the Collector stating that if orders like the one in Uttersanda were passed everywhere the struggle would come to an end, and it would be possible to inform His Excellency the Governor on the 10th instant—the day of the sitting of the Provincial War Conference—that the domestic difference in Kaira was settled. The Collector has replied to the effect that the order like the one in Uttersanda is applicable to the whole district. Thus the people's prayer has at last been granted. The Collector has also stated in reply to a query about Chothai orders that the orders will not be enforced against those who may voluntarily pay up. Our thanks are due to the Collector for this concession.

We are obliged to say with sorrow that although the struggle has come to an end, it is an end without grace. It lacks dignity. The above orders have not been passed either by generosity or with the heart in them. It very much looks as if the orders have been passed with the greatest reluctance. The Collector says:

"Orders were issued to all Mamlatdars on the 25th April that no pressure should be put on those unable to pay. Their attention was again drawn to these orders in a proper Circular issued by me on the 22nd of May and to ensure that proper effect was given to them the Mamlatdars were advised to divide the defaulters in each village into two classes, those who could pay and those who were unable to pay on account of poverty.

If this was so, why were these orders not published to the people ? Had they known them on the 25th April, what sufferings would they not have been saved from! The expenses that were unnecessarily incurred by the Government in engaging the officials of the district in affecting executions would have been saved. Wherever the assessment was uncollected the people lived with their lives in their hands. They have lived away from their homes to avoid attachments. They have not even enough food. The women have suffered what they ought not to have. At times, they have been obliged to put up with insults from insolent Circle Inspectors, and to helplessly watch their milch buffaloes being taken away from them. They have paid Chothai fines and, had they known the foregoing orders, they would have been saved all the miseries. The officials knew that this relief for the poor was the crux of the struggle. The Commissioner would not even look at this difficulty. Many letters were addressed to him but he remained unbending. He said, "Individual relief cannot be granted, it is not the law." Now the Collector says :

"The orders of April 25, so far as it related to putting pressure on those who were really unable to pay on account of poverty, were merely a re-statement of what are publicly known to be the standing orders of Government on that subject."

If this is really true, the people have suffered deliberately and through sheer obstinacy ! At the time of going to Delhi, I (Gandhiji), wrote to the Commissioner requesting him to grant or to issue orders to the above effect so that the good news could be given to His Excellency the Viceroy. The Commissioner gave no heed to the request.

"We are moved by the sufferings of the people, we perceive our mistake and in order to placate the people we are now prepared to grant individual relief", the officials could have generously said all this and endeared themselves to the people, but they have obstinately avoided this method (of winning them over). And even now relief has been granted in a niggardly manner, involuntarily and without admission of any mistake. It is even claimed that what has now been granted is nothing new. And hence we say that there is little grace in the settlement.

The officials have failed to be popular because of their obstinacy, because of their mistaken belief that they should never admit being in the wrong and because of their having made it a fetish that it should never be said of them that they had yielded to anything like popular agitation. It grieves us to offer this criticism. But we have permitted ourselves to do so as their friends.

But though the official attitude is thus unsatisfactory, our prayer has been granted and it is our duty to accept the concession with thankfulness. Now, there is only 8 per cent of the assessment remaining unpaid. It was a point of honour with us till now to refuse payment. Conditions having materially altered, it is a point of honour for a Satyagrahi to pay up the assessment. Those who can afford, should pay without causing the Government the slightest trouble and thus show that where there is no conflict between the dictates of conscience and those of man-made law, they are second to none in obeying the law of the land. A Satyagrahi some-times appears momentarily to disobey laws and the constituted authority, only to prove in the end his regard for both.

In making a list of those who are unable to pay, we should apply a test so rigid that no one can challenge our findings. Those whose incapacity for payment is at all in doubt should consider it their duty to pay. The final decision as to the incapacity for payment will rest with the authorities, but we believe that the judgment of the people will have its full weight.

By their courage the people of Kaira have drawn the attention of the whole of India. During the last six months they have had full taste of the fruits of observing truth, fearlessness, unity, determination and self-sacrifice. We hope that they will still further cultivate these great qualities, will move forward on the path of progress, and shed luster on the name of the Motherland. It is our firm belief that the people of Kaira have truly served their own cause, as well as the cause of Swaraj and the Empire.

May God bless you !

We remain Always in your service, M. K. Gandhi Vallabhbhai J. Patel.

Letter by Gandhi to Patel and Agitator

Sisters and Brothers of the Kaira District,

You have only recently finished a great Satyagraha struggle and come out victorious. You have displayed so much courage, tact and other good qualities in that fight, that I venture to advise you and earnestly press you to engage yourself in an even more important work of service to your Motherland.

You have shown how the people can oppose the Government without giving up courtesy, how they can pay due respect to the officials but still resist their orders and get what they want by peaceful means. And now I give you a chance to show to the world that you bear no hatred towards the Government though you fought a better fight against it only recently.

You are all Swarajists, and some are even members of the Home Rule League. 'Home Rule' itself implies maintenance of connection with the Empire as one of its partners. At present we are subjects of the Empire. We do not enjoy the rights and privileges of the Englishman. Our position is not like that of Canada, South Africa and Australia which are veritable parts of the Empire. India is a 'dependency'. We want the same rights as the Englishman enjoys, the same Colonial Status that S. Africa etc., have, and we want to have an Indian Viceroy at the head of our government. In order to acquire this status we must gain the power to defend ourselves and for that to arm ourselves and fight. We can never be respected as equals of the Englishman, as long as our safety depends upon our protection by British arms and we are afraid of their police force and soldiery. We must, therefore, learn to bear arms and gain the power to protect ourselves from any aggression. It is, therefore, our duty to join the army if we want to learn that art very quickly.

There can never be a friendship between a coward and a brave man. We are stigmatized as cowards. If we want to remove this stain, it is but meet that we show heroism on a battlefield by seizing this chance of recruitment.

It is certain that we want to be a partner in the Empire. Since it is so, we must, at any cost even at that of death, join in the defence of the Empire. If the Empire is destroyed, with it topple down all our hopes of freedom and equal partnership.

The easiest and the straightest way, therefore, of winning Swaraj is to stand shoulder to shoulder with the Britishers in the defence of the Empire. We have not the economic strength to help it by munificent donations. Besides, it is not money alone that wins a war. It is stupendous manpower that turns the scale. And India alone can create an impregnable wall of men against the German onslaught. If the Empire wins principally through the Indian army, it is clear that we can gain whatever rights we demand.

Some may object that the Britishers will play false with us afterwards, if we do not insist on getting our rights just now. Even in that case we can win them with the same power that we shall have acquired through the successful defence of the Empire. You cannot become its partner by harassing it. Harassment of the Empire at this critical hour can never bring for us the rights which its service can. Distrust of the rulers of the Empire is distrust of our own power and is a sign of weakness. Our rights must not depend upon the weakness or generosity of the rulers, but upon our own fitness, our own inherent power.

The Indian States are helping the Empire and they have their reward. And the rich are solidly supporting it and they too get the return they want. Neither of these have made any preconditions. Then there are the Indian soldiers who are fighting in order to maintain their families and to prove themselves worth their salt. They are awarded honours and prizes. All these classes belong to India but they cannot be called Swarajists. Swaraj is not their aim in life. It is not patriotism, nor the good of the country that impels them to help the war-effort. It is possible that if we entertain hatred and enmity towards the Empire, the men at its helm may employ all these three classes of Indians to crush us.

If we want Swaraj it is our duty to help the Empire and we too are certain to have our reward. If our intentions are honest, the Government will respond with equal honesty. Supposing for a moment that the intentions of the Government are mala fide, even then we must have faith in the purity of our own motives. There is no heroism in being good to those who are good to us. Heroism lies in returning good for evil. "The Government does not grant us Commissions in the army, does not repeal the Arms Act, does not even open Military Colleges to train Indians. How then can we help it ?" The objections are valid.

The Government commits a serious blunder in not introducing these reforms. The English people can rightly claim credit for many virtuous deeds. May God reward them fully in return. But the heinous crime, which in the name of the English people the English administrators have perpetrated in disarming India, will wash off all their good deeds unless officialdom wakes up to the crime betimes. God forbid, but if India comes to grief and if she passes under the tutelage of some other Power, her concentrated cry of distress will harm the British nation so seriously that it will be stained with shame and disgrace and the world will spit upon it for emasculating the thirtythree crores of Indians. But I believe that Britain's statesmen have realized this dire possibility and are even quite awake to it. Only that cannot at once transform the situation that they have themselves created.

Every Englishman, the moment he sets his foot on the Indian soil, is taught to keep himself proudly aloof from Indians and remain always conscious of his own greatness and superiority. This over-bearing attitude is in their very air. Officials at the top are trying to free themselves and their subordinates from this climate, but they do not succeed in clearing the mists. Were this not a time of crisis, we would have fought with them. But to sit tight and wait for the grant of Commissions at such a time is to cut the nose to spite the face. It may happen that we may go on waiting for the Commission order and let the opportunity to help the Empire slip through our fingers.

Even if the Government's motive in refusing or delaying the grant of Commissions etc. to us is to prevent us from helping the Empire through recruitment and other ways, we must, it is my conviction, make it a point to join the army.

The Government wants five lakhs of men as recruits to meet the challenge of the present times and is going to get them by any means. But if we provide these men ourselves, we would cover ourselves with glory, render valuable service and save our own people from the reportedly harsh and improper ways in which the recruiting campaign is conducted at present. It would be no small power that we would gain, if all recruiting work comes into our hands. From the above facts and arguments it will be seen that in helping the Empire by joining the army, we gain fitness for Swaraj, learn how to defend our country and recover to some extent our lost manliness.

I have faith in the innate goodness of the English nation. I must admit, it is only on that basis that I give the above advice. I believe that though that nation has done us much harm, it is to our advantage to remain in the Empire. Between the virtues and vices of that nation, to me for one it appears that the balance tilts in favour of its virtues. It is indeed painful to remain as subjects under the British people. The Britishers have the serious vice of making their subject peoples lose their self-respect. But they have also the virtue of treating their equals with great respect and loyalty. We have also seen that nation has often helped some other peoples subjected to foreign rule. If we become partners with them, we can take much and give much and this respectable status is likely to do great good to the world. If I did not possess this faith in the bonafides of the Britisher and if I felt it desirable to be totally independent of him, I would not only advice my countrymen not to help the British but would even instigate them to an open revolt and rouse national consciousness by inviting on myself the suffering and punishment of a rebel. At least at present we are not in a position to stand on our legs, independently of any other nation's help. I believe that our good lies in acquiring the position of partnership within the Empire, and in my tours I have seen that all Home Rulers believe likewise. The hope I entertain from the Kaira District and Gujarat is not for the recruitment of a few hundreds but of thousands.

If Gujarat wants to remove the stain of spineless, it must contribute thousands of recruits. In many conception of this would-be army of Gujaratis every class should be included. The educated and advanced classes as well as the illiterate and backward, Patidars, Barias, Vaghris and all others will, I hope, stand shoulder to shoulder in that army. As long as the educated and cultured classes—the elite do not come forward to join the army, it is useless to hope for any response from other classes.

I hope all healthy adults among the educated classes will join the army. They will be employed, if not in actual fighting at the Front, in numerous departments of work pertaining to a war. They can, for instance, nurse the wounded soldiers. I hope that those parents who have sons of a mature age will never hesitate to send them as recruits. It should be not at all a matter of grief but one of joy for a brave man to sacrifice his son in a war. The son's sacrifice at this crisis will be regarded as national service for the cause of Swaraj. It is my appeal to the women not to feel nervous about this appeal for recruitment, but to hail it enthusiastically. Their personal safety and the protection of their honour depend on the response to this appeal.

There are 600 villages in the Kaira District with an average population of more than a thousand. If such village gives at least 20 recruits, the district can contribute an army of 12,000 men. The population of the district is seven hundred thousand and so 12,000 men came to 1.7% of the whole population. Death annually claims a higher toll in percentage than this figure. If we are not prepared to pay even this price for the Empire, and for Swaraj, no wonder we would prove ourselves unfit for freedom. If, the recruits die on the battlefield they will make themselves, their village and their country immortal and twenty others will step into the dead men's shoes and defend the country.

If we really want to do this work, we cannot afford to be slow and lethargic. I appeal to the men and women of every village to select the strongest among their men and send their names to the recruiting centre. Meetings will be held in important villages to appeal to you for recruitment and to clarify the many points that will arise from the appeal. Volunteers also will move from village to village for the same purpose.

The following gentlemen have joined in this work:

Messrs. Vallabhbhai Jhaverbhai Patel (Bar-at-Law), Krishnalal Narsinghlal Desai (M.A.,LL.B.), Indulal Kanhaiyalal Yagnik (B.A., LL.B.), Hariprasad Pitambardas Mehta (Proprietor, "The Hitechhu" Press), Pragji Khandubhai Desai, Mohanlal Kameshwar Pandya, Ganesh Vasudev Mavlankar (B.A., LL.B.) Kalidas Jashkaran Jhaveri (B.A., LL.B.), Fulchand Bapuji Shah, Gokuldas Dwarkadas Talati (B.A., LL.B.), Shivabhai Bhailalbhai Patel (B.A., LL.B.), Raojibhai Manibhai Patel and several others.

Mohandas Karamchand Gandhi

Nadiad, dated 22.6.1918

Second letter by Gandhi to Patel and Agitator

It is a month today since the first bulletin was written. My colleagues and I have had many enlightening experiences during the period. Meetings were held at various places such as Nadiad, Karamsad, Ras, Kathlal, Jambusar etc. Hundreds of men and women were approached and frank talks were held. I beg to submit here the impressions we have gained through our experiences. Hardly a hundred men have enrolled themselves as recruits. When I compare the result with the time spent, a month, and with the many tours undertaken, I feel that this number is very small. If, on the other hand, I think of the present wretched condition of the people, I am surprised at even this number. Those who had never joined in any physical fight, who had never even brandished a walking stick against anybody have enrolled themselves. If then the class of physically and mentally fit but ignorant persons are persuaded to join, we can supply an unending array of soldiers.

The present times have clearly brought out the faults of the 'knowing' men. I use the word 'knowing' and not 'educated' purposely. If men and women of this class do their duty properly, they can successfully influence those classes which are illiterate but constitutionally fit to be soldiers. My experience reveals one great weakness of the elite. They do not possess sufficient national consciousness and do not take enough interest in national work. That is why the recruiting campaign becomes a difficult job. Those of them, therefore, who happen to read this bulletin must enrol themselves and exhort the illiterate and politically unconscious classes to do the same, if, of course, they have faith in this programme.

But I have seen some among them who do not believe in this work. This bulletin is specially meant to remove their doubts. I request them to read it carefully. It is a wise man's business to chalk out his line of action after a careful consideration of the actually prevailing situation. We must on no account help the British if we really wish to sever our connection with them, but I know of only a very few who say that they want to cut it off. And everyone can clearly see that even they cannot do so right today. Be that as it may, our salvation lies in helping the British just now. To help them is to help ourselves. Where our interests are identical with theirs, it is sheer folly to remember old scores and refuse to help the other party. If our village is attacked by dacoits and the whole village is in danger, we will forget all our internal feuds and animosities and rush to the rescue of our enemies within the village to drive away the outsiders. Exactly similar is the situation that faces us in this war today. Opposition to the common danger is not only the need of the hour but our imperative duty. Then there is another question that is raised : "How could it be our dharma to get our best men killed in the war ? All the Swarajists will be exterminated and how can we then fight and win Swaraj ?" Were this argument not advanced by some of the intelligentsia, I would have called it simply ridiculous. If the whole of India contains only 5 lakhs of Swarajists, it is clear we are not fit for Swaraj. But then the doubting Thomas says, "Whatever the number of Swarajists, the intelligent among them who actively agitate for Swaraj are definitely less than 5 lakhs, and these would be swept off.."

At first sight the statement is a convincing argument. Only, one important point is overlooked here. In the process of creating an army of 5 lakhs of men determined to lay down their lives, 50 lakhs will have come to know the implications of 'Swaraj', 'war' etc. We wish to raise the tempo of 5 lakhs of men to such a pitch that they would enrol themselves consciously and of their own free will. They will have consulted their friends and relatives before they do. These 5 lakhs will thus leave behind them lakhs of men with the same fiery enthusiasm as they possess. But the real point behind these objections is the fact that we have lost the power to fight altogether and with it all our bravery. We do not possess even the capacity to protect our women. In the name of dharma we have put on the shelf our karma (duty). We cannot face depredators even in broad daylight. It is only India among all the countries of the world where you can meet with the sight of 8 men raiding a population of 1000 and coolly looting and robbing the thousand without having to put up a fight. Not that the Indian villagers are physically so weak as to be unable to drive out the dacoits. But death is a nightmare to them. "Why should one risk his life by plunging in such a fight? Let the robbers have a free hand. It is the Government's business to deal with them and why bother oneself to meddle in what is the Government's function ? Let us save our bones". This is their mentality and they keep to their homes. These 'philosophers' remain passive and indifferent witnesses if the neighbours' house is burnt, if he is dishonoured and disgraced, or if he is robbed of his property. So long as this pseudo-philosophy is not uprooted from the Indian soil, there is not going to be any real peace in the country. It is an intolerable sight for a man of self-respect to see his village saved only by the Government policemen or privately employed chowkidars A splendid chance offers itself to save ourselves from this tragic plight. Recruitment will teach us how to bear arms, fire us with national consciousness and enable us to protect our villages.

'What will happen to our wives and children ?' is the question on everybody's lips. Over and above food and clothing, the soldier gets a minimum salary of Rs. 18 and his position and pay are raised according to the worth he displays. Besides, the Government provides for the maintenance of his wife and children, if he dies in the war. If he returns home, he is rewarded with prizes and honours. I believe that everything considered, the profession of a soldier is more paying than many others.

"But these advantages, you talk of, are only the monopoly of the Englishman. Which Indian ever gets them ?" This also is an argument I have heard from many. To them I will say that it is impossible for anybody to cheat us of the rights which Englishmen enjoy, even after a stupendous army of 5 lakhs of men is raised by our exertions. If that differentiation persists even then, it would only mean the weakness of those 5 lakhs and their leaders. An army of 5 lakhs, once created, is bound to gain equality with the British army and secure all the rights the latter enjoys. The very formation of that huge phalanx carries with it, as an inevitable consequence, the conferment of those rights.

"You say we must enlist without any preconditions. Others advise us to do so only after securing the promise of the grant of our rights. And there are others still who say we are not at all bound to help in the war and that we need not unnecessarily waste our energy and harm ourselves. We are lost in the maze of these three bewildering advices. To us, therefore, it seems that wisdom lies in sitting tight and doing nothing." In my opinion this is the language of the coward. As time passes, parties will be formed and they will hold varying views. You will have to sift them all, form your own views and act upon them. Let us not forget that you and we all have taken a solemn oath to win Swaraj. If for nothing else, for that sacred vow we must join the army. If we do not, I for one, go to the length of considering our indifference a breach and betrayal of our pledge.

Moreover, there is every danger of our being left out from taking part in the war and of the consequent postponement of the implementation of the Swaraj Scheme, if we insist at present on preconditions. In our very admission into the ranks automatically lies the safety of our country and of the grant of Swaraj. All parties are unanimously of the view that no harm whatsoever is going to be done to the attainment of Swaraj, if we enlist ourselves in the army. Considering the pros and cons of all the three views, therefore, I believe that the one that supports recruitment is the best. I hope the residents of the Kaira District will do their duty and give their names for enrolment in the army to the volunteers in the district or send them direct to the Ashram.

I hope our women will help in this work. I know of some of them who stop their husbands and sons from joining the army. If they only reflect a little more seriously, they will find that it is in their own interest to let their husbands and sons become brave men. And it is undoubtedly to the good of the country.

Yours in service,

Mohandas Karamchand Gandhi

Nadiad, 22-7-1918

DANDI MARCH

The march on foot undertaken by Gandhi and seventy-eight Congress volunteers was the most significant event in the history of the breach of salt law in our country. It was commenced in accordance with a fixed schedule to be carried on by them during the long journey ending at Dandi. Undoubtedly, it was a disciplined band of nonviolent satyagrahis who were to present a new model of satyagraha which later on converted into a bigger movement at all-India level.

On 12 March 1930 at 6-10 A.M. Gandhi came out of his room, calm and composed, accompanied by Prabhashankar Patani, Mahadev Desai and Pyarelal, his secretary. He offered prayers, looked at his watch and exactly at 6.30 A.M. commenced his march with seventy-eight volunteers.

With his usual gentle smile, betokening his unifying faith in the justice of the cause he was pursuing and in the success of the great campaign he had embarked upon, he headed the procession with quick and unfaltering steps.

'Like the historic march of Ram Chandra to Lanka, the march of Dandi would be memorable' exclaimed Motilal Nehru in a message. P.C. Ray called it the 'exodus of Israelites under Moses?

Jawaharlal Nehru called Gandhi, ' .... the pilgrim on his quest of truth, quiet, peaceful, determined and fearless who would continue that quiet pilgrimage regardless of consequences.'

The satyagrahis were to face a fatiguing journey through heat and dust of the Kheda villages. Thousands of men, women and children accompanied the marching column for a few miles and thousands lined the route and showered flowers, coins, currency notes and kum kum at the satyagrahis.

Following the commencement of his epic Dandi March, a tremendous wave of enthusiasm swept over the entire country. The historic day was celebrated all over India. Calcutta woke that morning amidst sounds of conch shells and shouts of 'Gandhiji ki Jai'. At a conference of the Congress leaders of Bengal a decision was taken to appoint immediately an ad hoc council to be called the Bengal Civil Disobedience Council, with the object of carrying out the programme outlined by Gandhiji. J. M. Sen Gupta appealed to all men and women of the province to enrol themselves as volunteers for the Civil Disobedience Movement. He said, 'Bengal is on trial. She had always been in the vanguard of the country's battle for freedom and cannot lag behind. Let us plunge head-long in the fight and regain the rights which are ours.'

In Bombay, a public meeting was held under the presidentship of K. F. Nariman. He exhorted the audience to get ready for the fight. The 'War Council' of the Bombay Provincial Congress Committee announced a it of 'iron-sides' to join the first detachment of volunteers from the town.

In Madras, at a public meeting at Tilak Ghat, prayers were offered for the success of Civil Disobedience campaign by the Madras District Congress Committee, Andhra Congress Committee, the Triplicate Congress Sabha and the political section of the Youth League. The meeting reiterated India's resolve to achieve Swaraj by nonviolent means under Gandhi's leadership by following his path.'

In Lahore, a band of Congress volunteers paraded the streets and raised shouts of 'Mahatma Gandhi Ki Jai'. In a mammoth meeting of the citizens of the town, held under the auspices of the City Congress Committee, Maulana Abdul Qadir, in opening the proceedings, said, 'The 12th of March would be a red letter day and it would figure in letters of gold in the future history of India'.

He hoped that the people of India, from that day onward would give practical demonstration of their determination to win freedom. He believed that as soon as the people of the Punjab would receive the news of Gandhi's arrest, they would suspend their business and work out the plan of the movement. In Peshawar, the 'Satyagraha Day' was observed by taking out a procession and holding a public meeting. Resolutions reiterating the pledge of independence and wishing Godspeed to the soldiers of freedom and congratulating Vallabhbhai Patel on his imprisonment were unanimously passed. Besides, a large number of volunteers were enlisted for the satyagraha.

Civil Disobedience Day was celebrated in Delhi in a meeting attended by about 10,000 persons, including a large number of ladies. Devdas Gandhi gave the detailed history of the salt tax and called it the most 'barbarous' tax which effected the poor classes, and pleaded for its abolition immediately. He also exhorted the people to observe complete but peaceful hartal if Mahatma Gandhi was arrested.

Allahabad, the nerve centre of U. P. politics, witnessed scenes of enthusiasm in connection with the celebration of the commencement of the satyagraha campaign. Jawaharlal Nehru hoisted the national flag over the building occupied by the offices of the A.I.C.C., the City Congress Committee and the All-India Spinners' Association, U.P. branch. A large gathering participated in the ceremony. While addressing the audience, Nehru said that the pledge of satyagraha laid stress on nonviolence which was the very basis of the Civil Disobedience campaign. He warned that only those who were convinced of the efficacy of that method either as a creed or as a policy in the present circumstances of the country, should take the pledge. He opined that nonviolence was not a convenient shelter either for cowards or for those who wanted to prepare for violence. He asked the nonbelievers in nonviolence to withdraw from the movement to give others a chance.

In Ahmedabad, a meeting of the Youth League was held in which a resolution was passed empowering the secretaries to enlist volunteers for Civil Disobedience Movement. About twenty-five names were enlisted on the spot including two secretaries and Miss Mridula Ambalal, daughter of a local mill-magnate.

The 'Dandi March Day' was observed in Nagpur by hoisting the national flag. A procession passed through the main bazaars of the town, and, thereafter, a public meeting was also held. Gandhi's letter to the Viceroy was read out and explained to the audience. An appeal for the enlistment of volunteers was also made. While exhorting the people to give the moment their whole-hearted support M. V. Abhyankar said, 'I shall perish in the struggle for Independence or live to enjoy freedom after its achievement? Similar celebrations were held all over the country and considerable enthusiasm was aroused with people for participating in the Civil disobedience Movement. For the first time, a new spirit for Swaraj-full and complete-was found bubbling everywhere. The Viceroy informed the Secretary of State on 13 March 1930, 'Most of my thought at the moment is concentrated upon Gandhi. I wish I felt sure what the right way to deal with him is.'

The same day Gandhi and his satyagrahis reached a small village, Aslali, where they were received well by the villagers. Gandhi emphasised the importance of salt and criticised the salt tax levied by the government. He stated, 'The poor destitute villagers do not have the strength to get this tax repealed. We want to develop this strength... We should make a resolve that we shall prepare salt, eat it, sell if to the people and, while doing so, court imprisonment, if necessary. If, out of Gujarat's Population of 90 lakhs, we leave out women and children, and the remaining 30 lakhs et ready to violate the salt tax, the Government does not have enough accommodation in jails to house so many people.' Next day, Gandhi, who was apprehensive of his arrest, informed Jawaharlal Nehru, 'The news given to me of my impending arrest was said to be absolutely authentic. But we have reached the second stage. We take the third tonight'

The second halt of the Dandi marchers was at Bareja, a village with a Population of 2,500. He emphasised the importance of khadi, its production and use by the villagers. 'Khadi is the foundation of our freedom struggle.... I request you to renounce luxuries and buy khadi from this heap before you.

'We have come forward to win our freedom from this tyrannical and oppressive Government. If we cannot put our own house in order in an organized manner, how shall we run the country's Government? I ask you, therefore, to learn order and organization.... This struggle against the Government on which we have embarked is not going to reach its conclusion with five, or twenty-five, or even millions of men getting killed. We have to look after other things also simultaneously.'

As Gandhi entered the Kheda district, memories-some sweet, some bitter-filled his mind. It was while working in this district that he became one with the lives of people. He had seen nearly all the villages of the district and had covered many of them on foot. He stated, 'I have come to Navagam in the middle of a battle... The Government found some pretext or other to arrest Vallabhbhai... Pressure was brought to hear on the Magistrate some how to serve a notice on Sardar and he was arrested. What could a poor Magistrate do where the entire atmosphere is vitiated?

When some headmen and matadars of Kheda district submitted their resignations as a protest against the oppressive policy of the government, Gandhi advised them, 'Remember that in the resignations, you have handed in I see God's hand. The Kheda District has made an auspicious beginning.'

At Vasana, where the villagers had gathered to accord reception to the marchers and listen to their leader, Gandhi explained that abolition of the salt-tax or remission of some taxes would not mean swaraj for them. Winning of swaraj was not going to be so easy as they might think. It was only a way to it and by following it they would reach the goal of freedom. He had a word of praise for the headmen of Navagam, Vavdi, Agam, Mahelaj and other villages who had tendered their resignations. 'Why should they stick to Headmanship for the mere five rupees a month that the government pays them? If the Collector summons a Headman, let him say, 'Give us back our Sardar. Grant us a remission in land revenue.'

At Nadiad, a town with a population of thirty-one thousand, Gandhi reminded the people, 'Bound by the chains of slavery, we are being crushed at present and we want to shake them off.' He wished all government servants to give up their jobs. A government job gave them the power to tyrannize over others. Finally, be asked them to enlist themselves as volunteers. And as soon as he got behind the bars or as soon as the All-India Congress Committee gave a call, they should come forward to offer themselves for being jailed. 'Then alone shall I believe that Nadiad has made its contribution to our struggle'.

In a letter to Jayaprakash Narayan which Gandhi wrote from Anand on 17 March, he explained, 'No where else have I observed such zeal for sacrifice as has been displayed by the Ashram women. At present the women are to a great extent managing the internal affairs of the Ashram. The chance of acquiring such experience will never be repeated. I would therefore advise you to send Prabhavati there. After my arrest the Ashram women too will court imprisonment. I think Prabhavati should join them. She is worthy in every respect.'

At Anand, an educational centre of Patidars, Gandhi demanded, 'In your hands lies the honour of the Patidars of Charotar. You are like salt in the sea of Patidars. If the salt loses its savour, wherewith shall it be salted? Salt is more sapid than either sugar or juggery. The latter may even cause jaundice, whereas a pinch of salt adds flavour to the meal. If Anand gives up its savour if courage and such other virtues which have been attributed to the Patidars are not displayed in Anand at this juncture, where else can one see them?.'

The students' services to the national cause were also applauded. They were advised to suspend their studies for as long as this struggle continued. Formerly, Gandhi had asked his students to leave schools and to set up national schools.

But this time he asked them to leave schools and come out on the 'battlefield' and become 'mendicants' for the sake of the country. But he did not ask them to give up their studies for good, but only to give up book-learning so long as the struggle lasted.

At Borsad, the reception of Gandhi and his satyagrahis was celebrated with the immediate announcement of the resignations of headmen, matadars and ravanias of twenty villages of the taluka. Over one hundred village officers of twenty-five villages submitted their resignations.

The government sources commented, 'Gandhi's attention is directed on two points *i.e.* resignations of patels and enrolling volunteers. Under his instructions local workers are trying to get more resignations under the threat of social boycott. They were warmly received by the village folk. They were keen to listen to Gandhi's discourse · He explained to them, 'Our patience has been severely tried. We must free ourselves from the yoke of this Government and we are prepared to undergo any hardships that we may have to suffer in order to secure swaraj, it is our duty as well as our right to secure swaraj.

'Today we are defying the salt law. Tomorrow we shall have to consign other laws to the wastepaper basket. Doing so we shall practise such severe noncooperation that finally it will not be possible for the administration to be carried on at all. Let the Government then, to carry on its rule, use guns against us, send us to prison, hang us. But how many can be given such punishment? Try and calculate how much time it will take a lakh of Britishers to hang thirty crores of persons.'

Gandhi once again exhorted the students to leave their institutions and join the struggle for independence. He desired that all students studying in the local high school and who were above the age of fifteen, and all teachers too, should enrol themselves. He pleaded that wherever revolutions had taken place, that is, in Japan, China, Egypt, Ireland and in England, students and teachers had played a prominent role. In Europe, war broke out on 4 August 1914, and when Gandhi reached England on the 6th of the same month, he found that students had left colleges and marched out with arms.

Gandhi further explained that his prostrating himself on the ground for the sake of removing the hardships of crores of people was of no avail. He had spared no efforts in drafting appeals.

He became a revolutionary when politeness and persuasion proved infructious. He indeed found peace in describing himself as a revolutionary and appealed that in a revolution of that nature which was calm, peaceful and truthful, people should get themselves enrolled regardless of the religious faith to which they belonged. He was confident that if they enlisted themselves with sincerity and if they could keep up their courage, the salt tax would have been abolished, this administration would have come to an end and all the hardships enumerated in the letter to the Viceroy as well as those which had not been enumerated would have to cease.

On 19 March, the party of satyagrahis reached Ras Taluka where Sardar Patel was arrested and sentenced to prison and in which he had carried on such a vigorous struggle in 1924 that the Government had finally to admit its 'error and mete out justice that should not have required a struggle. It is as if Sardar was sentenced to prison as a reward for having served you'.

During the short stay of Gandhi, some of the headmen and matadars had handed in their resignations. But Gandhi expressed unhappiness on the small number of resignations at Ras. In fact, the headman, talati and revania were the representatives of the government in the villages and it was through these persons that the latter carried on its administration. A village which was afraid of a handful of men and continued to act in a manner contrary to its own wishes, neither enhanced the prestige of the headman, the talati or the revania nor that of the villagers themselves. Sardar Patel had been making great effort to end this indignity.

Gandhi praised the services rendered by Sardar Patel. He also apprised the villagers of his mission. He explained 'Sardar neither made speeches nor came here to foment trouble. Neither the Magistrate nor you had acted any sort of trouble. The task for which Sardar had approached you was not a secret to anyone. A satyagrahi has no secrets .... What secret can a satyagrahi like Sardar have?' He had come there to clear the way for Gandhi and he had not come there to convey the message regarding salt. Gandhi was at a loss to know about the offence committed by Sardar Patel and wondered that a man of his stature should have been awarded a sentence of three months' jail and labelled it a matter of shame to the Sardar and to the government. Gandhi wished that a person like Sardar Patel should be sentenced to a term of seven years' imprisonment or be exiled. 'It would not befit the Government to sentence me to three months' imprisonment. Exile for life or hanging would be a punishment fit for a person like me. I am guility of sedition. It is my dharma to commit sedition against the Government. I am teaching this dharma to the people. A regime under which tyranny is being perpetrated, under which the rich and the poor are made to pay the same amount of tax on an item like salt under which exorbitant sums are being spent on watchmen, the police and the army under which the highest executive receives a salary which is five thousand times the income of the cultivator, under which an annual revenue of 25 crores of rupees is derived from narcotics and liquor, under which foreign cloth of the value of Rs. 60 cores is imported every year, and under which crores of persons continue to remain unemployed, it is one's dharma to rise against and destroy such a regime, to pray that fire may consume its policies.

Meanwhile, the A.I.C.C. held a meeting on the banks of the Sabarmati on 20 March. Besides the president Jawaharlal Nehru, it was attended by other prominent leaders like Maulana Azad, Sarojini Naidu, P. D. Tandon, Abbas Tyabji, Darbar Gopaldas, J. B. Kripalani, N.C. Kalelkar, Kasturba Gandhi, Ansuyabehn and Mrs. Ambalal.

Many members excused themselves from attendance on the plea that they were busy with preparations for Civil Disobedience Movement, in their own areas.

The leaders met under a sense of 'heavy' responsibility and the result was foregone conclusion.

By its principal resolution, the A.I.C.C. confirmed the Working Committee's resolution authorising Gandhi to launch Civil Disobedience Movement. It laid down the conditions under which the various provinces should start satyagraha on a mass scale.

The Provincial Congress Committees were given wide discretion about the manner, the form and the place of Civil Disobedience. It was open to them, to prepare their provinces for any form of satyagraha, best suited to them. But it was clearly laid down that the salt satyagraha should be undertaken in every province when it was possible. Other forms of satyagraha might be prepared for, but should be reserved for the second stage of the campaign. In case Gandhi was arrested, the Provincial Congress Committees should immediately determine to start Civil Disobedience, and if he was not arrested, they should await instructions which he might issue on reaching his destination. He would give the necessary signal and the Provincial Congress Committees would be informed immediately through the A.I.C.C. Office.

The Government of India felt much concern over the resolution of Congress. The Home Member suggested, 'it is essential that we should able to give timely warning owing to local Governments'.

He also suggested that the correspondence of the members of the Working Committee; the correspondence of the head office of the Congress and of all provincial Congress offices and provincial Congress Presidents and of any particular individual whose correspondence in local government concerned might regard as likely to yield 'specially important' information, should be censured.

It was barely ten days ago that Gandhi had begun his historic march and the actual campaign was yet to be started. The whole country was already in a state of forewent for a parallel to which one might recollect the 'hottest days' of the Noncooperation Movement of 1920-22. People in the provinces were planning to start the movement, and in some cases preliminary steps had already been initiated. In Bengal, for instance, which had for the moment, lost both its outstanding leaders, a 'War Council' had been formed. In the United Provinces, the Provincial Congress Committee had started a satyagraha committee consisting of prominent leaders, including the President of the Congress himself. Judging from the signs, the whole country appeared in the throes of an agitation of unprecedented magnitude.

The Civil Disobedience plans of Gandhi and the Congress leaders.

As the march proceeded, so the pressure of publicity and social boycott was built up and resignations began to occur in large numbers. By 22 March, approximate number of resignations were four from

Ahmedabad district: twenty-seven from Kaita (of whom sixteen were from Borsad taluka) seventeen from Broach, and two from Surat. But Surat soon became the most affected district by 5 April. One hundred and forty headmen had resigned and ten clays later, the figure had risen to two hundred and twenty seven.

Gandhi warned them, 'It will be regarded as cowardice to hand in one's resignation and then to withdraw it. There is no compulsion to resign. It is advisable to give up the post of Headman, looking upon it as something base, dirty and filthy.' The speech delivered by Gandhi at Broach on 26 March dealt with the communal question.

He explained that he had never dreamt that he could win swaraj merely through his effort or assisted only by the Hindus. He sought the assistance of Muslims, Parsis, Christians, Sikhs, Jews and all other Indians. He needed the assistance even of Englishmen. 'But I know too that all this combined assistance is worthless if I have not one other assistance, that is, from God. All is vain without His help. And if he is With this struggle, no other' help is necessary.

In a letter to Jawaharlal Nehru on 31 March Gandhi expressed his optimism about he forthcoming movement. 'Things seem to be shaping very well indeed in Gujarat... I feel you are right in attention to the salt tax for the time being. What more we can or should do. Unless you hear from me to the contrary, please take 6th April as the date for simultaneous beginning.'

At Jambusar, Kamaladevi Chattopadhyaya arrived to see Gandhi to remove the general impression that had gone abroad that as he had not included women in his first batch of volunteers, they might not be taken up at all. Gandhiji told her, 'If impatient mothers will be a little patient they will find ample scope for their zeal and sacrifice in this national struggle for freedom'.

She asked Gandhi what women with children should do. He said that he neither desired nor expected women to neglect their children. They might have to wait and bide their time, and thus be of use in some ways. Those women, however, who could make some satisfactory arrangements to have the children well looked after, should join the struggle. At Surat where Gandhi and the satyagrahis reached on I April, they received a big welcome. He called the salt tax as beastly, inhuman and a Satanic Law. 'I have not heard of such justice anywhere in the world where it prevails ... To bow to an empire which dispenses such justice is not dharma but adharma. A man who prays to God every morning at dawn cannot, must not, pray for the good of such an empire. On the contrary while praying or saying the namaaz he should ask God to encompass the destruction of such a Satanic empire, such an inhuman government. To do so is dharma.'

In a message to the nation in the issue of Young India dated 3 April 1930, Gandhi exhorted the people 'Remember 5th April', and scart mass Civil Disobedience regarding the salt laws. He advised them to observe nonviolence in the fullest sense of the term. This was to be the spontaneous action. The workers were required to merely guide the masses in initial stages. Later, the masses would regulate the movement themselves.

The congress volunteers would render aid wherever needed. They, however, would be expected to be in the forefront. They were advised not to take sides in any communal quarrel. Wherever, there was a violent eruption, volunteers were expected to die in the attempt to quell violence. Those who were to be engaged in Civil Disobedience were occupy themselves and induce others to be engaged in some national service, such as khadi work, liquor and opium picketing, foreign-cloth shops, village sanitation, assisting the families of civil resistance prisoners in a variety of ways.

Gandhi also expected that if there was a real response about civil resistance regarding the salt tax, people should by proper organisation secure boycott of foreign cloth through khadi and secure total prohibition. This would mean a saving of 91 crores per year, and supplementary work for the millions of unemployed. 'If we secure these things, we cannot be far from independence. And not one of these things is beyond our capacity. Thus at each village, where the party stopped, Gandhi spoke briefly, telling the villagers that a great ordeal was at hand. He filled his political appeal with exhortation relevant to village life, such as khadi, cow-protection, cleanliness and untouchability. His appeal was not for money but for change of attitudes: he called on village officials to resign their posts which buttressed the exploitive regime. As he journeyed, he continued to give press interviews and to write to Navajivan and Young India, spreading his massage of swaraj and giving instructions for the conduct of the campaign during the days ahead.

Out of twenty-five days, which the journey took, the party of satyagrahis had walked for twenty-two days, excluding three days of Gandhi's silence. On his way, Gandhi passed by forty villages and towns and everywhere he addressed the audience. The whole countryside was awake to the call of the Mahatma.

At least fifty thousand persons heard his stirring message to the nation: his speeches were generally impassioned and always brave and there was a tone of pathos which had gone home to the hearts of the listeners. Despite all the fatigue and other hardships of the journey, he never allowed himself any comfort that was denied to the last man of his 'army'.

The satyagrahis reached Dandi on 5 April. Sarojini Naidu had already arrived there to welcome them. When interviewed by special correspondent of The Bombay Chronicle, Gandhi said, ' Government, perhaps, deserves congratulations for their policy of non-interference which is not exactly in keeping with their proved capacity for provoking popular sentiment.'

Next day he was to break the salt tax law. If the Civil Disobedience Movement become widespread in the country and the government tolerated it, the salt law, Gandhi declared, might be taken as abolished. He indeed had no doubt in his mind that the salt tax stood abolished the very moment that the decision to break that salt laws was reached.

'If they arrest me or my companions tomorrow, I shall not be surprised. I shall certainly not be pained. It would be absurd to be pained if we get something that we have invited on ourselves.'

Gandhi advised the people to make salt freely in every home, as our ancestors used to, and sell it from place to place, and they should continue doing so wherever possible till the government yielded, so much so that the salt in government stocks would become superfluous. 'If the awakening of the people in the country is true and real, the salt law is as good as abolished'.

Gandhi highlighted the importance of Dandi and praised the efforts of the people of the taluka. He explained,' Dandi was chosen not by a man but by God. How otherwise could we have chosen for the battlefield of satyagraha such an out-of-the-way place-a place where no food grains are to be had, where there is scarcity of water, where thousands can assemble only with difficulty, walking ten miles from the railway station, and where if you are travelling on foot, you have to negotiate creeks full of slush and mud? The truth is that in this struggle we have to put up with suffering. You have made the road from Navsari to Dandi famous throughout the world by arranging for free drinking-water at frequent intervals all along it... Dandi should be a sacred ground for us, where we should utter no untruth, commit so sin. Everyone coming here should come with this devout feeling in his heart.'

'If you have not yet gone out to remove salt, let the whole village get together and go. Hold the salt in your fist and think that you are carrying in your hand salt worth Rs. 6 Crores. Every year the Government has been taking away from us Rs. 6 Crores through its monopoly of salt.'

Gandhi and his volunteers broke the salt laws at 8-30 A.M. on 6 April 1930 by taking a lump of natural salt which was deposited in a small pit. Hundreds of persons witnessed this scene. Sarojini Naidu stood by Gandhiji's side, and, as the symbolic gesture was made, she cried, 'Hail Deliverer'.

Gandhi, while picking up a lump of salt in his hand, said, 'With this, I am shaking the foundation of the British Empire.' Not a single policeman or excise officer was present there. While talking to the representative of the free press, Gandhi said, 'Now that the technical or ceremonial breach of the Salt Law has been committed it is open to any one who would take the risk of prosecution' under the Salt Law to manufacture salt wherever he wishes and wherever it is convenient. My advice is that the workers should everywhere manufacture salt to make use of it and to instruct the villagers to do so.'

'Thus the war against the salt tax should be continued during the national week. Those who are not engaged in this sacred work should devote themselves to a vigorous propaganda for the boycott of foreign cloth and the use of Khadar. They should also endeavour to manufacture as much Khadar as possible.'

After Gandhi had addressed the meeting on 6 April about two tolas of salt which was taken by him in the morning and also cleaned by him, was auctioned for Rs. 525/-to Seth Ranchhod Shodhan, a mill-owner of Ahmedabad.

Gandhi's march on foot, form village to village through Gujarat which was his home and where his influence was greatest, aroused considerable interest and excitement. It has in fact appealed to the imagination of multitudes of people who were emotionally swayed by the dramatic turn of events. Throughout the march, Gandhiji went on preaching his cult of truth and nonviolence to the multitudes that gathered from far and near and he did not hesitate to impose the strictest discipline on the satyagrahis that flocked to his banner. The salt became the symbol of India's will to freedom. The same day the salt laws were broken throughout India at least by five million people at over 5,000 meetings. The entire countryside became acutely conscious of the struggle for Swaraj which was intensifying. The Dandi march received world-wide publicity. Soon the Civil Disobedience Movement spread simultaneously in western, northern, central, eastern and southern regions of India.

Militant Nationalisms: Regional Patriotisms and Indian Heroes

The papers on this panel address the place of militant nationalism in India and the ways in which three distinct regional movements constitute postcolonial imaginaries about Indian nationalism. All three papers deal with paths taken by Indian nationalists; paths that when compared to the mainstream nationalist agenda espoused by the Gandhi-led Congress can be described as incomplete or at best marginal. Nonetheless, the visions embodied in these nationalisms resonate as important narratives to which Indians are attached.

Rochona Majumdar analyzes the significance of multiple stories circulated by many in different parts of India that Netaji Subhas Chandra Bose did not die in the plane crash in Taiwan and had allegedly "returned" in the guise of a mendicant(s). Neeti Nair locates Bhagat Singh in the anti-colonial movement in the Punjab and points to the potential of and limits to dissent that were exemplified by his death. Finally, Durba Ghosh's study on the participation of women in a revolutionary movement was largely underground during the nationalist movement examines the worship for heroes whose promise was never realized. The affection and reverence that many have for these figures who held radical views suggests that the hegemonic vision of Indian nationalism as nonviolent might be one we should reconsider.

The panel seeks to address issues of the transition from the colonial to the postcolonial by exploring the ways in which remembrances of heroes are shaped by the socio-political exigencies of the postcolonial state.

Bhagat Singh as 'Satyagrahi': a 'Clash of Principles' and a 'Question of Humanity'

As 'prince among martyrs', Bhagat Singh has either been eulogized in locally produced monographs or relegated to a footnote in 'national' histories devoted to Gandhi's role in the making of India's Independence. This paper argues that he was central to the resolution of many of the divisions that racked the Punjab.

Far from being advocates of illegitimate violence, Bhagat Singh and his co-conspirators gained unprecedented popularity during their practice of hunger-strikes and nonviolent civil disobedience within the walls of Lahore's prisons in 1929-1930. Although they failed in their final goal at causing a shift in the Congress' 'national' program, we dwell on a moment when the 'clash of principles' that necessitated their death by hanging, brought them the support of every group in the Punjab Congress and the entire non-official bloc in the Central Legislative Assembly.

By labelling them 'murderers' and 'terrorists', and invoking their history of violence, the British sought to dismiss their nonviolent demands for rights as 'political prisoners.' The same politics of labelling assisted Gandhi and his followers from not facing the fundamental contradiction in the Congress' anti-colonial strategy.

Revolutionary Women, Nationalist Heroes: Kalpana, Kalyani, Kamaladevi and the Narratives of Violent Resistance

This paper examines the ways in which three women's lives have been narrated and remembered in Bengal in the postcolonial period. It questions conventional historical narratives that link nonviolence and women's participation in twentieth-century South Asian politics by examining a regional movement and the narratives and memories that have sprung up around it.

Bengal's history of political violence against the colonial government began in the aftermath of the 1905 partition, when Bengal was divided for administrative purposes. The well-known swadeshi campaign was accompanied by a campaign of political violence, which included assassination attempts, robberies, bombings and vandalism. These groups were restrained by the colonial government through a program of arrests, censorship and detentions that began in 1916 and carried on through the 1920s.

By the 1930s, political parties who engaged in political violence had regrouped, including women for the first time. Many of these women were educated, elite daughters of important civil servants and professionals. Defying the stereotypes that colonial police officials had of high-caste Hindu women as secluded, compliant, and politically unaware, these three women – Kalpana Dutt, Kalyani Das Bhattacharje, and Kamaladevi Chattopadhyay – joined and participated in an underground revolutionary movement that planned to overthrow British rule by supporting acts of violence.

After India was granted its independence in 1947, all three of these women produced memoirs, oral histories, and contributed to stories detailing their insurgent exploits. Occupying a special place in Bengal's telling of its contribution to the nationalist struggle, these women produced themselves as a particular type of female nationalist hero who fulfilled, rather than betrayed, the promise of Bengali womanhood.

Immortality of a Mortal: Netaji's Death and its Aftermath

In August 1945, Netaji Subhas Chandra Bose, nationalist leader from Bengal and the founder of the Indian National Army died in a plane crash in Taiwan. Or did he? As numerous historians, politicians, and thousands of ordinary Indians from all parts of the country asked, expressing skepticism about Netaji's demise in the alleged plane crash. A large number of books have been written investigating the events leading up to the crash. Doubts about his death were first voiced on November 7, 1946, to Jawaharlal Nehru, Sardar Vallabhbhai Patel and others of the interim government that was preparing India for independence. The first government enquiry committee convened to investigate whether Netaji had really died in the crash was in 1956. Since then numerous other committees have met to critique and refute the findings of the 1956 committee, namely the One Man Inquiry Commission headed by G.D.Khosla in 1970 and most recently the Mukherjee commission which ended in 2005. Born in 1897, Netaji would have been 108 years old if in fact he was alive in 2005. Although this seems highly unlikely many Indians have until very recently clung on to the hope that the nationalist leader is still alive. This main question animating this paper is thus: Why has the Netaji myth had such a tenacious grip over the psyche of the Indian masses? To elaborate this primary question a little more one could ask, in what ways did people imagine Netaji's return? In order to understand the longevity of the Netaji myth, this paper will attempt to link Bose's afterlife to the nationalism he espoused during his lifetime.

Gandhi and Congress: Secular Saints or Pious Hypocrites?

Congress' role during all this seemed to be of consistently under-estimating the ML threat. If the party leadership had shrewdly held out an olive branch early in the process, Jinnah and his group could have been bought off very easily. By the time, the ML threat was realized through the referendum results, both ML and Congress leadership balked at a compromise: ML because they saw much more to be gained in Pakistan, Congress because they saw that too much power would have to be conceded at the centre. In particular, Vallabhbhai Patel, with his virulently anti-Muslim rhetoric, successfully organized the 'refuseniks' inside Congress. Nehru's suave manner, rapport with Lord and Lady Mountbatten, and Gandhi's ascetic image, all helped to sway the British to be more partial to Congress' demands. Although, Nehru and Patel were the chief opponents of Jinnah, those interviewed indicated that Gandhi was seen as a target for Muslim frustrations during the partition period. In particular, Gandhi professed love for all religions, but did not allow his relative to marry a Muslim. When Noakhali's Saha family was hit by riots, Gandhi went to visit the area. The local Muslims were furious at this double standard, and gave him a very hostile reception.

This new anti-Gandhi sentiment among Muslims was strongest in Noakhali itself. Shafayath Hossain described how attempts were made to block the railroad to prevent Gandhi from advancing. But the Noakhali Muslims' "shining hour" was in the form of a huge affront they delivered to the man who was "revered worldwide as a latter-day saint...To Muslims though, especially after Noakhali, he was something completely different. I mean look, he wouldn't let his own blood marry a Muslim, and he would talk all the time about communal harmony." Gandhi always took a goat with him on his travels in order to drink goat's milk. Within an hour of his arrival in Noakhali, his goat was stolen in the midst of the crowd. The story goes that, the goat was then cooked and fed to the local people. Clearly, Gandhi had not succeeded in winning the hearts and minds of all Indians.

MA Sami had an actual meeting with Gandhi, which was similarly unpleasant: "Gandhi I didn't like at all. An absolute hypocrite. I met him once, in 1940. I went to the nikethan, his secretary was this lady......______. I said my name is Mohammed Abdus Sami, really emphasizing the first part. Because usually I would say Sami, people would think Swami— they would think I was a Hindu. So I wanted her to know I was a Muslim. Now you know, thakur ghore ke, bole ami kola khai ni. She says, well Mr. Sami, we don't really believe in conversion. Now this meant, they were thinking that I was wanting to get close to Hindu dadas, to walk a little like you, improve myself. So I said, why not, you mean to tell me that you do not want to convert. You talk to someone, you try to make them see your point, that is converting to your views. So you know, she saw that, ore baba, e tho thyador chele [Oh goodness, this is a tricky fellow]. Quickly became very careful. Said to me, oh you want to see bapu, he is about to take his walk, you can talk to him there.

So there was a thatch type thing. A very thick white mattress, and there he sat, surrounded by these pretty girls, his apsaris you know. Wearing that nengti and resting on two women, a sight. He started saying, ah yes, you are a Bengali, please be comfortable, speak in your own language. But meanwhile he had already reached inside his dhoti and pulled out his watch. Never mind Bengali, I didn't even have a chance to speak.

He said, well now I have to go for my walk. So you know, I understood exactly what was what. I thought, acccha, thik ache— all right. Oh then I said to one of the others, can I get a glass of water. So he [Gandhi] had already started going away, but he had heard me. He pointed in the distance and said, there is the motka, you can drink it from there. And you know what, not one single person there moved to help me. I had to walk all the way there and get it myself. So I got a very valuable lesson."

The Partition

Comment: India's Independence was accompanied by one of the biggest catastrophies in the history of South Asia, the partition of the country into Pakistan (West & East) and India. Partition led to a massive loss of lives and forced many to evacuate their lands.

East & West Punjab, North West Frontier Province, North India and Sind were engulfed in an orgy of violence for months. Mammoth migrations of Muslims from India and Hindus from Pakistan took place, shattering both communities down to their core. Nearly, 5,00,000 people died in the holocaust and 55,00,000 people were forced to migrate from their abodes. When the 'trains with dead' bodies arrived in Delhi due to 'train massacres' it further aggravated the situation with narrations of ghastly incidences of the slaughter on both side of the border. What did the partition lead to? The 'communal politics' which was meant to be buried by the partition only assumed more menacing proportions in all the three countries (India, Pakistan, Bangladesh). The breakup of erstwhile Pakistan into Pakistan and Bangladesh buried the 'Two Nation Theory'. Relations with Bangladesh, which was born with help and support from India, are not particularly 'friendly'. Gandhi's optimism that partition is a temporary phenomenon and the withdrawal of the British, in due course, would restore the old relations, is still a distant dream. Lohia's idea of 'India-Pakistan' federation stands rejected by the people of both the countries.

Hindu communal politics has drawn heavily from the existence of the 'enemy' country 'Pakistan', using it as the whipping boy to arouse communal passions by attributing to it the source of most of the problems which India faces (Kashmiri militants, Bombay bomb blasts, etc.). To justify and rationalise these attributions a number of myths and claims were manufactured and spread about the whole Partition tragedy by these communal forces. These are given immense prominence and with the emergence of the whole communal project of Hindutva they have become highly ominous. It is imperative to therefore not only explode these myths but to expose the communal propagandists and their macabre mis-interpretations and distortions of historical events like the Partition. The belief that Partition would once-and-for-all put an end to communal politics remains a dream. It was finally buried with the Indo-Pak War of 1971 that led to the creation of Bangladesh, *i.e.* East Pakistan as a separate, Muslim-majority State separating from the other Muslim majority state, West Pakistan.

Today, despite a rich heritage of shared values, etc., both countries continue to be locked in a state of semi-war preparedness, with mutually reciprocating mistrust and hatred. The ruling classes of these countries have done their utmost to keep their people apart; attributing to the other the cause of most of their internal, domestic problems. They have impeded inter-border movements and prevented the people from visiting each other to exchange mutual good faith and goodwill. Cultural exchanges and scope for trade, etc., have been strangulated despite enormous potential. The Partition tragedy ironically has only vitiated the situation. Communal violence has been errupting with increasing ferocity. The violence reached its acme in the pre-planned demolition of the Babri Masjid, engineered by the dominant arrowhead of Hindutva, the Sangh Parivar. Likewise, in Pakistan, the Jamat-e-Islami has also been spewing venom with equal virulence. Both these communal forces survive and thrive on the division that were the cause and the result of the so-called Two-Nation Theory. The onslaught and virulent propaganda only stifles the democratic ethos of society and terrorises the weak and disadvantaged sections of society. Moreover, the communal propagandists consciously blank out the positive role of the common people among the Muslims who had also shaped the course of national politics with all its limitations. Communal Organisations

The colonial economy had generated multiple trends in politics. "Instances of local conflicts between Hindus and Muslims can certainly be found occasionally in past centuries, just as there are numerous instances of Shia-Sunni clashes and caste quarrels. But communal riots do seem to be rare down till 1880s. That communalism in large measure sprang from elite conflicts over jobs and political favours has long been a truism...". Thus the early phase of communal politics was dominated by merchants and money-lenders. Feudal lords and rich peasants, mostly Hindus, were the main beneficiaries of the placement in the emerging bureaucracy. The reasons for this were: a) a section of Hindu community was in a position to take advantage of modern education, b) the 1857 rebellion against the British under the Muslim leadership of Bahadur Shah Zafar and, c) the existing anti-Muslim prejudices of the British. The British with their 'Divide and Rule' policy decided that the only way they could prolong their supremacy over the country was by dividing the anti-colonial movement. Accordingly, their game plan recognised the communal, Muslim minority elite as the sole representative of their community rather than sections of the Muslim leadership outside the fold of the League but who were members of the Congress opposing the communal politics of the League. The British underplayed the 'broad' secular character of Congress and overlooked the presence of Muslim leaders within it. Besides, as and when it suited their interests they over-emphasized the relevance of the Muslim League.

Colonial Machinations and Communal Politics. One of the events that embittered intercommunity relations was Lord Curzon's decision to partition Bengal by dividing it into Muslim majority East Bengal and Hindu majority West Bengal, apparently for administrative purposes. The underlying motive, however, was to suppress the nascent nationalist trend. The move was strongly opposed by Hindu communalists and even the Congress. The Muslims for their part fearing that their community interests are at stake pressed for a separate electorate, which was acceded to by the British. Lord Dufferin had encouraged them to consider themselves as a separate entity. Citing Dr.Ambedkar, Seervai notes that Lord Dufferin even went to the extent of suggesting a separate electorate for the community and a reform of the Councils to wean away the Muslims from the Congress. Meanwhile the Muslim League had already been established in opposition to the Punjab Hindu Sabha and Hindu Mahasabha with similar goals.

The Montague-Chelmsfold (Montford) Reforms which were implemented in 1921 introduced a 2-tier administrative set-up. The Governor and the Council had charge of 'reserved subjects' while ministeries responsible to legislators in charge of 'transferred subjects', were given to Indians. Constituencies were also of two types: 'general and 'special'. The former was again split into 'general' and 'reserved' with far reaching impact since minority groups ('reserved' sections) enjoyed the allocation of specified number of legislative seats in areas where they were substantially represented. Thus, communal representation in the Indian political ethos got institutionalized for the first time.

Meanwhile Turkey sided with the Germans in the War that had broken out in Europe and the Indian Muslims turned away from the British, a development which Tilak took advantage of to influence its leaders to join the Congress. After the Khilafat movement, which brought in large numbers of Muslims in the anti-imperialist struggle,the Non-Cooperation Movement was launched. Differences over reservations for Council seats and other political differences led to communal riots. Meanwhile, Lala Lajpat Rai wrote a series of 13 articles in the Tribune demanding partition of Bengal and Punjab maintaining that Hindus and Muslims can no longer live together.

Yet another important factor in the formation of Pakistan was the effort to draw up the Indian Constitution in the wake of the Simon Commission. Muslim leaders asked for a separate Sind Province, parity of North West Frontier Province (NWFP) with other states, 1/3 representation for Muslims in central legislature, and proportional representation in Punjab and Bengal assemblies. The Congress proposals came in the form of Motilal Nehru Report, which had recommended that India to be a federation based on linguistic provinces, provincial autonomy, elections based on joint electorates, and seats in central and provincial legislatures reserved for minorities in proportion to their population. This Report initially accepted the Muslim demands of a separate Sind Province and reforms in NWFP. But even the two demands which Nehru

Committee had accepted were later withdrawn under the pressure of Hindu Mahasabha and other Hindu communal leaders within Congress. Deeply perturbed by this turnaround over their demands, Jinnah voiced his displeasure in no uncertain terms. However, under the false assumption that the Muslim League represents all Muslims, he responded by demanding 1/3 representation for 25% of Muslim population to ensure that no legislation can be passed which is against Muslim interest, since 2/3 majority is needed to pass the major legislations.

Clearly, the real issues that exacerbated the divide were the role of the elites of both communities. Jinnah's demands were in favour of the Muslim landlords and merchant class. Moreover, he further expanded the four demands to fourteen demands on similar lines that severely impeded Hindu-Muslim unity.

In the meanwhile the Round Table Conferences held between 1931-32 in London, to consider Dominion Status for India, achieved little. In 1932 Gandhi restarted the Civil Disobedience Movement. At the same time however Gandhi made an effort at reconciliation with the Muslim leaders but it was foiled by Hindu leaders like B.S.Munje and Madan Mohan Malviya who together, according to Sir Tej Bahadur Sapru, were responsible for the collapse of these negotiations. Consequently this led to the Sir Ramsay MacDonald's Communal Award towards which the Congress was merely a mute spectator.

5

Patel and Indian Independence

Vallabhbhai Jhaverbhai Patel, one of the six children of Jhaverbbai Patel and Ladbai was born at Nadiad in Gujarat. There is no record of his date of birth. The generally accepted date, October 31, 1875, of which the source is his Matriculation certificate, was chosen by Vallabhbhai himself while filling in a form. The family was an agriculturist one, of the Lewa Patidar Community and could in terms of economic status be described as lower middle-class. It was poor and had no tradition of education. Vallabhbhai's childhood was spent away from books, in the ancestral fields at Karamsad. He was already in his late teens when he passed out from the Middle School at Karamsad and went to the High School at Nadiad from where he matriculated in 1897. Even as a young boy Vallabhbhai displayed qualities of organization and leadership that marked him out for his future role. Once as a sixth-form boy he organized a successful strike of his classmates that lasted for three days to teach a lesson to one of the teachers who was unduly fond of the rod. Vallabhbhai must have inherited these attributes from his father who, it is said, had fought in the Mutiny under the Rani of Jhansi and was subsequently taken prisoner by Malharrao Holkar.

Vallabhbhai was a mature young man of twenty-two when he matriculated. Owing to the impecunious circumstances of the family higher education was not within his reach. The next best thing was to take a course in law and set up as a country lawyer. This he did and established a small practice at Godhra But an attack of plague, which he contracted while nursing a friend, made him leave the town and after spending some time in Nadiad, he moved on to Borsad in 1902, a town in the Kheda district where at that time the largest number of criminal cases in Gujarat were recorded. Vallabhbhai became quite popular here as a defence lawyer. Vallabhbhai now wanted to go to England and qualify as a Barrister. From his practice at Borsad he had earned enough for his expenses there but owing to certain circumstances he was not able to make the trip at once. His brother Vithalbhai desired that he should complete education in England firm and not Vallabhbhai readily acquiesced in this. His wife, Zaverbai, died early in 1909 after an operation for some abdominal malady. When news of the bereavement reached Vallabhbhai, he was cross-examining a witness in a murder case at Anand. With an impregnable composure for which he became known later, he did not show grief but went on with the cross-examination in hand.

He finally sailed for England in 1910 joined the Middle Temple. Here he worked so hard and conscientiously that he topped in Roman Law, securing a prize, and was called to the Bar at the end of two years instead of the usual period of three years. On his return to India in 1913, he set up practice in Ahmedabad and made a great success of it. He had ready wit, a fund of common sense and a deep sympathy for those who were the objects of the British officials' wrath and were caught in the clutches of the law, which was not the uncommon in the Kheda district. He came to enjoy a position in public life that his eminence as a Barrister. He accepted Mahatma Gandhi's leadership, having been tremendously impressed by the fearless lead that Mahatma Gandhi gave to right public wrongs. In 1917 he was elected for the first time as a Municipal in Councillor Ahmedabad. From 1924 to 1928 he was Chairman of the Municipal Committee. The years of his association with the, Municipal administration were marked by much meaningful work for the improvement of civic life. Work was done to improve water supply, sanitation and town planning and the Municipality came to be transformed from being a mere adjunct to the British rule into a popular body with a will of its own. There were also calamities like plague in 1917 and famine in 1918, and on both occasions Vallabhbhai did important work to relieve distress.

In 1917 he was elected Secretary of the Gujarat Sabha, a political body which was of great assistance to Gandhiji in his campaigns. The association with Mahatma Gandhi became closer during the Kheda Satyagraha in 1918, which was launched to secure exemption from payment of the land revenue assessment since the crops had failed. It took three months of intense campaigning that was marked by arrests, seizures of goods and chattels and livestock and much official brutality before relief was secured from an unwilling Government. Gandhiji said that if it were not for Vallabhbhai's assistance "this campaign would not have been carried through so successfully".

The five years from 1917 to 1922 were years of popular agitation in India. The end of the war was followed by the Rowlatt Act and still further curtailment of individual freedom. And then followed the Khilafat movement with massacres and terror in the Punjab. Gandhiji and the Congress decided on noncooperation. Vallabhbhai left his practice for good and gave himself up wholly to political and constructive work, touring in villages, addressing meetings, organizing picketing of foreign cloth shops and liquor shops. Then came the Bardoli Satyagraha. The occasion for the Satyagraha was the Government's decision to increase the assessment of land revenue from Bardoli taluka by 22 per cent and in some villages by as much as 50 to 60 per cent. Having failed to secure redress by other means the agriculturists of the taluka decided, at a Conference on February 12, 1928, to withhold payment of land revenue under the leadership of Vallabhbhai Patel. The struggle was grim and bitter. There were seizures of property and livestock to such an extent that for days on end, people kept themselves and their buffaloes locked in. Arrests followed and then brutalities of the police and the hired Pathans. The struggle drew the attention of the whole country to it. Patels and Talatis resigned their jobs. Government revenues remained unrealized. The Government had ultimately to bow before popular resolve and an inquiry was instituted to find out to what extent the increase was justified and the realization of the increased revenue was postponed. It was a triumph not only of the 80,000 peasants of Bardoli but more particularly of Vallabhbhai personally; he was given the title of "Sardar" by the nation.

About this time the political situation in the country was approaching a crisis. The Congress had accepted its goal of Purna Swaraj for the country, while the British Government through their policy of pitting one interest against another and through constitutional tricks were trying to stifle the voice of freedom and doing everything they could to perpetuate their rule. The boycott of the Simon Commission was followed by the launching of the famous Salt Satyagraha by Gandhiji. Vallabhbhai Patel though he had not committed any breach of the Salt Law, was the first of the national leaders to be arrested. He was in fact arrested on March 7, 1930-some days before Gandhiji set out on the march to Dandi. He was released in June. By then Gandhiji, Jawaharlal Nehru and other leaders were in jail and the tempo of the struggle in the country was rising. In a few months Vallabhbhai was back in prison.

In March 1931 Vallabhbhai presided over the 46th session of the Indian National Congress which was called upon to ratify the Gandhi-Irwin Pact, which had just then been concluded. The task was not an easy one, for Bhagat Singh and a few others had been executed on the very day the Congress session opened and delegates, particularly the younger sections, were in an angry mood, while Jawaharlal Nehru and Subhas Bose were not happy with the terms of the Pact. But the Congress finally put its seal on the Pact with one voice. Civil Disobedience was suspended, political prisoners were released and the Congress agreed to participate in the Round Table Conference.

The Round Table Conference failed. Gandhiji as also the other top leaders were arrested and a policy of repression followed. Vallabhbhai Patel was lodged with Gandhiji in Yeravada Jail and they were together there for sixteen months-from January 1932 to May 1933. Vallabhbhai then spent another year in the Nasik Jail. When the Government of India Act 1935 came, the Congress, though generally critical of the Act, decided to try out those of its constitutional provisions that seemed to grant to India a measure of self-government and to take part in the elections for Provincial legislatures that were envisaged under it. In seven of the eleven Provinces Congress majorities were returned and Congress Ministries were formed. Vallabhbhai Patel, as Chairman of the Congress Parliamentary Sub-Committee, guided and controlled the activities of these Ministries.

Not for very long, however, for, on September 3, 1939 when Britain declared war on Germany, the Viceroy without consulting either the Central or the Provincial Legis latures, proclaimed India as having entered the war as an ally of Britain. The Congress could not accept this position and the Congress Ministries resigned. Gandhiji launched Individual Civil Disobedience opposing India's participation in the war, and the Congress leaders began to court arrest. Vallabhbhai Patel was arrested on November 17, 1940. He was released on August 20,1941 on grounds of health. Then the All India Congress Committee passed the famous Quit India resolution in Bombay on August 8,1942, and Vallabhbhai, along with the other members of the Working Committee, was arrested on August 9, 1942 and detained in the Ahmednagar Fort while Gandhiji, Kasturba and Mahadev Desai were detained in the Aga Khan's Palace. The Sardar was in jail for about three years this time.

When, at the end of the war, the Congress leaders were freed and the British Government decided to find a peaceful constitutional solution to the problem of India's Independence, Vallabhbhai Patel was one of the chief negotiators of the Congress. When India attained Independence he became the Deputy Prime Minister and was responsible for the Home, States and the Information and Broadcasting portfolios. It was in this capacity that he was called upon to tackle the most intricate and baffling problem of the States' integration into the Union of India. And it is here that his tact, his powers of persuasion and his statesmanship came into full play. He handled the question as only he could have handled it, managing, in less than a year's time, to reduce the Princely States from 562 to 26 administrative units and bringing democracy to nearly 80 million people of India, comprising almost 27 per cent of the country's population. The integration of the States could certainly be termed as the crowning achievement of Vallabhbhai Patel's life. But for him, this may not have been achieved easily and quickly.

As Minister of Home Affairs, he presided over efforts to bring back order and peace to a country ravaged by communal strife unprecedented in its history. He accomplished this task with the ruthless efficiency of a great administrator. He sorted out the problems of partition, restored law and order and dealt with the rehabilitation of thousands of refugees with great courage and foresight. He reorganised our Services which had become depleted with the departure of the British and formed a new Indian Administrative Service, to provide a stable administrative base to our new democracy.

While Gandhiji gave to the Congress a programme for a broad-based action, it was Vallabhbhai who built up the Party machine to carry out that programme. No one before Vallabhbhai had given adequate thought to the need to have an effective organisation, but Vallabhbhai realised this need during his campaigns and devoted his organisational talents and energy to the building up of the strength of the Party which could be geared to fight in an organised and effective manner. His grip over the Party organisation was complete.

Vallabhbhai Patel was thus one of the chief architects and guardians of India's freedom and his contribution towards consolidating the freedom of the country remains unrivalled. He died on December 15, 1950, leaving behind a son, Dhayabhai Patel, and a daughter, Manibehn Patel. -Morarji Desai

I am not interested in loaves and fishes, or legislative honours. The peasantry do not understand them, they are little affected by them. I believe that Gandhiji's eleven points mean the substance of Swaraj. That which does not satisfy them is no Swaraj. Whilst I would respect the rights of landlords, rajas, maharajas and others to the extent, that they do not hurt the sweating millions, my interest lies in helping the downtrodden to rise from their state and be on a level with the tallest in the land.

Thank God the gospel of Truth and Non-Violence has given these an inkling of their dignity and the power they possess. Much still remains to be done. But let us make up our minds that we exist for them, not they for us. Lot us shed our petty rivalries and jealousies, feuds and let everyone realise that the Congress represents and exists for the toiling millions and it will become an irresistible power...

From the Presidential Address-Sardar Vallabhbhai Patel.

I.N.C. Session, 1931, Karachi.

Tying Bharat Mata up in knots!!

One of the greatest economists the world has ever known and one who is in the run for Nobel Prize for revolutionary economics-Sitaram Yechury, has come out with the following statement in his recent avant-garde article titled "Tying Bharat up in knots" in the Hindustan Times: "The culmination of the RSS's countrywide celebrations marking the birth anniversary of its longest serving Sarsanghachalak, M S Golwalkar comes ominously close on the eve of the 5th anniversary of the 2002 genocide in Gujarat. These celebrations triggered the eruption of communal violence in a number of places in recent weeks. In Karnataka, the whipping up of communal polarization is being systematically undertaken. Reports of clashes have come in places like Mangalore, Bangalore, Chickmagalur, various cities in Madhya Pradesh which is also a B J P-ruled State. Similar reports are coming from Indore, Jabalpur and Mandsaur. The latest are the reports of widespread communal disturbances coming from Uttar Pradesh with violence rocking Gorakhpur, Maharajgund, Kushinagar, Basti and Assamgur. These centenary observations need to be seen in the context of the recent Lucknow session of the B J P where it adopted a strident communal pitch calling for the propagation of "PRAKHAR" Hindutva. "Am I running amuck? No. The fact is that if I have to be admitted as an Honourable and Esteemed Member of the Pseudo-Secular Corps of the Mafia of Mass Media in India, I have to begin this article only this way and in no other way.

The Godra incident has become the favourite hobby horse of pseudo-secular politicians belonging to the Congress, the CPI (M), the CPI, the R J D, The Lok Janshakthi, the D M K and all the "lie loveless upon my faithless arms" allies forming part of the UPA coalition Government in New Delhi. As one of the known VIP minions of the CPI (M), Sitaram Yechuri has no other option but to bark loudly along with the rest of the pack. What amazes me is the fact that while Sri Guruji Golwalkar (1906-1973) passed away in 1973, the Gujarat riots took place 29 years later in 2002. But for Communists like Sitaram Yechuri, Time stands still.

No one can dispute the fact that because of the wanton outrage committed by the terrorist Muslims at Godra Railway Station, Narendra Modi was swept back to power by the united and determined voice of Gujarat. Even after his resounding victory in the elections, politicians like Sitaram Yechuri, ably abetted or assisted the anti-national and anti-social journalists belonging to the pseudo-secular mafia of mass media in India have been crying hoarse about the communal frenzy in Gujarat let loose by Narendra Modi and his Government.

The simple question to be asked is what has Sri Guruji Golwalkar Centenary to do with incidents of unprovoked violence let loose by the Islamic terrorists in India? It is well known that Sitaram Yechuri and his CPI (M) to which he belongs are known for their Islam-embracing, Christianity-coveting and Hindu-hating brand of electoral vote bank politics. Sitaram Yechuri"s hatred for Hinduism and Sanatana Dharma in general and Sri Guruji Golwalkar in particular comes out in the following baseless and fraudulent typical Communist Party (CPI-M) statement in his article: "Following the ban of the R S S after the assassination of Mahatma Gandhi, Golwalkar entered into an agreement with the Government seeking its withdrawal while assuring that the R S S would not play any political role in the future".

This great and self-righteous champion of Bharat without Bharat Mata-in effect a betrayer of BHARAT MATA-seems to be blissfully ignorant of the letter sent by Sardar Vallabhbhai Patel to Sri Guruji Golwalkar in September 1949. In his letter Sardar Patel had referred to Communist machinations, which at that point of time meant the anti-national machinations of great communist leaders like P C Joshi, B T Ranadive, S A Dange, G Adhikari, P Sundaraiah, Somnath Lahiri, E M S Namboodripath, D S Vaidya and many other known Communist traitors right from the days of "Quit India Movement".

These are the political progenitors of pseudo-patriots like Sitaram Yechuri and others of his ilk today. To come back to Sardar Patel's words in his letter to Sri Guruji Golwalkar in September 1949: "In answer to the call of the times alone, please take a decision. I and all my co-workers have been striving from the very start to cooperate with you to bring the situation under control and make our Motherland invincible. ... I am thoroughly convinced that the R S S men can carry on their patriotic endeavour only by joining the Congress and not by keeping separate or opposing".

When Sri Guruji Golwalkar was illegally detained without a trial from November 1948 to June 1949 under the notorious "Bengal State Prisoners Act of 1818" (which Mahatma Gandhi and Nehru and the Congress Party had severely condemned as a Black Law before our independence), more than 80,000 Swayamsevaks of the R S S offered their peaceful Satyagraha throughout India and they were all detained without any trial in November 1949. "The Statesman" of Calcutta in its issue dated 22 January 1949 wrote in its Editorial: "The leaders of the R S S deserve to be praised for the manner in which they conducted the agitation and there is an imperative and urgent public need for the ban on the R S S to be removed immediately. The youth power of the country is being laid to waste by clamping them behind bars. They are idealistic, physically fit, imbued in the spirit of sacrifice and have the capacity to enhance the prestige of the country. How is it proper to keep such youth power in jail?"

As a true Communist wedded to the cause of his own brand of truth and falsehood, Sitaram Yechuri may be "voluntarily" ignorant of the fact that the Minister for Home and Revenue, Government of Bombay, gave the following reply in the Bombay Legislative Assembly on 14 October 1949 in his reply to questions raised by Sri Lalubhai Patel from Surat District. The Minister said:-1) The lifting of ban on R S S was unconditional and 2) Sri Guruji Golwalkar had given no undertaking to the Government whatsoever". Against this background, I would request Sitaram Yechuri in my capacity as an unknown, superstitious, obscurantist, saffronized, communal, half-literate and half-savage Paganish Hindu, (but to Yechuri's dismay, in no way an official part of the Sangh Parivar!) to explain as to what he means when he says that Sri Guruji Golwalkar "gave an undertaking" to the Government regarding the non-participation of the R S S in the field of politics!

T.R. Venkatrama Sastri, former Advocate General of Madras in the 1920s (and not in the sucking days of Congress Party in post-independent India where such posts came to be conveniently bought and sold), has clearly recorded that no undertaking was ever given by Sri Guruji Golwalkar to Government of India either before his release in June 1949 or after it. For the elucidation of the ignorant and corrupt pseudo-secular leaders of India who are swarming our beleaguered nation today like a swarm of poisonous insects and stinging bees, I would like to clarify that it was T R Venkatrama Sastri who met Nehru and Sardar Vallabhbhai Patel on his own in 1949 and proved to both of them with facts and figures that the detention of Sri Guruji Golwalkar and the ban of the RSS were unwarranted, illegal, anti-national and anti-social.

K M Munshi was a Cabinet Minister in the Government of Jawaharlal Nehru in 1949. He wrote in the "Organizer" dated 4 October 1949: "Sri Guruji Golwalkar, the R S S Chief, is now on an all-India tour. The ovation which he received in Delhi for instance, is an indication that R S S. has come to stay. It is no use ignoring the fact". In the same article, comparing the R S S with CPI, K M Munshi wrote: "CPI is the enemy of Indian nationalism, tied to the chariot wheel of the USSR. R S S is fanatically nationalist, worshiping Bharat Mata with high-powered emotion, looking to ancient India alone for inspiration. CPI seeks to undermine the foundation of well-ordered life in order to bring about an upheaval. R S S builds up the foundation of an unyielding discipline to take over, should the nationalist movement fail before the CPI.

CPI attracts young men by providing a romantic background of revolutionary zeal and young women-possibly a more dangerous-element by offering an alluring breakaway from normal disciplined life. R S S attracts young men by the lure of spectacular organizational life and a fanatic hatred of what they deem anti-Hindu. I do not know whether it has ever attempted to enlist the young womanhood in India. To CPI, Lenin, Stalin and USSR are the FATHER, SON and HOLY GHOST. To R S S, India is a Divine Mother, at whose altar self-immolation is bliss. What is USSR to CPI, ancient Bharat is to R S S. The Church of CPI is "MATERIALISM"; the Church of R S S is "DHARMA" buttressed with ancient traditions."

It is very clear that all the pseudo-secular parties in India like the Congress, the CPI (M), the CPI and others have been completely rattled by the massive public support that people have given to the organizers of the Sri Guruji Golwalkar Centenary Celebrations in all parts of India from February 2006 to February 2007, cutting across caste, colour, creed and faith. Men like Yechuri are in the line of men like Hitler, Goering and Goebbels who were described appropriately by Winston Churchill as "Repositories of some of the most virulent forms of soul-destroying hatred.

Yechuri's hate for "things Hindu" in general is greater than his known and naturally whipped-up hate for Bourgeois Dictatorship!! Whether Sitaram Yechuri likes it or not, the people of India have clearly shown during the Centenary Year of Sri Guruji Golwalkar that they have their full and indivisible faith in the mission of the R S S. Like the immemorial waters of the sacred Ganga, the R S S keeps rolling along-let it roll, let it roll on, full flood, true, benignant, inexorable, into broader lands and better days.

Kashmir and the Trauma of Partition

During several decades- the end of the last century and the beginning of the present-the European population was being severely disciplined by industry. All phases of social education were dominated by the principle of the productivity of labour. This yielded stupendous results and seemed to open up new possibilities to people. But actually it only led to war. It is true that through the war humanity has been able to convince itself, in the face of the crowings of anaemic philosophy, that it is not degenerating after all; on the contrary, it is full of life, strength, bravery, enterprise. Through the same war, it realized its technical power with unprecedented force. It was as if a man, to prove that his pipes for breathing and swallowing were in order, had begun to cut his throat with a razor in front of a mirror.

LEON TROTSKY

Divide and Rule

The partition of India was one of the greatest crimes of British imperialism. This act was not intended to defend the interests of Muslims or Hindus but to split and wreck the national liberation movement, which they had failed to defeat by force of arms. After the Second World War the world saw an enormous upswing of the colonial revolution. This was perhaps the biggest movement of the oppressed people in human history. This was an enormous awakening of the colonial peoples of China, Africa, Latin America the Middle East, Indonesia, India, and Pakistan. This was an inspiring movement in which countless millions of former colonial slaves rose up against their masters, fighting for their national emancipation. The reasons why Marxists supported the colonial revolution are obvious. It was a revolutionary movement, a blow against imperialism, and it aroused the masses and advanced the class struggle.

The partition of the subcontinent into India and Pakistan, apart from being a reactionary political act, caused one of the biggest bloodbaths of innocent human beings in history as well as extreme suffering for millions. It created mayhem for the whole of society. The memory of partition is still painful for those wounded by it.

Altogether, some half a million people were killed before the end of 1947. Many more were uprooted: four and a half million Hindus and Sikhs migrated from the West Pakistan to India, six million Muslims in the opposite direction. While there were relatively less killings in Bengal, some one million people were displaced there. In the year 1700 A.D. roughly when the British arrived, India's share of world income was 22.6%. At the end of the direct British rule it was reduced to 3.8% just after independence.

It took the British more than three hundred years to build up their Indian empire. They dismantled it in just over seventy days in 1947. The true weakness of the British was not widely appreciated. In fact, after the terrible winter of 1946-47 Britain was on the verge of financial catastrophe. In February 1947 the Attlee Cabinet had to adopt a policy of a drastic reduction of overseas responsibilities. The widespread revolt amongst the soldiers of the British army also weakened its capability of maintaining direct military control of its colonies. This was the background to the Mountbatten Viceroyalty (March 22 to August 15, 1947), which not only brought the British Indian Empire to an end but also saw the first stage of India and Pakistan's dispute over Kashmir.

The basic plan for the dividing up of the British Indian Empire was drawn up in four hours by V.P Menon and accepted by the British Cabinet after a discussion lasting all of five minutes. The haste with which partition was executed guaranteed that there would be serious problems the successors to the British Raj would be left to deal with.

Such traumatic surgery was unlikely to heal without complications. One side effect was the exacerbation of communal tensions in the subcontinent, resulting in massacre and migration on a colossal scale: another was the set of circumstances that resulted in the outbreak of the Indo-Pakistan conflict over Kashmir.

It is an extraordinary historical fact that at the time of partition, when most parts of the subcontinent (especially Bengal and Punjab two nationalities cleaved apart) were in the throes of communal slaughter and religious bigotry, Kashmir was relatively safe from this frenzy. But due to its geographical proximity violence from the carnage in Punjab did eventually spill over into Jammu.

The division first unleashed a 'holocaust' of communal killing, as well as mass migrations of Hindus and Sikhs eastward, and Muslims to the west. Some of the Punjabi refugees found their way to Jammu and Kashmir, carrying with them harrowing tales of killings, rape, etc. The presence of these refugees served to incite and intensify communal violence. In Jammu Province, to where the majority of Hindus had fled, there was a backlash by their co-religionists against the Muslim inhabitants. Lamb writes that by August 1947:

The communal situation in Jammu, the one part of the state where there was a large non-Muslim population, had deteriorated rapidly with bands of armed Hindus and Sikhs (including members of the RSS, Hindu extremists, Akali Sikhs and others) attacking Muslim villages and setting in train a mass exodus. It has been estimated that in August, September, and October 1947 at least 500,000 Muslims were displaced from Jammu: perhaps as many as 200,000 of them just disappeared. Many of these then fled to Kashmir and Poonch, adding their tales of woe to those of the Punjabi Muslims who had preceded them. The predictable consequence was another communal backlash, this time by Muslims against Hindus and Sikhs.

The Poonch Revolt

In Poonch a rebellion against Dogra rule, based essentially on economic grievances (food prices and taxes), was encouraged to take on a 'Muslim vs Hindu' character a result of the killings in Punjab and Jammu. Further encouragement came from the direction of the North-West Frontier Province (Pashtonkawa). Pathans angered by reports of Muslim deaths went to Poonch seeking revenge against

Hindus and Sikhs. Poonch had come under the direct control of Maharaja Hari Singh in 1935-36, but the former jagir's population had never reconciled themselves to Dogra rule. Ethnically they had few links with Jammu: they were much closer to Punjab. The Muslims of Poonch, notably the Sudhen tribe, had served widely in both the British Indian army and in the Jammu and Kashmir forces. In 1947, following the end of the Second World War, some 60,000 ex-servicemen had returned to Poonch. These men possessed both military experience and arms.

In June 1947, a revolt broke out over the state government's exorbitant taxes. Some 10,000 Poonchis decided to march on Poonch City in protest at high food prices. Before they reached the city they clashed with state troops at Bagh. The government ordered the inhabitants to surrender their weapons. This was largely ignored. The situation was exacerbated on August 14, when Muslims attempted to celebrate Pakistan Day (also Kashmir Day) in defiance of a government ban. In addition, with the killings in Punjab after partition and the arrival of a large number of Muslim refugees in Poonch the conflict took on a communal aspect. By September the revolt had acquired a degree of organisation under Muhammad Ibrahim Khan (the Muslim representative for Poonch in the Praja Sabha and a Muslim Conference member), and had evolved into a secessionist movement. In October 1947, the 'Government of Azad Kashmir' declared the area independent of Dogra rule, and set up its capital in Muzaffarabad.

Once underway, the Poonch rebellion received support from a number of sources: defectors from the Jammu and Kashmir forces, former Indian National Army soldiers, and Punjabi Muslims from Jhelum. Initially most of the support came from Pathans of the North-West Frontier Province. The government of Pakistan was at first very reluctant to become involved. In fact it refused to recognize the Azad Kashmir government. However, by September it was providing unofficial aid to the rebels. Looking at the wider picture, the communal violence in Punjab and later in Jammu and Kashmir generally served to harden the prevalent opinions of the three major groups. The state's Hindu community was even more convinced that it had no future under Muslim rule; if the Maharaja could not retain control, they wanted to accede to India. The Muslim Conference supporters moved closer to joining Pakistan, though some still favoured an independent Muslim state.

Degeneration of CPI Leaders

The movement in Kashmir was inreality directed against the despotic and brutal rule of the Dogra Maharajas. In other words the class struggle was more prominent in the movement than religious and nationalist sentiments. Had there been a genuine revolutionary Marxist party and leadership, Kashmir could have given a lead to the national liberation struggle that was pulsating throughout British India in the last months of the Second World War. The Communist Party had a modest presence in Kashmir. Unfortunately a position of conciliation with the British imperialists during the later part of the war was adopted by the central leadership of the CPI (Communist Party of India). This was at the behest of the Stalinist bureaucracy in Moscow, which was pursuing its own agenda of compromise with imperialism to forward the "national interest" of the Soviet Union. These policies of the CPI leaders had a drastic impact on the significant forces of communism in all parts of India, including Kashmir.

At the beginning of the Second World War, and especially after the Stalin-Hitler pact, the CPI launched an intensive anti-war campaign. It called the war an imperialist war, and the CPI was at the forefront of anti-British agitation. This was a golden opportunity for the CPI to present itself as a revolutionary alternative to the masses. At the start of the anti-war campaign, the CPI took the courageous step of organising mass strikes against the war. The first ever anti-war demonstration of workers in the world took place in India on October 22, 1939 with a one-day protest and general strike in which 90,000 people participated. The main slogans of the demonstration were "Defeat this treachery against the human race", "Down With The Imperialist War", "Long Live The Freedom Of

India", etc. The British colonialists increased state repression. Thousands of CPI workers were put in jail during this anti-war agitation. Congress was polarized, and a number of leftist groups, including those around Dr. Subhash Chandra Bose, identified with the CPI. While the process of unity amongst the left on the basis of the anti-war and anti-British posture of the CPI was forging ahead, changes in Moscow's policy struck a devastating blow. On June 22, 1941 Hitler attacked the Soviet Union. The Stalinist bureaucracy made a 180-degree turn on its policies and analysis of the forces in the international arena. The masters of the Kremlin, having cômpletely abandoned a revolutionary international perspective, were totally unaware that Hitler was preparing a devastating blow against them. This is what disarmed the Soviet Union in the face of its terrible foe. From the outbreak of the Second World War right up until June 1941, when Hitler attacked the Soviet Union, Nazi Germany received a large increase in exports from the USSR.

Stalin tried to make a deal with the imperialist powers between 1944 and 1945 at the Big Three Conferences at Tehran, Yalta and Potsdam. His humiliating capitulation at the altar of imperialist diplomacy sealed the fate of several Communist Parties and revolutions in a number of countries. The CPI paid a heavy price for the opportunist turn. Apart from the attitude of appeasement towards the British, it started to develop a conciliatory attitude towards the national bourgeois leadership. In reality, large sections of the CPI were absorbed into Congress.

The CPI cadres should have exposed the real class interests of Nehru, Jinnah and Gandhi to the toiling masses. They should have striven to overcome and eliminate the images of the bourgeois leaders from the minds and consciousness of those who were taking part in the struggle to overthrow the Raj. Their main aim should have been to recruit the socialist youth and militants who were in Congress into the CPI and create a mass movement of the workers and peasants to put an end to imperialist rule.

The change in the CPI's position on the war created disillusionment amongst the masses and confusion and apathy in the party ranks. One of the most prominent Communist leaders of India, E.M.S Namboodripad, admitted the damage done to the Communist Party by its sudden U-turn in its attitude towards war. In his book "B.J.P/R.S.S: In The Service Of Right Reaction", he wrote: "In the first phase of the war the Communists had launched a countrywide movement in demand for total independence. In the second phase they felt a change in the character of the war, the result of the attack of Nazi Germany on the Soviet Union. It had become a 'peoples' war. The CPI leadership opposed the 'Quit India' demand, and isolated themselves from the movement."

The policy zigzags, the wavering and the political ineptitude of the CP leadership at local levels also created a vacuum, which was filled by accidental and populist individuals in the subcontinent, hence we see a plethora of parties and leaders come and go, eventually abdicating the political arena for Congress and the Muslim League.

However, in Kashmir, the National Conference and the Abdullah Dynasty filled the vacuum created as a consequence of this absence of a conscious revolutionary leadership. As we described earlier the oppression and the class antagonisms had reached an explosive level. As history has shown several times, any event can trigger an explosion when the contradictions in society have reached a critical point.

In July 1931 mass anger burst open the accumulated contradictions. The anger that had been simmering and slowly building against the Maharaja exploded through this breach. Given the political vacuum, Sheikh Mohammed Abdullah was able to intervene with a reformist programme for the oppressed Kashmiris. In this intervention he cleverly articulated the problems of the peasants, workers and the artisans. He launched a movement of civil disobedience. Several activists were arrested and jailed in Hari Parbat Fort. The first reforms in Kashmir came as a direct consequence of this movement. Initially the party Sheikh Abdullah had set up was the Muslim Conference in 1930 (which still exists mainly in the

Pakistani controlled Kashmir). But the class character of the movement had an impact and the party changed its name to the National Conference in 1939. It adopted a red flag with a white plough in the centre. The slogan given to the peasants was "when the plough moves, it tears apart the enemy".

Problems of Populism

Since its inception the National Conference was a petit bourgeois populist party with socialist rhetoric. However, to prop-up and expand its mass base, it had to wage a consistent struggle against the despotic rule of the Dogras.

In 1944 Sheikh Abdullah announced his blue print for the future of Kashmir. The clear class character and pressure of the movement amongst the Kashmiri masses is evident from the statement of the NC leaders themselves. Sheikh Abdullah himself proclaimed, "Wherever I looked I saw a relentless struggle between the oppressor and oppressed. I yearn to become their saviour and sacrifice my life in their cause".

Abdullah described the class-base of the new party in his autobiography: Our movement had been thrown open to all religious groups. It became imperative to develop new political and economic rallying points. We had learnt from experience that the real reason for conflict was not religion but a clash of interests between different classes and groups. The primary objective of our movement was to oppose oppression and support the oppressed.

The aim of the socialist creed was explained in the document titled in "New Kashmir": To perfect our union in fullest equality and self-determination, to raise ourselves and our children forever from the abyss of oppression and poverty, degradation and superstition, from medieval darkness and ignorance, into the sunlit valleys of plenty ruled by freedom, science and honest toil.

Pyare Lal Hindu, Minister of Law under the Sheikh Farooq Abdullah, describes the situation in 1944: The battle for political freedom (had to) mean the battle for economic emancipation....

once he (Sheik Mohammed Abdullah) got this programme adopted as the charter for political and economic emancipation of our state, a swift change swept the countryside till it culminated in the historic slogan of quit Kashmir in 1946...

But in spite of this populist programme they made several compromises and capitulations to the rulers under the Raj. It was later proved that even reforms to this system could not deliver the masses from misery or create social stability.

Sir Gopalswami Ayyangar was Prime Minister of Jammu and Kashmir from 1935 to 1943.

The British describe him as 'a strong Hindu and a strong nationalist with not unsympathetic leanings towards the congress."' Iffat Malik elaborates,

In August 1942, Sheikh Abdullah began organizing strikes, processions, etc., in support of the congress movement in India. Through subordinate officials, Ayyangar advised him not to attack the Maharaja or the British. Heeding this advice Abdullah limited his followers' activities to expressing support for Congress. As a result unlike in British India there were no significant arrests in Jammu and Kashmir. In November 1942, Ayyangar held a meeting with Abdullah, the first after several years: 'after which the latter made more protestations of his loyalty to His Highness, and rumours of constitutional reform in Kashmir began to become prevalent...Shortly afterwards the Kashmir Government entrusted the work of issuing Rice ration ticket and permits for fuel in Srianagar to Committees composed almost entirely of non-officials. The National Conference was represented on these committees at the instance of the Kashmir Government but no representative of the Muslim Conference were appointed'.

Although they rejected the religious segregation of the subcontinent and opposed a theocratic state, this was not good enough. They did not understand that post-British India could not achieve genuine democracy, secularism, or "socialism" under the capitalist system. Despite the glaring need for a socio-economic transformation of the subcontinent, the National Conference and its leadership lacked a clear revolutionary perspective and the ideological foundation to carry it through. They were basically radical bourgeois liberals and their programme was restricted to the demands of the national democratic revolution.

The leadership of the National Conference was ideologically closer to the Congress and the Gandhi-Nehru leadership, so they teamed up with them. They were opposed to joining "theocratic" Pakistan .At the same time they were in the struggle against the Dogra Monarchy. According to the Independence Act, the rulers of the princely states were given the right to decide on joining one of the dominions or remaining independent. The Dogra ruler Hari Singh was ambiguous and wavered.

Intrigues and Treachery

In mid-September, Jinnah instructed his secretary, Colonel William Birnie, to go to Kashmir and arrange for him to spend two weeks of resting and relaxing. Choosing Kashmir for his holiday was entirely natural. To Jinnah, as to most of his countrymen, it seemed inconceivable that Kashmir, with the population over three quarters Muslim, could become any thing but a part of Pakistan.

The British officer, nonetheless, returned five days later with a story that stunned Jinnah. The Maharaja Hari Singh had refused Jinnah permission to set foot on his soil, even as a tourist. This gave Pakistan's leaders their first indication that the situation in Kashmir was not evolving as they had complacently assumed. Forty-eight hours later, Jinnah's government sent a secret agent into Kashmir to evaluate the situation and determine the Maharaja's real intentions. The report he brought back told them that Hari Singh had no intention of acceding to Pakistan. In mid-September, Liaqat Ali Khan, the Prime Minister of Pakistan, arranged a secret meeting of a select group of collaborators in Lahore to decide how to force the Maharaja's hand. The collaborators immediately dismissed the idea of an outright invasion. The Pakistani army was not ready to start a war over Kashmir that could escalate into a war with India.

Two other options were considered. Colonel Akbar Khan, a Sandhurst graduate with a taste for conspiracy, outlined the first. He proposed that Pakistan should supply the arms and money to foment an uprising of Kashmir's dissident Muslim population. The preparation would require several months, but would result in forty or fifty thousand Kashmiris descending onto Srinagar to force the Maharaja to accede to Pakistan.

The second option was far more intriguing. Its sponsor was the chief minister of the Northwest Frontier Province, and it would involve Pakistani tribesmen. The gathering closed with a stern warning from the Prime Minister that the operation must be a complete secret and that the finance would be provided by secret funds from the Prime Minister's office. Neither the officers of Pakistan's army, her civil servants nor the British officers and administrators in the service of the new state were to be given access to this secret. Just before five o'clock on the afternoon of October 24, 1947, Major General Douglas Gracey, who had replaced General Messervy as Commander-in-Chief of the Pakistan army, got his first intimation of what had happen in Kashmir through a secret intelligence report. It gave the raider's strength, armaments, and their location. Gracey did not hesitate. He immediately went to his predecessor's private quarters and communicated precious information to the man who commanded the only force that could deny Kashmir to the raiders... the Commander-in-Chief of the Indian army, Lieutenant General Sir Rob Lockhart, a Scot and Sandhurst classmate of Gracey. Lockhart was stunned by his old friend's report. He in turn communicated it to two more people, both of them British: Governor General Mountbatten, and Field Marshal Auchinleck.

Mountbatten received the news as he was getting ready for a banquet in honour of Thailand's foreign minister. When the last guest had left, he asked Nehru to stay behind. The Prime Minister was shocked by the news.

The Governor General was to discover another side of Nehru on Kashmir. The cool detached intelligence, so admired by Mountbatten was replaced by an instinctive, emotional response driven by passions that even the Kashmiri Brahmin could not control. "As Calais was written upon the heart of Queen Marry", Nehru would cry out to him one day to explain his attitude, "so Kashmir is written upon mine".

The following afternoon a DC3 of the Royal Indian Air Force landed on the abandoned dirt strip of Srinagar Airport. It carried VP Menon, the civil servant who had presided over so many princely accessions to India, Colonel Sam Manekshaw of the Indian army, and an air force officer.

As soon as they returned to Delhi, V.P Menon and the two officers that had accompanied him to Srinagar made their report to another meeting of the cabinet's Defence Committee. Their words were sombre. The Maharaja was ready at last to present Kashmir to India, but the Pathan raiders were only thirty-five miles from Srinagar and could at any moment seize the only airport in Kashmir on which India could land her troops. While the frenzied preparations for the operation were underway, Lord Mountbatten ordered V.P Menon to fly to Jammu. He carried with him, awaiting only Hari Singh's signature, the Act of Accession, which would provide a legal framework for India's invasion.

V.P Menon was back in his Delhi home late in the evening of that same Sunday, twenty-six October. Alexander Symon, Britain's Deputy High Commissioner joined him for a drink a few minutes after his return. Menon was jubilant. He poured them each a stiff drink . As they sat down, an enormous smile spread across his face. He raised his glass to Symon. Then he pulled a piece of paper from his jacket pocket and waved it gaily towards the Englishman. "Here it is," he said. "We have Kashmir. The bastard signed the Act of Accession and now that we have got it, we will never let it go."

Mehr Chand Mahajan had been a member of the Radcliff Boundary Commission in Punjab. Hari Singh appointed him Prime Minister of Jammu and Kashmir on the recommendation of Sardar Patel. In Alistair Lamb's opinion Mahajan's appointed task was to see through accession to India. This impression is confirmed by

Mahajan's visit to New Delhi on 11th October 1947, just before formally taking office as Prime Minister, when he called on Sardar Vallabhbhai Patel, Jawaharlal Nehru and Mahatma Gandhi. "V.P Menon (Sardar Vallabhbhai Patel's right hand man in matters of the accession of states to the India) ensured that Mahajan did not seek an interview with any senior Pakistani politician or official before assuming office."

Lamb writes that the Indian Government was making preparation for military intervention long before the instrument of Accession was signed: The first volume of Sardar Vallabhbhai Patel's correspondence which was published in 1971, makes it clear that both Sardar Vallabhbhai Patel and Baldev Singh were heavily engaged in the planning of some kind of Indian military intervention in Jammu and Kashmir, if only on a contingency basis, by at least 13 September 1947; and that by the third week of October a substantial foundation for such an operation had been laid. Much later in March 1951, Nehru admitted in a statement to Parliament that India would have sent her troops into Jammu and Kashmir even if Hari Singh had not signed the instrument of Accession: 'irrespective of accession we would have had an obligation to protect the people of Kashmir against aggression'.

On March 26, 1935 Maharaja Hari Singh had leased the Gilgit Wazarat, north of the Indus and its dependencies, to the British for a period of sixty years. However, in April 1947, after just twelve years, Mountbatten decided to hand the area back to direct Jammu and Kashmir control before the subcontinent became independent. This handover took effect on August 1, 1947. Hari Singh's Governor, Brigadier Ghansara Singh, reached Gilgit one day before this transfer. The local population, who had not been consulted about the handover, had no desire to return to Dogra rule. The local military force, the Gilgit Scouts, shared these sentiments. Faced with impending mutiny plus a Pathan tribal incursion, the Scouts' British Officer, Major Brown was to put the entire region under Pakistani control. Ghansara Singh was placed under house arrest and, on November 3, 1947 Brown announced Gilgit's accession to Pakistan.

Insurgency and the First Indo-Pak War

The Pathan tribesmen crossed the Jehlum River into Kashmir on the night of October 23-24,1947. Instead of marching straight to Srinagar, they indulged themselves in arson and plunder in Muzaffarabad and nearby towns. The plan was to capture Srinagar by October 26, in time for Eid celebrations. However, they fell short of their target, getting only as far as Baramulla (though they did manage to cut off the power supply to the Kashmiri capital). This gave the Indian army crucial time to amass troops and push back the raiders advance to Srinagar and beyond. Hence the history of the subcontinent took a strange twist. More than two thirds of Kashmir was taken by India and the other one third of mostly rugged terrain came under Pakistani control.

Indian troops, replacing National Conference supporters in the defence of Kashmir, succeeded in halting the tribal advance before Srinagar was captured. They also launched a counter-offensive, recapturing Baramulla. Once India had sent her forces into Jammu and Kashmir, Pakistan's Governor General M.A. Jinnah wanted to send his country's regular troops in as well. But such a move was blocked by the Pakistan Army's acting Commander-in-Chief, General Sir Douglas Gracey, who feared that it would spark off a war between the two new states (the two armies were still under the same supreme command). Jinnah still attempted to send help to the pro-Pakistan "Azad Kashmir" forces, for example encouraging Pakistan regulars "on leave" to make their way to the state. In May 1948, Gracey reversed his earlier decision, and Pakistan "officially" sent its troops into Jammu and Kashmir.

A series of offensives and counter-offensives ended with Pakistan controlling Gilgit (which had "acceded" to that country on 3 November 1947), Baltistan, part of the Vale, most of Poonch, and the Mirpur area of Jammu. Indian forces controlled Ladakh, most of the Kashmir and Jammu provinces, and a small part of Poonch. By the end of 1948 the war, which had so far been confined to Jammu and Kashmir, threatened to spread to "proper" India and Pakistan. Such an escalation was avoided by the declaration of a ceasefire, partly the result of the intervention of the United Nations which took effect on January 1, 1949. The ceasefire line was defined in an agreement between Indian and Pakistani military representatives on July 27, 1949 and remained unchanged until the 1965 Indo-Pakistan War.

By the time the war ended, the Jammu and Kashmir State had been divided into three separate administrative regions. The first, consisting of Gilgit and Baltistan (the Northern Area), was controlled directly by Pakistan. These regions had, for all intents and purposes, been integrated into that country. The second region, known as Azad Kashmir, consisted of part of the Kashmir province, most of Poonch and the Mirpur district of Jammu. This was controlled by a far from united group, which included Poonch Muslims (mostly Sudhans), and former Muslim Conference exiles such as Mirwaiz Yousaf Shah and Ghulam Abbas. In theory, Azad Kashmir was independent, *i.e.* it was not part of Pakistani territory. In practice however, it had very close links with Pakistan, and was heavily dependent economically and militarily on Karachi (then capital of Pakistan). These links severely restricted its ability to act as a separate entity. The third part of the state was that held by the Indian troops. Sheikh Abdullah, the leader of the National Conference, was freed from the jail of Hari Singh in September by the Nehru government and he was staying with Nehru in Delhi. He put his weight behind the decision to send Indian troops to "secure" Kashmir. In October 1947, in accordance with the terms of accession to India, Maharaja Hari Singh appointed Sheikh Abdullah as the head of an emergency government. Though Mehr Chand Mahajan stayed on as Prime Minister, real power was in the hands of Abdullah. In June 1949, the Maharaja was "persuaded" to appoint his son Karan Singh as regent, and leave Kashmir for what turned out to be permanent exile in India.

The Facade of Legality

Sheikh Abdullah was installed as the head of the new government of Kashmir on October 31, 1947. This Government included his close lieutenants Mirza Afzal Beg, Bakshi Ghulam Mohammed, Sham Lal Saraf, and GM Sadiq. His subservience to India was to such an extent that in an interview published on November 5, 1947 in Hindustan Times, Sheikh Abdullah had said, The grave of Pakistan will be dug in the valley of Kashmir".

Nehru, convinced of the legality of India's case, took the problem to the United Nations on December 31, 1947. He would later come to regret this decision. The Indian constitution awarded Kashmir special status through Article 370. Even until the 1951 elections, with the landslide victory of the National Conference, Nehru and Abdullah were confident that due to the popularity of the NC, even if a referendum were held in Kashmir, it would vote to accede to India. That is why he accepted the UN resolution calling for a plebiscite in Kashmir.

When Nehru and Liaqat Ali Khan met again in Delhi toward the end of December 1947, Nehru informed him of his intention to refer the dispute to the UN under Article 35 of the UN Charter, which allowed any member "to bring to the attention of the Security Council a situation whose continuance is likely to endanger the maintenance of International Peace!" The Pakistani Prime Minister was unhappy with the accusatory tone of the reference but supposed he would have to accept it since the earlier it was brought before the UN the better.

On December 31, 1947 Nehru formally wrote to the UN General Secretary. In January 1948 the Kashmir issue was debated in the United Nations Security Council at Lake Success, New York with representatives from both India and Pakistan. Much to the annoyance of the Indians, on January 16, 1949 Sir Zafarullah Khan Pakistani Foreign minister, delivered a five-hour speech in favour of Pakistan's position and against the continued rule of the Dogras over Kashmir:What is not fully known is the depth of misery to which they have been reduced by a century of unmitigated tyranny and oppression under the Dogra rule until it is difficult to say which is a greater tragedy to a Kashmiri: his life or his death.

On January 20, 1948 the Security Council passed a resolution that establish a commission which became known as the United Nation Commission for India and Pakistan (UNCIP).

A further resolution was adopted on April 21, 1948 that called the Government of Pakistan, To secure the withdrawal from the state of Jammu and Kashmir of tribesmen and Pakistani nationals not normally resident therein who have entered the state for the purposes of fighting."

The Government of India was Requested

"To reduce its forces to the minimum strength after which the circumstances for holding a plebisciteshould be put into effect "on the question of the accession of the state to India or Pakistan."

On August 13, 1948 another resolution adopted by UNCIP once more stated that the final decision on the future status of Jammu and Kashmir "Shall be determined in accordance with the will of the people".

Nehru was already talking about the partition of the state on lines previously talked about, *i.e.* Western Poonch, Gilgit, and Chitral, most of Baltistan would all go to Pakistan. However, this suggestion was unacceptable to Liaquat Ali Khan, the main spokesman after Jinnah's death in September 1948.

The ceasefire finally imposed on January 1, 1949 was signed by General Gracey on behalf of Pakistan and General Roy Bucher on behalf of India, two British officers on behalf of the respective Dominions to whom the British had granted independence sixteen months earlier.

The terms of Article 35 under which India had referred the issue to the UN did not give the UN any mandate to impose a solution, only to make recommendations. Then as now, the Indian government considered itself to be in legal possession of the state of Jammu and Kashmir by virtue of the Instrument of Accession of October 1947 signed by the Maharaja and the then governor general, Lord Mountbatten.

The Ruler of a State... could, if he wished to join, sign an instrument of Accession in which he transferred to the appropriate Dominion what were deemed the three major powers, those over Defense, External Affairs and Communication. On the other hand the state of Jammu and Kashmir had signed an agreement with Pakistan on August 15, 1947 that prevented the state from entering into any kind of negotiation or agreement with any other country.

According to the provisions of the 1947 agreement it was possible for a state deliberating accession or in the process of acceding while certain issues remained unresolved to sign with one or both of the Dominions what was termed as 'Standstill Agreement.' This would permit the continuation of various essential services even if their constitutional basis was now uncertain.

In October 1963 the Government of Pakistan once more referred the question of Kashmir to the Security Council and in the spring of 1964 the issue was debated for the 110th time in fifteen years.

The fact is that of the innumerable UN resolutions on Kashmir not one makes any specific reference to the "third option", that of the independence of the Kashmiri people. After its early diplomatic initiatives in the 1950s and 1960s the United States has kept aloof from resolving the Kashmir issue till now.

To sow illusions in the UN and in the idea that it could solve the Kashmir issue and liberate its people is to betray the liberation struggle that the Kashmiri masses have fought for several generations. It is a defeatist policy designed to pacify the movement and maintain the status quo. The great Greek philosopher Solane once said, "Law is like a spider's web, small and weak things get stuck in it, the big one's pierce through it."

This is all the more true for bourgeois international law and the character of the so-called United Nations. It is a symbol of legalistic and diplomatic hypocrisy. Lenin once called the League of Nations a "thieves' kitchen". The United Nations, if anything, is the greatest deceiver of all.

Kashmir is the oldest unresolved dispute on the agenda of the United Nations. It is still unresolved. Many later disputes put to the United Nations have not been resolved either. Two hundred and eighteen resolutions have been passed against the atrocities and the occupation of Palestinian land by the state of Israel. Not one of these resolutions has been implemented. The recent imperialist invasion of Iraq is a glaring example of the impotence of the UN. The problem is that most conflicts around the world cannot be resolved on a capitalist basis. Hence, as a deviation or a delaying tactic, these politically decadent leaders refer them to the UN. Such is the case with Kashmir. The United Nations is financed by imperialist and reactionary bourgeois states. How could it dare confront them or impose any decision against their vested interests? The UN is simply the gossip club of the rulers of oppressive regimes that rule through an exploitative system. The UN was a rotten compromise between Imperialism and Stalinism in the past, now it is an instrument for justifying and legalising the economic and military aggression of imperialism, especially that of the United States.

The liberation of Kashmir will not come from UN resolutions or the charity of the imperialist masters. It will come through the revolutionary struggle of the Kashmiri masses, which they have carried on with such courage and bravery for so long. With all these sacrifices they have a huge treasure of experience of struggle. From this will emerge the exact path to take, in order to achieve their freedom.

POST-INDEPENDENCE ERA

Struggle for Andhra State

The Andhras were struggling for the formation of a separate Andhra Province since the period of British, but could not succeed. When India attained Independence on the 15th of August, 1947, Andhras hoped that their long-cherished desire would be realised soon. Inspite of several renewed efforts put forth by the Andhra leaders before the Prime Minister Jawaharlal Nehru and the Deputy

Prime Minister Sardar Vallabhbhai Patel, the desire for a separate Andhra State remained as a dream itself.

The Dar Commission, appointed by the Government of India under the Chairmanship of S.K.Dar did not recommend for the creation of States on the linguistic consideration. This report of the Commission created such an adverse reaction in Andhra that the Congress leaders felt it prudent to assuage the ruffled feelings of the Telugus. An unofficial Committee, consisting of Jawaharlal Nehru, Vallabhbhai Patel and Pattabhi Sitaramaiah, popularly known as the J.V.P. Committee, was constituted by the Congress. The Committee in its report submitted to the Working Committee of the Indian National Congress in April, 1949 recommended that the creation of linguistic provinces be postponed by few years. However, it suggested that Andhra Province could be formed provided the Andhras gave up their claim to the city of Madras (now Chennai). This report provoked violent reaction in Andhra as the Telugus were not prepared to forego their claims to the city of Madras.

Under the prevailing situation, a Partition Committee was formed under the Chairmanship of Kumaraswami Raja, the then Chief Minister of Madras. Andhra was represented by Tanguturi Prakasam, B.Gopala Reddi, Kala Venkata Rao and N.Sanjiva Reddy. The Partition Committee could not arrive at an agreed settlement. Prakasam disagreed with the views of other members and gave a dissenting note. The Government of India, took advantage of the dissenting note of Prakasam and shelved the issue. To express the resentment of the Andhras, Swami Sitaram (Gollapudi Sitarama Shastri), a Gandhian, undertook a fast unto death, which created an explosive situation in Andhra. However, Swami gave up his 35-day fast on the 20th of September, 1951, on the appeal made by Vinoba Bhave. Nothing came out of this fast except the increasing distrust of the people of Andhra towards their own leaders and the Government of India.

In the First General Elections of 1952, Andhras expressed their resentment towards the Congress leaders by defeating them at the polls. Out of the 140 seats from Andhra in the Madras Legislative Assembly, the Congress could secure only 43, while the Communist Party of India bagged as many as 40 seats out of the 60 it contested. In the Madras Legislative Assembly itself, the Congress could secure only 152. The non-Congress members in the legislature, numbering 164 formed themselves into a United Democratic Front (U.D.F.) and elected T.Prakasam as their leader. But the Governor nominated C.Rajagopalachari to the Legislative Council and invited him to form the ministry.

After Rajagopalacharya became the Chief Minister of the Madras State, he tried to divert the Krishna waters by constructing Krishna-Pennar Project for the development of the Tamil area. The Andhras agitated against this as they feared that the Project spelt ruin to Andhra. The Government of India appointed an expert Committee under the Chairmanship of A.N.Khosla, who pronounced that the project in its present form should not be proceeded with and suggested the construction of a project at Nandikonda (the site of the present Nagarjunasagar Project). The report of the Khosla Committee vindicated the apprehensions of the Andhras regarding the unfriendly attitude of Rajagopalacharya's Government towards the Andhras. The desire of the Andhras to separate themselves from the composite Madras State and form their own State gained further momentum.

At this juncture, Potti Sriramulu, a self-effacing Gandhian, began his fast unto death on the 19th of October, 1952 at Madras. Though the fast created an unprecedented situation throughout Andhra, the Congress leaders and the Government of India did not pay much attention to it. On the 15th of December, 1952, Sriramulu attained martyrdom. The news of Sriramulu's death rocked Andhra into a violent and devastating agitation. The Government of India was taken aback at this popular upsurge. On the 19th December, 1952, Jawaharlal Nehru announced in the Lok Sabha that the Andhra State would be formed with the eleven undisputed Telugu districts, and the three Taluks of the Bellary district, but excluding Madras City.

On the 1st of October, 1953, Andhra State came into existence. It consisted of the districts of Srikakulam, Visakhapatnam, East Godavari, West Godavari, Krishna, Guntur, Nellore, Chittoor, Cuddapah, Anantapur and Kurnool, and the taluks of Rayadurg, Adoni and Alur of the Bellary district. On the question of Bellary taluk, it was included in the Mysore State on the recommendation of L.S.Mishra Commission.

Kurnool became the capital of the new State, under the terms of the Sri Bagh Pact of 1937 between the leaders of the Coastal Andhra and Rayalaseema. T.Prakasam became the first Chief Minister of the Andhra State and C.M.Trivedi was appointed Governor of this new State. With the inauguration of the Andhra State by Nehru, the forty year old dream of the Telugu people to have a separate State of their own was partly fulfilled. They looked forward to the formation of Visalandhra with Hyderabad City as the Capital.

POLICE ACTION IN HYDERABAD STATE

Andhras were very much agitated over the developments in the State of Hyderabad during the years 1946—48. The Nizam was very anxious to become independent and he insisted that Hyderabad should be the third dominion. He tried to achieve his ambitious desire with the help of Khasim Razvi of the Ittehadul Muslimeen and its storm-troopers, the Razakars. Meanwhile, the Hindus of the Hyderabad State who accounted for 93 per cent of its population, launched the 'Join India' movement with the cooperation of a few patriotic Muslims for the integration of the State with the rest of the country. The State Congress leaders, led by Swami Ramanand Tirtha, invoked themselves whole-heartedly in the movement. As the State Congress was banned by the Nizam, its leaders conducted their activities from places like Vijayawada and Bombay. The Communists on their part organised village defence squads to protect the villagers from the attacks of the Nizam Police and Razakars.

All negotiations between the Nizam's Dominions and the Indian Union proved abortive. The Nizam Government did not agree to the accession of the Dominions to the Indian Union. The activities of the Majlis Ittehadul Muslimeen and the Razakars within the Dominions were posing a threat to peace and harmony. The growing violence of the Razakars seriously jeopardised law and order. The Government of India, tried to make the Nizam see reason and sign the Instrument of Assession with India. After tortuous negotiations, the Nizam finally entered into a 'Stand Still Agreement' on November 29, 1947, with India for one year to maintain status quo, which existed between the British and the Nizam before August 15, 1947. This agreement of the Nizam was only to gain time to procure military hardware from different parts of the world and smuggle them into Hyderabad. In the meanwhile, the Nizam sent a delegation to the U.N.O. to refer the Hyderabad case to the Security Council.

With the growing violence by the Razakars and the Nizam's attempts to get himself independent, the Government of India decided to curb these tendencies by launching a 'Police Action' against the Nizam. On the 13th of September, 1948 'Police Action' on Hyderabad commenced. The Indian Army, led by Major-General J.N.Chaudhuri entered the State from five directions and the military action was a brilliant success. On 18th September, 1949, Nizam's forces surrendered and Mir Laik Ali, the Prime Minister of the Nizam, and Khasim Razvi were arrested. On September, 23, the Nizam withdrew his complaint in the Security Council. The merger of Hyderabad Dominions into the Indian Union was announced. Major-General J.N.Chaudhuri took over as Military Governor of Hyderabad and stayed in that position till the end of 1949. In January 1950, M.K.Vellodi, a Senior Civil Servant, was made the Chief Minister of the State and the Nizam was designated 'Raj Pramukh'. After the 1952 General Elections, the first popular ministry headed by B.Rama Krishna Rao took charge of the State.

EMERGENCE OF ANDHRA PRADESH

The creation of Andhra State in October, 1953 strengthened the general demand for linguistic States. Andhras had also long cherished demand for the formation of Visalandhra, since the people of Hyderabad State were unanimous in their demand for the trifurcation of their State. Andhras hoped that the outlying Telugu areas in Orissa, Madhya Pradesh, Mysore and Madras be incorporated in the greater Andhra. The States Reorganisation Commission, with Syed Fazl Ali as the Chairman, set up by the Government of India in December 1953, who heard the views of different organisations and individuals, was though convinced of the advantages of Visalandhra, however, favoured the formation of separate State for Telangana. This report of the S.R.C. led to an intensive lobbying both by the advocates of Telangana and Visalandhra. The Communists reacted sharply and announced that they would resign their seats in the Hyderabad Legislative Assembly and contest elections on the issue. In the Hyderabad Legislative Assembly, a majority of the Legislators supported Visalandhra.

The Congress High Command favoured Visalandhra and prevailed upon the leaders of the Andhra State and Telangana to sort out their differences, who, thereupon, entered into a 'Gentlemen's Agreement'. One of the main provisions of the Agreement was the creation of a 'Regional Council' for Telangana for its all round development. The enlarged State by merging nine Telugu speaking districts of Adilabad, Nizamabad, Medak, Karimnagar, Warangal, Khammam, Nalgonda, Mahabub Nagar and Hyderabad, into Andhra State with its eleven districts of Srikakulam, Visakhapatnam, East Godavari, West Godavari, Krishna, Guntur, Nellore, Chittoor, Cuddapah, Anantapur and Kurnool, totalling 20 districts* was named 'Andhra Pradesh' with its capital at Hyderabad. It was inaugurated on the 1st of November, 1956 by Jawaharlal Nehru. Neelam Sanjiva Reddy became the first Chief Minister of Andhra Pradesh, who later rose to the position of the President of India. Burgula Ramkrishna Rao, last of the Chief Ministers of Hyderabad State was elevated to the Office of the Governor of Kerala. C.M.Trivedi continued to be the Governor of Andhra Pradesh.

As stated above, on the formation of Andhra Pradesh on the 1st of November 1956, Neelam Sanjiva Reddy became the first Chief Minister of the new State. Consequent on his becoming the President of the All India Congress Committee, he resigned the post of Chief Minister on 10th June, 1960 and was succeeded by D.Sanjivaiah, a talented young man from the Scheduled Castes. After

1962 General Elections, Sri N.Sanjiva Reddy again became the Chief Minister of the State on 12th March, 1962. But, he relinquished the Chief Ministership in 1964 on moral grounds consequent on the adverse verdict of the Supreme Court in Kurnool Transport Nationalisation case. He was succeeded by Sri Kasu Brahmananda Reddy on 29th February, 1964. He was in the office till 30th September, 1971. His long innings witnessed development of the city as well as the State in many ways. True the Telangana agitation erupted during his time paved way for rectification of defects and implementation of measures to develop Telangana.

POLITICAL CRISIS IN 1969 AND 1972

During the years 1969 and 1972, Andhra Pradesh was rocked by two political agitations popularly known as the 'Telangana' and the 'Jai Andhra' Movements respectively. Telangana agitation was started by the people of the region when they felt that the Andhra leaders had flouted the Gentlemen's Agreement which facilitated the formation of Andhra Pradesh. The influx of the people from the coastal region into the city of Hyderabad created many social tensions. Slowly the discontent spread among the Telangana officials and the unemployed youth who felt that they were exploited by the people of the Andhra region. The discontent manifested itself when a student of Khammam went on a hunger-strike in January 1969 demanding the implementation of the safeguards for Telangana provided in the Gentlemen's Agreement. Slowly the agitation spread to Hyderabad and other parts of Telangana. In the beginning, the movement demanded the implementation of the safeguards agreed upon earlier, but later it wanted the separation of Telangana from Andhra Pradesh.

The agitation took a new turn when the Congress legislators from Telangana supported the movement. Dr.Channa Reddy entered the fray and formed the Telangana Praja Samiti to lead the movement. But by November 1969, there was a split in the Praja Samiti when dissident Congress legislators realised that the Prime Minister Indira Gandhi was not in favour of separate Telangana. The movement slowly petered out. In September 1971, Brahmananda Reddy, the then Chief Minister, resigned his position to make room for a leader from Telangana to become the Chief Minister. On the 30th of September, 1971, P.V.Narsimha Rao became the Chief Minister. The Telangana Praja Samiti was dissolved and its members rejoined the Congress.

Sardar Shri Vallabhbhai Patel, the Iron Man of India, who was much grieved on seeing the ruins of the old Somnath Temple took a pledge on November 13, 1947, on the sea-shore nearby, to reconstruct the Temple. This pledge was realised when Dr. Rajendra Prasad, the first President of India, performed the Pran-Pratishtha Ceremony of the Jyotirlinga on May 11, 1951 in the Garbh - Gruh of the Somnath Temple which was being reconstructed at that time. The vast gathering of the people greeted this happy and historic occasion with joyous cries of "Jay Somnath" which expressed their unassailable faith and devotion. To commemorate this great event, Shree somnath Trust is celebrating the whole year from May 11, 2000 to May 11, 2001 as Shree Somnath Jyotirling Pran-Pratistha Golden Jubilee Year. The inaugural functions like Mahabhishek-Mahapooja, Sahasra Deep Arti, Shobhayatra of Lord Somnath, Sant-Padarpan on the newly constructed Pradakshina Path, inauguration of Illumination of the Temple and inauguration of the Golden Jubilee day and the Golden Jubilee Year celebrations were held from May 8 to May 13, 2000. A commemorative publication "Yugvarti Punarnirman" and Golden Jubilee Web-Page on the Somnath website were also released.

Installation of idols of deities - Ganesh and Hanuman, in the extended portion of the Ahalyabai Temple; Atirudra Yagna; Plantation of Bilva Van; Bhoomi Pujans for Morarji Desai Ghat, Sankirtan Hall and Krishna Moksha Dham; Inauguration of "Sound and Light" of the Somnath Temple; grand Maha Shivratri celebration, as well as Dance and Music festivals; Presentation of Shivnam Pothis to Lord Somnath; Historians' meet on Sardar and Somnath and Purnahuti of the Suvarnajayanti Mahotsav on May 11, 2001, are other major programmes, which from part of the year - round celebrations of the Golden Jubilee of Shree Somnath Jyotirlinga Pran - Pratishtha.

KASHMIR: THE BITTER TRUTH

India That the Princely States of India, including Jammu and Kashmir State, were on the agenda of the partition of India in 1947, is a travesty of history and a part of the diplomatic offensive, Pakistan has launched to mislead the international opinion about its claim to Jammu and Kashmir. The matter of the fact is that the lapse of Paramountcy was a consequence of the dissolution of the British empire in India and the political imperatives of the authority, the British Crown exercised over the princely States. The withdrawal of the Paramountcy was not a concomitant or a consequence of the Indian partition, and neither the June 3 Declaration of 1947, nor the independence of India Act, embodied any provision by virtue of which the partition of India affected the Princely States or the British Paramountcy.

The British colonial empire in India was divided into two separate and different political organisations, the British India constituted of the British Indian Provinces and the India of Princes. The British India was directly governed by the British Government through the Governor-General of India, with each of the Provinces in charge of a Provincial Governor, who in the old British tradition, administered the Provinces, with the help of the Indian Civil Service.

The Princely States were ruled by local potentates, who had carved their independent fiefs and kingdoms in the long and atrocious process of the British expansion in India. Five hundred and sixty two in number, the Indian States formed a conglomerate of widely disparate identities in their territories, population and government. The Princes were British feudatories, who accepted the supremacy of the British Crown, which was symbolized in the person of the Crown Prince, or the Viceroy of India. The relations between the British Crown and the States were governed by what the British called, the "Paramountcy'. Paramountcy in real terms, described the extent of the authority the British exercised over the States.

Apparently, the rulers of the States were vested with the powers to rule their States, but in actual practice, the States were administered by the British officers, whose functions were determined by the

Viceroy, the Political Department of the Government of India and the British Residents posted in the States. The Princes represented the best of the oriental splendour, with their treasuries held by the British, and their privy purses plentifully provided. The Partition of India, which loomed larger on the horizons after the failure of the Cabinet Mission and the campaign of "Direct Action" launched by the Muslim League, suddenly pushed the States into the fore-front. Interspersed in the British Indian Provinces, the States were spread over more than one third of the territory of India and constituted about a hundred million people, almost a quarter of the population of India. The British, the Muslim League as well as the Indian National Congress, for their own interests, did not favour the inclusion of the Princely States, in the constitutional reforms, the Indian liberation movement idealised. The British held the States as a personal preserve, protected the Princes against their people and harnessed the resources of the States to promote the interests of their empire. The Princes, of their privileges and unrestricted power over their subjects, supported the British, to isolate themselves from any constitutional change which prejudiced their position.

The Indian renaissance evoked a widespread response in the Princely States, and the liberation movement in India received as much support from the people of the States as it did in the British Indian Provinces. In fact, the revolutionary struggle, which followed the Swadeshi Movement in the aftermath of the stormy session of the Indian National Congress at Calcutta in 1906, grew in the States, where numerous revolutionaries received quarter.

The Congress leaders, however, on the insistence of the Princes and the Muslim League, withdrew its movement from the States, and till almost the end of the British rule, refused to integrate the people's movements in the States avowedly inspired by the liberation of India, with the national struggle against the British in the Provinces. The Congress leaders were neither prepared to displease the Princes, who were the mantle of Indian nativity, nor did they dare to disregard the Muslim League leaders, who made the exclusion of the hundred million people of the Princely States, a precedent condition to any compromise on the constitutional reforms in India. The League leaders knew that the inclusion of the people of the States, predominantly Hindu, would reduce the weightage of the Muslim population in the British India in any future scheme of constitutional change. Throughout the long decades, the Indian national movement evolved, the Congress leadership remained divided on the anti-imperialist struggle in the States and the All-India Congress Committee did not formalise its opinion on the States till the Udaipur session of the All-India States People's Conference held in 1946. By that time, however, much precious time had been lost. The States had almost been isolated from the mainstream of the national movement and stood vulnerably exposed to the machinations of the British, the Muslim League and the Princes to balkanise India.

The Muslim League policy on the States was more involved and shifting, which concealed the designs of the League to grab the Muslim ruled Hindu majority States as well as the Muslim majority States for the separate Muslim State of Pakistan, the League demanded for the Muslims in India. The All-India States Muslim League, an appendage of the Muslim League, constituted to coordinate the Muslim movements for Pakistan in the States, demanded in 1940, the integration of all such Indian States in the Muslim homeland of Pakistan as were ruled by the Muslim rulers as well as all such States .as were inhabited by Muslim majorities. The Lahore Resolution of the League, claimed a separate homeland for the Muslims in India, which was constituted of the Muslim majority Provinces of Sindh, the Punjab, Bengal, Northwest Frontier, the Chief-Commissioner's Province of Baluchistan and the Hindu majority Province of Assam for its geographical contiguity to Bengal, besides the Princely States which were either ruled by the Muslim rulers or populated by Muslim majorities.

The Congress awoke to the dangerous consequences of the isolation of the States almost after it had virtually accepted the partition, when it realised that the British, in collaboration with the Muslim League, were conspiring to break up India into several imbecile political entities with the Muslim State of Pakistan strategically placed at their epicentre. That was precisely what Jinnah, Conrad Corfield, and the Political Department of the Government of India visualised as the future constitutional composition of India. The Cabinet Mission Plan also, by and large, envisaged the division of India into several political identities which were confined within the territorial jurisdiction of a united Indian Dominion. The Cabinet Mission precisely accepted the separate identity of the Princely States and rejected any proposition to transfer the Paramountcy to the federal government. The Mission insisted upon the agreements between the federal authority and the Princely States, as a basis for any future relations between the States and the Indian Union which would follow their accession and withdrawal of the Paramountcy.

At the time, when the British and the Muslim League settled down to decide the fate of India, the Congress turned to the people in the States, whom they had neglected throughout the long history of Indian struggle against the British. Once again the Congress leaders fell prey to their own indecision and made a half-hearted plea for the right of the people of the States to determine their future. Not backed by conviction, the Congress demand made little impression upon the British and the League. The Princes were disparaged and opposed the right of the people in the States to determine their future. The League leaders turned the bend at the most appropriate time and in an astute move, pledged their support to the British designs to exclude the States from the constitutional arrangements envisaged by the partition and the withdrawal of the Paramountcy, to restore to the Princes, the powers which the British Crown exercised over them. The Muslim League realised that most of the States were populated by Hindu majorities and any arrangements to transfer Paramountcy to the two Dominions, would definitely place them in India. After the lapse of the Paramountcy, the Muslim League shared the optimism of British about independence of the States and their eventual alignment with the Muslim State of Pakistan, as a counterweight against India.

The Congress resolve, having been broken by the partition and the Congress leaders, still groping for a new rationale of the Indian freedom, after their basic commitment to the unity of India was abandoned, did not stick to their demand for the right of the State's people to determine the future disposition of the States. Instead they acquiesced, without demur, with the British proposals to terminate the Paramountcy and restore the Princes the powers to decide their future affiliations with the two successor Dominions of India and Pakistan. The States were thus removed from the agenda of the Indian partition on the insistence of the British, the machinations of the Muslim League as well as the unconditional acceptance of the lapse of Paramountcy by the Congress.

The conspiracy proved to be deeper and though the British Government refused to accord the status of British Dominions to the Princely States, it left the door open for separate negotiations with their rulers. Mountbatten informed the Princes, that he would forward to the British Government any requests from anyone of them to establish direct relations with Great Britain. When Jinnah met Mountbatten, a day before the acceptance of the partition plan was announced, he was triumphant. He had after all, carved out a Muslim State and also destroyed the bond of unity between British India and the Princely States. Jinnah did not conceal his satisfaction on the vivisection of India, which the Partition Plan, in fact envisaged." His delight was unconcealed", Mountbatten reported to London. "The Long campaign" the Viceroy mentioned in his report, "was virtually over There would be no Hindu government of an undivided India."

In fact, not only Jinnah, but the entire Muslim League accepted the creation of Pakistan on the terms the British offered. In the League Council, the Muslim League accepted by 400 votes to 8, the separation of the Muslim majority regions and the British provinces into an independent and separate Muslim State. The League Council did not include the Princely States in the settlement with the British which created Pakistan.

So clear was the line drawn in the Partition Plan, between the division of the British India Provinces and the Princely States, that the Secretary of the State for India, refused to accept any interference with the lapse of the Paramountcy or its consequence on the States or the two Dominions. The Viceroy wrote to the Secretary of the State to insert a clause into the Indian Independence Bill, limiting the powers of the Princely States which would revert to them with the lapse of the Paramountcy. The Secretary of State, straightway rejected the suggestion to the satisfaction of both the Political Department of the Government of India as well as Muslim League. The British as well as the Muslim League, sought the reversion of Paramountcy to the Princes, as a part of the transfer of power, to leave any future alignments in India, in which the Princes would participate to be determined primarily by them, of course, with the Muslim State of Pakistan backing them up in what they decided to do.

The partition plan, envisaged by the June 3 Declaration, did not apply to the Indian States, which were left out of its procedure as well as its consequences. States were never placed on the agenda of the Partition of India, and therefore, the claim made by Pakistan to complete the agenda of the partition, by forcing India to cede the Muslim majority State of Jammu and Kashmir to it, has no historical or political relevance. Neither Pakistan nor India, laid any claim, to any Princely State on account of the partition, which was strictly limited to the agreement between the British, the Congress and the Muslim League to divide the boundaries of the British India and create the State of Pakistan.

The transfer of powers of India in 1947, involved the division of the British Indian Provinces, into two dominions, India and Pakistan and the liberation of the Indian States from the British Paramountcy. The two processes were distinctly separate and underlined political change, which led to different consequences. The Provinces were reorganised into two independent dominions; the States were released from the obligations of the Paramountcy and the rulers of the States were empowered to adhere to either of the two Dominions, irrespective of the communal division, the Indian partition underlined. The State Departments of India and Pakistan, headed by Sardar Vallabhbhai Patel and Sardar Abdur Rab Nishtar respectively, opened negotiations with the Princes, for separate political settlement, with them. Neither Patel nor Nishtar demanded, at any time, the adherence of any State to either of the Dominions on the basis of the partition of the British India. Sardar Abdur Rab Nishtar offered whole-hearted support to the independence of the

States, including the State of Jammu and Kashmir and strongly opposed any political arrangements, which were sought to be reached with the Princes on the basis of the division.

The Hidden Hand

It was again the invisible hand of the British, which sought to alter the balance and this time, it was no other person than Mountbatten himself, who, perhaps, having realised the force of the States People's movements for unity with India, sought to prepare the ground for a division of the Princely States between the two Dominions on the basis of the partition. Mountbatten realised that none of the Princes, whose States were geographically situated within the territories of the Indian Dominion, would be able to hold out against the will of his subjects and the States would sooner or later join the Indian Dominion. He did not share the optimism of the British officers in India and at home and the leaders of the Muslim League, to save the Muslim rules States from India. Instead he feared that the tide of the events would wipe off the Princes and India would absorb the States, perhaps sooner than anticipated. He was more concerned about the Princely States, situated within the proposed boundaries of Pakistan, among which the ruler of the Kalat State, refused to accede to Pakistan. He was also apprehensive of the Jammu and Kashmir State, which would be left with contiguous borders with both the Indian Dominion and Pakistan and of which the ruler was not favourably disposed towards settlement with Pakistan. His fears about Jammu and Kashmir were confirmed by Hari Singh, the ruler of Jammu and Kashmir, who refused to accept his advice to arrive at an agreement with Pakistan.

Mountbatten went to the extent of ensuing India a viable border with Pakistan and played safe in the division of the Upper Bara Doab, and favoured the inclusion of the districts of Amritsar and Gurdaspur in India. On the States, Mounbatten had a different commitment, which was dictated by the interests of the British empire. By the close of the month of July 1947, while the partition had begun to assume effect, Mountbatten was convinced that the borders of India should be confined to the Punjab, leaving the northern frontier of Jammu and Kashmir in safer and more friendly hands of Pakistan.

In his last address, he delivered to the Princes on 25 July 1947, in Delhi, Mountbatten spelt out certain broad guidelines for them to follow in the determination of the future disposition of their States. He advised the Princes to accede to either of the two Dominions on the basis of the geographical contiguity of their States and the composition of their population. In his endeavour to extend the partition to the States, he utilised V.P. Menon, who had a few months earlier prepared the blue-print for the partition of India, which formed basis of the transfer of power.

The Muslim League leaders scoffed at the advice of the Viceroy to the Princes and secretly counselled the Muslim Princes to ignore his address. They communicated to the Princes their readiness to support them in their independence. The Indian leaders, with V. P. Menon pulling the strings from behind, walked into the trap and entrusted the task of the negotiation with the Princes to Menon and Mountbatten. Mountbatten, deliberately avoided to take a bold initiative on the Muslim-ruled States and Jammu and Kashmir to bring about their integration with India. Junagarh acceded to Pakistan; Hyderabad refused to join India and Jammu and Kashmir was pushed into the oblivion. Menon succeeded where the going was easy, with Mountbatten adding an element of diplomatic intrigue to an otherwise versatile comedy which the Princes enacted to accede to India. Mountbatten provided a long handle to Pakistan which that country is still using in Kashmir with devastating effect.

The British were no votaries of the Indian Unity and in the negotiations with the Indian leaders, preceding the acceptance of the partition of India, they kept the door open, for the Princes, to form a third, fourth and even a fifth estate in India, which in the new balances of power, between the two Dominions. Conrad Corfield and the Political Department of the Government of India as well as the Secretary of the State, were determined to keep the States apart from the division of the British India and the transfer of power to the two Dominions.

The record indeed is straight. The lapse of Paramountcy released the Prince from the British tutelage and they were ensured the right to determine the future of their States by the British which assumed effect with their withdrawal from India. Pakistan had no right to any claim the Princely States which did not form a part of the British India. The Indian leaders in fact should have decisively claimed the States as a part of the colonial empire liberated from the British tutelage. They knew that Princes were only the shadows of their British masters, and they would neither dare to join Pakistan nor remain out of India after the British had boarded their ships for home. The only factor, which the Dominion of India could not overlook in regard to the States was the geographical location of several Princely States, within the territories, of which Pakistan was proposed to be constituted. No Government of India could have consciously taken the responsibility of seeking islands of territory inside the boundaries of Pakistan with all the military responsibility any such possession would entail. The Indian leadership, understandably made no efforts to save the State of Kalat, where the ruler refused to accede to Pakistan and sought the help of the Indian leaders to save him from being swallowed by the League. Kalat was eventually smothered into submission by the continued pressure of the British, who backed Pakistan to acquire the States contiguous to its territories which incidentally, included Bahawalpur as well. Jinnah and the other leaders of the Muslim League had greater stakes in the States ruled by the Muslim Princes than they had in the Muslim majority of the Jammu and Kashmir State. They sought to keep the option open for the Muslim rulers to join Pakistan. And they did not close the option for the ruler of Jammu and Kashmir either. In fact, they offered to support Maharaja Hari Singh, in case he decided to opt for the independence of the State. Hari Singh saw through the game and refused to be used as a pawn in the British-League plan to keep the Muslim ruled States out of India.

Accession to India

The Jammu and Kashmir state was contiguous to both India and Pakistan and had hundreds of miles of contiguous border with

East Punjab and the Punjab Hill States, which had already decided to join India. Pakistan's propaganda has considerably clouded the real facts of the division of the Punjab. The division of the East Punjab from the west Punjab was not subject to the whims and caprices of the League leaders. They could not be ceded all the territories in the Punjab on which they laid their hands. They perpetrated a myth that the inclusion of the district of Gurdaspur in the East Punjab, contrary to their claims, was aimed to open up Jammu and Kashmir to India. The division of the Punjab was entrusted to an independent Boundary Commission which the British constituted and which was headed by an Englishman, Sir Cyril Radcliffe, a lawyer of considerable repute. Besides its Chairman, the Commission constituted of four other members, two of them Din Mohammed and Mohammed Munir who represented the Muslims, Mehar Chand Mahajan represented the Hindus and Teja Singh represented the Sikhs whose culture, history and religious heritage were inextricably linked with the Punjab.

The Commission could not follow standards different in demarcating the Muslim majority regions in the west of the Punjab and the Hindu majority regions in the east of the Punjab. Pathankot, was a Hindu majority Tehsil and it could not have been included in West Punjab by any stretch of imagination. The district boundaries were not strictly adhered to by the Boundary Commission as the basis of the division of the Punjab and there was evidently no reason why a Hindu majority Tehsil, which was contiguous to the Punjab Hill States should have been excluded from the East Punjab.

Pathankot apart, the whole of the district of Gurdaspur was strategically important not only from the viewpoint of a defensible Indian border, a major consideration, the Boundary Commission recognised in demarcating the boundaries of the East Punjab form the West Punjab but also in view of the future of the district of Amritsar which would be almost isolated into an island of Indian territory in the West Punjab. Amritsar was by no means a Muslim majority district and it could not be separated from the east Punjab for its significance to the Sikh Community. Amritsar symbolised the principal centre of the Sikh religion. Sikhs were by far the more important of the parties to the partition of the Punjab, because, a major part of their population was uprooted from the West Punjab where their main assets and lands were located and secondly the most sacred of their religious shrines were situated in the Muslim majority districts, which could not be retained in the East Punjab Gurdaspur formed the most strategic flank of the district of Amritsar.

The ruler of the Jammu and Kashmir State, Maharaja Hari Singh, had his own interests in the final delimitation of the new boundaries of the east and the west Punjab. Several of the Hindu leaders in the Punjab, among them notably Sir Shadi Lal and Bakhshi Tek Chand, kept him intimately informed of the proceedings of the Boundary Commission. The British were apprehensive about him, but through many of his British contacts, he had managed to convince the Political Department that he would not take any precipitate action, which would bring him into conflict with Pakistan. Hari Singh, did not hide his interest in a balanced order with India and Pakistan and open access to the two Dominions. He conveyed to the British Resident and the Political Department a veiled threat that he would be forced to deal directly with the Indian Government, if any attempts were made to isolate his state in the boundary demarcation of the Punjab, irrespective of the consequences his actions would have.

The Muslim Commissioners, Justice Din Mohammed and Justice Mohammed Munir insisted upon the division of the Upper Bari Doab, with a view to assume control over the Ravi Canal head-works at Madhopur and encircle the district of Amritsar and also cut off the fair weather track between Madhopur and Jammu. The Radcliffe award was announced three days after the transfer of power. Expectedly Gurdaspur was included in the east Punjab. Pakistan raised a hue and cry on the decision of the Boundary Commission, though the accredited Muslim members of the Commission had committed themselves to accept the award.

The actual game plan of Pakistan to grab the Muslim ruled States with the support of the British and the Muslim majority States with the support of their Muslim subjects unfolded on 14 August, 1947, the day power was transferred in Pakistan and the Nawab of

Junagarh, a Hindu majority State situated in the midst of the Kathiawar States, acceded to Pakistan. Pakistan had secured the accession of all the Princely States, situated within its territorial limits, including the State of Kalat, which had resolutely resisted accession to the new Muslim State. A secret understanding had also been reached with the Nawab of the Hyderabad, to support him against India till the Nawab was able to accede to assume independence and then align himself with Pakistan.

The Indian leaders failed to respond to the threat Pakistan posed to the Kathiaward States and instead of trying immediate counter-action against the Nawab of Junagarh, they feebly complained to Pakistan against the decision of the Nawab and proposed that the final disposition of the Junagarh State be determined by a reference to the people of the State. The bogey of referendum was actually raised by Mountbatten to enable him to execute his design; to divide the States on the basis of the partition.

The Congress leaders walked into the trap. Perhaps, unsure of the British reaction and unable to face Mountbatten, they did not dare take advantage of the people's wrath against the rulers of Junagarh and Hyderabad. In Hyderabad, feverish preparations were afoot to declare the independence of the State and a secret understanding had already been reached between the Nawab of Hyderabad and the League leaders, which assured the Nawab, the support of Pakistan for an independent Hyderabad. Contrary to the avowedly prò-Pakistan stand of the rulers of Junagarh and Hyderabad, Hari Singh maintained scrupulous silence on the issue of accession. Hari Singh told the Viceroy as well, and in plain terms, that he would take such a decision on the accession of the State as would be in the interests of his people. Indeed, Mountbatten denounced him for his indecision and accused him of stupidity in reacting to the situation in a way which the British did not approve. Hari Singh offered a standstill agreement to both the Dominions on 12 August 1947.

India had a claim to all the three States, mainly because of their geographical contiguity to the Indian Dominion and their strategic importance to its security and territorial integrity. Neither the partition nor Pakistan was a factor in this determination of the future of

Junagarh and Hyderabad which were embedded in the heart of the Indian Dominion and Jammu and Kashmir, which formed the traditional frontier of India in the north.

The indecisiveness of the Congress leaders to act promptly in Junagarh had a far-reaching impact on the Kathiawad States. Some of the rulers warned the Government of India that its prestige in Kathiawad had been irreparably impaired by its inability to save Junagarh and the two smaller States of Babriawad and Mangrol. The warning administered a jolt to the Indian leaders. Mountbatten Laughed in his sleeves, for he realised that Pakistan had assumed the initiative in using Junagarh as a pawn for a bargain on Jammu and Kashmir as well as Hyderabad. Pakistan followed the course Mountbatten had visualised. Acceptance of a plebiscite would, in effect mean the deferment of the accession of Hyderabad and Jammu and Kashmir and the continuation of the status-quo in Junagarh indefinitely, for how would the proposed plebiscite be conducted and by whom, more specially in a situation when the Nawabs of Junagarh and Hyderabad, were under no obligation to accept an agreement between the two Dominions which impinged upon their rights. The Indian leadership was broken into factions which were led by decrepit and small men, who had lost the courage to face the problems, the partition had created. Nehru put himself at the mercy of the Viceroy, who exhibited determination to tackle the problems of the partition, which Nehru himself, was hardly prepared to face. Gandhi had obsolete views on the States and had lost contact with the stupendous developments, which rocked the Princely India.

Inside the Congress, the debate on the viability or otherwise of nonviolence and non-intervention, immobilised whatever initiative India still possessed to retrieve the situation in the States of Junagarh, Hyderabad and Jammu and Kashmir, which were still outside the fold of the Indian Dominion. For India, the question of the Princely States was crucial, after the Muslim majority provinces and regions of the British India had seceded to form a separate Muslim State.

The further separation of the States into a third confederacy, Jinnah had visualised, was bound to balkanise India sooner or later.

Junagarh with a long sea-coast, which provided it access to Pakistan, posed a grave threat to whole Kathiawad peninsula Hyderabad was in the heart of India, and was boiling in internal distrust, which had dangerous portent for the country in the south. Jammu and Kashmir formed a part of the warm Himalayan hinterland, and if it was lost to Pakistan, the whole of the Indian frontier in the north, would suddenly disintegrate. The Jammu and Kashmir State was crucial to the existence of India and not Pakistan, the one basic fact, the Indian leadership failed to emphasise.

After the transfer of power in India, the Dominion Government of India extended the time for accession, to the two States of Jammu and Kashmir and Hyderabad, which had offered a standstill agreement, to continue the relationship already subsisting between the States and the British India. The standstill agreement was of the same standard pattern, which the State Department of India had evolved for all the States. The standstill agreements, it needs to be noted, had no political implications and were restricted to the continuation of arrangements, which had governed the relation between the Princely States and the British Government of India.

While Pakistan kept the fire hanging in Jungarh, it prepared fast to deliver another stunning blow to India. On 21 October 1947, hardly fourteen days after Pakistan had sternly warned India against any intervention in Junagarh. It launched a massive invasion of the Jammu and Kashmir State. Thousands of armed tribesmen and irregulars, led by the crack Tochi Scouts, easily identified by their brown tunics, stormed into the State, with the twin objective of occupying the Kashmir Valley and attacking Jammu from across the Sialkot border to cut off the only communication line connecting the State with Madhopur in the Punjab, which the State Government had ordered to be repaired into a more serviceable highway for communication with India. Even at that time, Pakistan claimed that the invading forces were the Muslim subjects of the State, who had risen in revolt against the Dogra rule and the Afridi and the other tribesmen had only joined their brethren in the war of their liberation.

Bibliography

Alter, Stephen: *Amritsar to Lahore: A Journey Across the India-Pakistan Border*, Philadelphia, University of Pennsylvania Press, 2001.

Alva, Joachim: *Leaders of India,* Bombay, Thacker & Co., Ltd., 1943

Arabinda Poddar : *Tagore : The Political Personality*, Kolkata, Indiana, 2004.

Aziz, K. K.: *Complete Works of Patel*, Islamabad, National Commission on Historical and Cultural Research, 1978.

Bapat, S. V.: *Tilak Sukti Sangraha*, A Kesari Prakashan, Pune, 1926.

Campbell-Johnson, Alan: *Mission with Mountbatten*, London: Hale, 1982.

Chaudhary, M.: *Partition and the Curse of Rehabilitation*, Calcutta, Bengal Rehabilitation Organization, 1964.

Erdosy, George: *The Indo-Aryans of Ancient South Asia*, New Delhi, 1955.

Ghoshal, U. N.: A *History of Indian Political Ideas.* London, 1966.

Lumby, E. W. R.: *The Transfer of Power*, London, Allen, 1954.

Menon, V. P.: *The Transfer of Power in India*, Bombay, Orient Longman, 1957.

Naik, J. P.: *Political Content of Education*, Socio Research Publications Centre, Calcutta, 1917.

Prasad, Lal Bahadur : *Indian Political System and Law*, New Delhi, Shree, 2005.

Roy, Ramashray : *Gandhi and Patel : A Study in Contrast*, Delhi, Shipra Pub., 2006.

Stanley A. Wolpert: *Tilak and Patel: Revolution and Reform in the Making of Modern India,* Berkeley, 1962.

Yasin, Mohammad : *Indian Politics : Processes, Issues and Trends,* New Delhi, Kanishka, 2004.

Zaidi, A. Moin: *Evolution of Muslim political Thought in India,* New Delhi: S. Chand, 1975-79.

Index

K

L

M

N

O

P

Q

R

S

T

U

W

❑❑❑